Combined Operations

Combined Operations

A Global History of Amphibious and Airborne Warfare

Jeremy Black

ROWMAN & LITTLEFIELD
Lanham • Boulder • New York • London

Published by Rowman & Littlefield
A wholly owned subsidiary of
The Rowman & Littlefield Publishing Group, Inc.
4501 Forbes Boulevard, Suite 200, Lanham, Maryland 20706
https://rowman.com

Unit A, Whitacre Mews, 26-34 Stannary Street, London SE11 4AB,
United Kingdom

British Library Cataloguing in Publication Information Available

Library of Congress Cataloging-in-Publication Data
Names: Black, Jeremy, 1955– author.
Title: Combined operations : a global history of amphibious and airborne warfare / Jeremy Black.
Other titles: Global history of amphibious and airborne warfare
Description: Lanham, MD : Rowman & Littlefield, [2017] | Includes bibliographical references and index.
Identifiers: LCCN 2017023130 (print) | LCCN 2017023719 (ebook) | ISBN 9781442276949 (ebook) | ISBN 9781442276925 (hbk. : alk. paper) | ISBN 9781442276932 (pbk. : alk. paper)
Subjects: LCSH: Combined operations (Military science)—History. | Amphibious warfare—History. | Air warfare—History.
Classification: LCC U260 (ebook) | LCC U260 .B55 2017 (print) | DDC 355.4/609—dc23
LC record available at https://lccn.loc.gov/2017023130

Printed in the United States of America

For Lisa Thomas

Contents

Preface

Combined operations are a key element of military capability and conflict in the modern world. They also have a long history. This book offers this history as well as looks at the present-day position and considers the likely future situation. To do so, we address the global scale. Moreover, there is particular attention to the two powers that practiced combined operations most intensively and that greatly developed joint capability and potential. These were, successively, the two leading naval powers from the 1690s to the present: Britain and the United States. This attention also throws much light on circumstances as far as other states were concerned, and not only those allied with Britain and/or the United States, and those who experienced their attacks or had to consider the possibility of such an attack. At the same time, this focus will not lead to a lack of necessary coverage of other powers.

Combined operations have been very differently defined, not least between as well as within the United States and Britain, and that remains the case today. I have been fortunate to be able to discuss the topic with many serving military and with many other scholars, and it is readily apparent that there remains no agreed definition. Among those offered were in the senses of combined arms (e.g., cavalry and firepower), combined different types of unit (e.g., under the Romans, legions and auxiliaries), and combined alliances (e.g., American and British during the Second World War as in Operation Overlord in Normandy in 1944). "Combined Operations" was also the name used for the British headquarters overseeing commando operations in the Second World War that was established in 1940. Varied definitions and (related but also distinct) uses of the term in particular countries, and in different languages, alternatively clarify or complicate the situation. Each approach has its value.[1]

Here, however, a particular approach is taken that seems most appropriate to what is both a significant and a distinctive type of military activity and one that is of great importance to military capability and, therefore, in international history and in the development of specific countries. The working approach is that of a unit of any size, of troops for operations onto land (including Marines), and the sea or air units available for its transport and firepower. For most of history, combined warfare, as defined in this book, was a matter of amphibious assaults, which have been described as the oldest form of naval warfare as raiding from boats long preceded clashes between vessels.

In the twentieth century, these operations were enhanced by improved ship engines, greater speed, and the capability to transport large amounts of matériel and troops to faraway places, while supplemented by air power, so that combined operations also took the form of air-land cooperation. Furthermore, the combination of air, land, and sea forces ensured the development of what Winston Churchill, the British prime minister, in a radio broadcast in 1943, termed "triphibian" warfare, a useful term that never caught on, and that followed Home Secretary Herbert Morrison's use of the term "triphibious."[2]

As a result of this expansion in the potential of combined operations, the range of capabilities and operations that has to be covered rose greatly in the twentieth century. These points help explain the coverage in this book. In particular, there is more space devoted to the twentieth than to other centuries. The situation today richly explains the significance of the subject, but it is also very important to be aware of historical roots and, more significantly, antecedents that throw much light on subsequent developments. The nonlinear nature of change helps explain why situations in history are not past in the sense of being without present or future meaning.

This book offers certain repeated themes, notably those that recur as problems with combined operations. These are mostly general problems in war and in no way unique to combined operations, but they take on special dimensions in this particular context. The level of coordination required, and the need for skill in all parts, and especially in a closely defined space-time setting, posed particular requirements for planning and execution. Moreover, the extent to which these could be readily disrupted by opposition increased the level of expertise, bravery, and luck required. Command and control and planning and logistical issues are all key elements, but each is accentuated for combined operations. As far as command and control, who is in command, the admiral or the general? How are units at sea, on land, and possibly in the air to be coordinated effectively, whether or not radio has been invented? What if it is foggy or dark? How is contact to be maintained with units? With planning, there is a need for detailed, accurate intelligence on the terrain, the sands, the winds, enemy fortifications, and other elements. There is only limited room for improvisation if the landing is at the wrong place or the vital equipment needed did not get ashore. Such problems have to be solved beforehand or, generally, not at all.

Logistics are a problem in every war, but in combined operations, it is necessary to bring considerable matériel and, if there is travel far from base, it must be aboard seaworthy ships, which for long periods could not go close to the shore unless by means of access via a port. To land directly on the beach is possible with galleys and with modern powered landing craft, but during the period in between, it was problematic—although in the Baltic and the Mediterranean, galleys remained in use until the eighteenth century. When forces land, it takes time before they can move out of their beachheads and start living off the land, so it is necessary to bring provisions. Moreover, there is a need to construct field fortifications on the beach, to destroy those of the enemy, and also to reshape the situation to ease the movement of stores. As a result, it is necessary to bring engineers.

Bureaucratic competition between the services makes everything more difficult. For most of history, this was not a problem, but by the late eighteenth century, there were already distinct government structures and career systems in most advanced states, and this situation impeded cooperation between services. The situation was further aggravated in the nineteenth century with the rise of military staffs, the increase in professional pride, the escalation in the costs of armaments, and the general expansion of public bureaucracy.

* * *

My work greatly reflects the stimulus and assistance of others. First, I have benefited from the opportunity to teach military history for more than three and a half decades at the Universities of Durham and Exeter and more generally. Second, for this book, I particularly profited from opportunities to speak at the Naval War College in Newport, Rhode Island; to give the keynote at a workshop on "Learning from Operational History Cases" held in the Royal Danish Defence College; and to visit Afghanistan, Belize, Brunei, Canada, China, Costa Rica, Cuba, Denmark, Estonia, Finland, France, India, Italy, Japan, Latvia, Malaysia, Nicaragua, Norway, Panama, the Philippines, Portugal, Russia, Spain, Sri Lanka, Sweden, Tunisia, Ukraine, and the United States.

Third, the two anonymous reviewers who commented on the proposal were most helpful. So also were those who gave their time and expertise to comment on earlier drafts of all, or part, of the book, notably Anne Louise Antonoff, Gunnar Åselius, Christopher Bell, Pete Brown, Stan Carpenter, Stephen Church, Mark Danley, Robert Davis, Paul Gelpi, Richard Harding, Albert Nofi, Ciro Paoletti, Martin Robson, Ian Speller, Mark Stevens, David

Trim, Greg Unwin, and Heiko Whenning. I also profited from advice on particular points from Virginia Aksan, Alejandro Amendolara, Rodney Atwood, Leopold Auer, Michael Axworthy, Pradeep Barua, Harry Bennett, Paola Bianchi, Michael Clemmesen, David Cohen, Richard Connell, Huw Davies, Hervé Drévillon, Paul Dukes, Charles Esdaile, Olavi Fält, Marcus Faukner, John Ferris, Karl Friday, Howard Fuller, John Gill, Blake Goldring, David Graff, Gregory Hanlon, Richard Harding, Guillaume Lasconjarias, Mark Lawrence, Nick Lipscombe, Peter Lorge, Eduardo De Mesa, Alexander Mikaberidze, Stephen Morillo, Jonathan Oates, Ryan Patterson, Karsten Petersen, Kaushik Roy, Nicholas Sarantakes, Don Stoker, Richard Toye, Javier Veramendi, Arthur Waldron, Peter Wilson, Jonathan Wise, Erbin Xu, and Carlos Alfaro Zaforteza. I alone am responsible for any errors that remain.

The collaborative nature of the project is further exemplified by the important role of my editor, Susan McEachern. She has provided the necessary mix of enthusiasm, skill, and wisdom that makes for a great editor. The book is dedicated to Lisa Thomas, a friend with whom I have worked producing historical atlases for more than twenty years. This book is another legacy of our friendship.

Abbreviations

Add	additional manuscripts
AWM	Canberra, Australian War Memorial, manuscript collection
Beinecke	New Haven, Connecticut, Beinecke Library
BL	London, British Library, Department of Manuscripts
CAB	Cabinet Office papers, British
CIA	Central Intelligence Agency, United States
DUKW	boat-shaped trucks (D = model year, U = amphibian, K = all-wheel drive, W = dual rear axles)
HL	San Marino, California, Huntington Library
JMH	*Journal of Military History*
LC	Washington, Library of Congress, Manuscript Division
LCA	landing craft, assault
LCM	landing craft, mechanized
LCT	landing craft, tank
LH	London, King's College, Liddell Hart Library
Lo	Loudoun papers
LST	landing ship, tank
LVT	landing vehicle, tracked
NA	London, National Archives, formerly Public Record Office
NAM	London, National Army Museum
NATO	North Atlantic Treaty Organization

NWCR	*Naval War College Review*
PLA	People's Liberation Army, China
RAF	Royal Air Force, British
RUSI	*Royal United Services Institute Journal*
SRO	Edinburgh, Scottish Record Office
USMC	United States Marine Corps
WO	War Office papers, British

Chapter One

Combined Operations to 1500

Combined operations were a norm for much of history for riverine as well as coastal societies. This reflected the relative speed and ease of transport provided by water, as opposed to land, and also the extent to which so much of the world's population lived on or close to the water. The situation obviously varied geographically, especially if shifting the view from the coasts to the continents, and the perspective accordingly that can be adopted is far from fixed. There were also differences between operations in particular maritime environments and notably between sea and river ones. Nevertheless, waterborne forces were important to military history in many regions.

Moreover, the significance for military history, and, indeed, the history of the world more generally, of the writings of Greek and Roman historians ensured that amphibious capability became a topic that was to the fore. This was particularly so because the seminal historical work, that by Thucydides, was devoted to the Peloponnesian War (431–404 BCE). This conflict involved many combined operations, notably by the Athenians—successfully against the Spartans at Pylos and disastrously against the Sicilian city of Syracuse—and also led to the juxtaposing, as a structural factor, of the capability of the land-based Spartans as opposed to the Athenians with their focus on naval power. The latter contrast was to be frequently cited across history when discussing other powers and circumstances, and possibly excessively so. At any rate, Thucydides offered the earliest accounts of amphibious operations and supplied good examples of the problems involved. His work continues to serve as an important text in service academies, for example in the American Naval War College.

THE NATURAL ENVIRONMENT

From the outset, humans have competed with other animals and fed, housed, and protected themselves as a result of these struggles. Such competition largely took place on land, generally close to freshwater, although there was also activity on rivers, lakes, and seas. This was the case with hunting animals that lived there, notably fish but also mammals, such as seals and whales, as well as birds. There was also the significance of the transport opportunities provided by such waterways in order to move more swiftly and securely and to transport goods. It was easier to transport on boat than by foot. Transport on rivers and along coasts was often the sole means to move cargo, especially when a road system and bridges did not exist. Thus, hunter-gatherer societies were not land-bound. The earliest evidence of the use of boats relates to the migration from Southeast Asia to Australia approximately sixty thousand years ago. Humans were able to colonize all the continents bar Antarctica within a time frame which represented a major evolutional breakthrough not matched by other species.

The dominance of humans over other animals was aided by the development of more successful weapons, many of which were useful for operating on the water, notably harpoons, spear throwers, and bows and arrows. All were used in Europe from approximately 35,000 BCE. Skill in hunting animals had wider consequences. For example, in northern Canada, the Dorset culture of the Paleo-Eskimos of the eastern Arctic was overwhelmed from about 1000 BCE by the Thule people of northern Alaska, whose kayaks, float harpoons, and sinew-backed bows made them more effective hunters of whales.

The development of agriculture, as humans moved from harvesting wild cereals to cultivating crops, was linked to growing social organization, and states followed. Ants have a similar social structure, but were not able to spread so fast and were not able to control their environment as humans could. In all this, the natural environment shaped possibilities for humans, not least in the way in which conflict was waged. This was also the case as far as naval power and sea-based conflict were concerned. For example, effectively inland seas, such as the Baltic, Black, and Mediterranean, lacked the large tidal range of oceans, which eased campaigning on them. Furthermore, the presence or absence of islands where freshwater could be taken on was important to naval operations, although reliance on rainwater helped the Polynesians cover great distances in the Pacific and the Vikings to do the same for lesser, though still major, distances in the North Atlantic.

There was also a major difference between coastlines that provided anchorages and supplies, notably freshwater, and those that did not, for example much of those of modern Namibia and Kamchatka. The relationship between coastal and distant waters could also be significant, as could the impact of the seasons, especially winter storms and/or ice. Although the technology and context have varied greatly, the constraints and impact of geographical factors, including the configuration and physical features of the coast, the depth of the water, and the intensity of the tides, remain extremely important.[1]

The most significant maritime environments were coastal waters. They were the prime areas of agriculture, industry, trade, and fishing, since much of the population (and marine life) lived in coastal regions. As a result, such regions were the target for attack.

The development of "states" created multiple opportunities for such operations. On the one hand, it was possible to support large naval forces able to carry out major amphibious assaults. The archeological remains of the naval dockyard at Carthage remain impressive as a demonstration of the importance of anchorages. Moreover, this development fostered an awareness of distinct branches of the military, and this awareness led to consideration of how best to obtain cooperation between them. At the same time, the settlements and trade of such states proved very tempting targets for predatory seaborne forces, such as the "Sea Peoples" who allegedly caused a crisis for the Bronze Age eastern Mediterranean in the twelfth century BCE, including for the Egyptian empire, the Hittite empire in modern Turkey, and Mycenaean Greece, although the Egyptians defeated an invasion by them in about 1175 BCE.

Rowing was the key means of propulsion for many ships, notably in riverine and coastal waters and in lakes and inland seas. The situation was different for high-seas travel, as it was not possible out of ready reach of the land to carry a large number of rowers. This was also a factor for mixed sail/oar ships as the rowers would have still to be fed and watered while the sail was used. A reliance on rowing in many coastal waters, notably the Mediterranean due to lack of wind there, had clear implications for combined operations. The necessity for considerable manpower for rowing meant that all, some, or none of this manpower could be landed for combat. Alternatively, ships could be used in combination with troops that they carried. Athenian triremes and those of other peoples had soldiers—"Marines"—in their complement.

At the same time, there were important operational constraints. The necessity for considerable manpower to row ships greatly limited their cruising range, as they had to stop to take on more freshwater and food. As a result, vessels rarely abandoned the coastline and generally beached every night. Galleys normally preferred to move in sight of the land, and a galley had to land frequently in order to refill its water barrels. Seven days was the maximum if the weather was not too hot, if the galley had not moved too much and too fast, and depending on the number of troops it was carrying. Operations across nearby waters were the key element as it was necessary to supply and support large forces and to protect them from the risk of storms, as well as from being becalmed. In contrast, an invasion at a great distance was not easy and was certainly more risky. From classical times, the Mediterranean was regarded as a sea that was not fit for shipping from early October to April. Galleys were docked in their home ports as soon as autumn came and were disarmed. During the difficult season, it was exceptional to use galleys.

THE CLASSICAL WORLD

Combined operations played a major role in the classical world, notably in the Persian invasions of Greece in 490 and 480 BCE. The first led to the defeat by the Athenians at Marathon of a recently landed army sent by Darius I, but the second involved a far more substantial force on both land and sea. Naval power gave the Persians considerable flexibility. In 480 BCE, in a reminder that combined operations could take many forms, a massive fleet provided a pontoon-style bridge for the invaders across the Hellespont as they crossed from Asia to Europe, not far from the planned destination of the 1915 Gallipoli campaign. The fleet then supported the Persian army under its ruler, Xerxes I, as it moved south along the Greek coast, not least escorting the supply ships, the presence of which was a response to serious logistical problems for the invasion. The historian Herodotus noted that it was unclear what advantage the Greeks could derive "from the walls built across the Isthmus [of Corinth] while the king [Xerxes of Persia] was master of the sea." This reflection captured the awareness that combined operations offered the possibility to outmaneuver defenses, in this case by landing in the Peloponnese, while the fleet could also be used to blockade Greek trade.

It was the defeat of the Persian fleet at Salamis in 480 BCE that changed the situation by lessening the prospect of successful Persian combined operations. Xerxes returned to Anatolia (Asian Turkey) with the remnants of his navy and part of his army. He left a force in Greece that still had to be defeated, as it was on land at Plataea in 479 BCE, but it was now exposed.[2]

Combined operations were also important in the Peloponnesian War later that century. Moreover, the significance of islands in the Greek world, notably in the Aegean Sea, was such that combined operations were necessarily important. This was also the case for non-Greek opponents, as with the capture of the Aegean island of Delos in 88 BCE by Menophaneses, a general of Mithradates VI, king of Pontus.

Moving beyond the Aegean, combined operations were also significant for Alexander the Great of Macedon. Although the Macedonians were a land power, they benefited from their ability to deploy allied and captured naval forces in combined operations, such as the capture of the Phoenician port of Tyre in 332 BCE. This was a key episode in Alexander's defeat of the

Persian navy on land, one that involved the capture of a series of ports including Halicarnassus, Sidon, Byblos, and Miletus. This campaign entailed combined operations at a number of levels, including the tactical as, to attack Tyre, Alexander complemented his local naval strength with the building of a mole (causeway) along which his siege engines could move.[3]

More generally, while naval power was mainly used for the projection of land forces and for logistics, each was a crucial aspect of what therefore became combined operations. Warships provided transport and firepower platforms for operations on land and sea, although the physical force of a *ballista* (land bombardment catapult) throwing a decisive projectile would have challenged ship hulls. Indeed, the range and throw weight of ship-based weapons were limited and low prior to the age of gunpowder. This made it difficult to damage seriously a land target, although they were very effective against other ships.

Rome for long did not place an emphasis on naval power but eventually had to do so in order to contest the Carthaginian position in the central and western Mediterranean. The consequences in terms of combined operations were wide-ranging. Indeed, one aspect was seen at sea: in battle, the Romans rammed their opponents and then used the plank-like *corvus*, which had a spike that attached it to the enemy ship, to form a bridge between ships and thus enable rapid boarding of the enemy vessel. War at sea was thereby transformed into land battle afloat. However, the *corvus* appears to have been a one-war wonder. Used to advantage in battles in the First Punic War, the *corvus* was not employed thereafter, possibly because it had been linked to the loss of many Roman ships in storms.[4]

At the operational and strategic levels, Rome, by 200 BCE, had exploited her naval strength to project troops successfully against Carthage into Sicily, Spain, and finally North Africa. This represented a key way to defeat Carthage by denying it strategic depth. In contrast, Hannibal, the Carthaginian general, invaded Italy by land, crossing the Alps from southern France.

The capability for force projection by sea was closely linked to the ability to deploy effective armies, as with the successful Roman conquests of Greece in the second century BCE, Julius Caesar's expeditions against Britain in 55 and 54 BCE, and the invasion of Britain from 43 CE. In 55 BCE, Caesar did not move from his precarious beachhead in Kent. The Romans were victorious in hard fighting, but the damage done to their ships by equinoctial gales and the scale of the resistance led Caesar to come to terms with the local tribes. In 54 BCE, he invaded anew with a larger force, benefiting from his opponents' naval weakness, which meant that they could not contest the passage of the English Channel. The local tribal leader was defeated and a settlement imposed. In 43 CE, approximately forty thousand troops landed unopposed and the Britons were defeated. This was not the only area for Roman combined operations in this period. In 12 BCE Drusus, the father of Claudius, the emperor in 43 CE, took an army up the North Sea coast of modern Holland and northwest Germany and subdued the Batavians and other tribes. His campaign included a landing at the mouth of the Weser River.

Combined operations were also significant to the civil wars within the Roman Empire and were demonstrated at the close of the greatest by Augustus's conquest of Egypt after his naval victory at Actium in 31 BCE. Such operations were also important to piracy and to its counter. Pirate attacks were directed not only against shipping but also against coastal settlements. In turn, campaigns against piracy, such as the successful large-scale one mounted in 67 BCE by Pompey, were in large part directed against pirate bases.

Some legions were versed in combined operations, with the Roman navy working with the army and under the command of the latter. At the same time, all Roman legions had a certain combined operations capability, as with the advances across the Rhine and Danube Rivers, notably that of the Danube by the Emperor Trajan in his conquest of Dacia (Romania). Thus, it is not necessary to think in terms of an organic ship complement attached to the legion in order to refer to them as capable of combined operations. Instead, the legions were like American army units in the Pacific during the Second World War. For the legions, the ships provided protection as well as transport.

There were also Roman "Marines" on two fleets, at Misenum near Naples and at Ravenna on the Adriatic coast, as well as with lesser fleets around the empire. Always noncitizens, and often former slaves, "Marines" and sailors were considered inferior to soldiers. The legionary soldier with his heavy armor and equipment would not have been very mobile in ship-to-ship fights and would drown fast if forced to swim. "Marines" would not have been so armored.

A *liburna* typically carried forty Marines as well as its crew. The *liburna* had been copied by Agrippa during his campaign against the Liburni (Dalmatians) around what later became the city of Zara on the Adriatic coast of modern Croatia. He saw that their ships were swift and quite good in the coastal area where islands were scattered everywhere and where the waters could be suddenly shallow. Their distinctive feature was that they had a round hull and were swift and thin. *Liburna* were used in Augustus's victory over Mark Antony at Actium.[5] Roman "Marines" were principally intended for ship-to-ship warfare—to prevent hostile boarders during battle and to board opposing ships, not to participate in amphibious warfare on land. The units belonged to the ship on which they were based.

The Byzantine (Eastern Roman) successors of the Roman Empire also had an impressive combined capability. This was seen in the reconquest, under Justinian I, of "barbarian" kingdoms, notably that of the Vandals, much of Italy, Sicily, Sardinia, Corsica, Tunisia, and southern Spain, in 533–555 CE.

For China, some literature of the Spring and Autumn Period (770–476 BCE) mentions the transport of troops across the sea or rivers, but pictures, in the shape of bronze wares, only come from the Warring States Period (475–221 BCE).

THE MIDDLE AGES

The attackers of the Roman world included groups that crossed seas and rivers (e.g., the Vandals crossing from Spain to North Africa), but most of the assailants focused on overland operations. However, the Angles, Saxons, and Jutes, who conquered England from the fifth century CE, relied initially on amphibious power projection, in their case across the North Sea.

The Vikings (Danes, Norwegians, and Swedes), from the eighth to the eleventh centuries, attacked by sea and river. The main burden of the Viking attack was on the British Isles, northern France, and the Low Countries. There were also attacks elsewhere, for example, a major raid of Spain and Portugal in 844, in which the Vikings sailed up the Guadalquivir River and sacked Seville; the raiding of Italy and North Africa in 860, in which Pisa was sacked; and raids across the Black and Caspian Seas. With limited land available for colonization in Scandinavia, the Vikings were possibly motivated by opportunities for raiding and settlement in more prosperous and fertile (because warmer and wetter) lands that were vulnerable to the amphibious assaults that the Scandinavians could mount so well. Viking longboats, with their sails, stepped masts, true keels, and steering rudders, although shallow and open, were effective oceangoing ships able to take to the Atlantic. The Vikings do not appear to have suffered from disease in the way that Renaissance galley and galleon crews did. This was probably due to the ships being open, with no decks, and thus better ventilated. The Viking diet was also heavily reliant on oily fish, so that they were better able to cope with both hygiene and dietary issues.

However, thanks to their shallow draught, the longboats could be rowed in coastal waters and up rivers, even if there was only three feet of water. Thus, in Ireland, where the wealthy monasteries attracted attack, the numerous rivers and lakes facilitated Viking movement. In modern terms, these ships were conceivably the first effective "littoral combat ships."

The size of the Viking ships was optimal for both rowing and the use of sail. Bigger ships would have relied on one or the other. Viking ships did not carry catapult-type "artillery," which would have led to problems with draught and stability. The Vikings were dedicated raiders and tended to avoid sieges or fights with strongly entrenched forces. They were armed similarly to the Roman "Marines."

The initial Viking successes were due to their mastery of the amphibious assault. Surprise, concentration of force at the point of landing, and the ability to withdraw before relief arrived all proved important. The Viking tactic of securing island bases, such as the Isle of Sheppey in England, for use as raiding bases was also highly successful. As their successes grew, so did the scale of their endeavor. It is worth noting that the scope of their operations included the successful penetration of the great Russian river systems, leading to the establishment of the trading city of Novgorod and the opening of trade and mercenary service with Constantinople (now Istanbul), the capital of the Byzantine Empire. The scale of Viking fleets was impressive, although their armies were smaller than those of the Romans.

Viking capability posed a major challenge to opponents. It was possible to improve the defenses of rivers, as with the fortified bridges built in France under Charles the Bald (c. 843–877) in order to obstruct Viking passage upriver. No such defense was possible for coastlines. The response of the emirate of Cordoba in southern Spain to Viking raids was similar to that of Alfred the Great in southern England in the late ninth century: to build a fleet to oppose the Vikings and to improve fortifications. Both expedients proved successful.

Defeated on land in England in the tenth century, the Vikings conquered it in the 1010s. In 1016, King Cnut of Denmark and his fleet appeared in the River Thames. As their passage upstream was blocked by the troops on London Bridge, Cnut reportedly dug a channel around the southern end of the bridge in Southwark and dragged his ships along it in order to encircle the city fully. London was then besieged, but the city resisted and Cnut moved off, only to win a decisive victory and gain control. In 1052, Earl Godwine of Wessex used a fleet on the Thames as part of his successful overawing of King Edward the Confessor.

In turn, in 1066, combined operations, again with the final verdicts settled on land, were directed against England. The Norwegian king, Harald Hardrada, an experienced warrior and sometime commander of the Varangian Guard (the Viking bodyguard of the Byzantine Emperor), launched an invasion of northern England that, in manpower terms, was as large as the Norman invasion of the south of England later in the year. Harald's defeat at Stamford Bridge was due to his overconfidence after his initial success and the positioning of his army at some distance from his ships.

The vagaries of the weather and their impact on combined operations are instructive in 1066. King Harold of England had his fleet in position on the south coast for much of the summer, anticipating an attack by William, Duke of Normandy. The weather, however, kept the Normans penned up in their ports until late in the season, by which time Harold had stood his fleet down.

The change in the weather simultaneously allowed the Norse fleet of Harald and the Norman fleet to sail against England. Had William landed first, it is likely there would have been a different outcome. In the event, although delayed by the weather, the invasion fleet of William successfully crossed the Channel and the army subsequently delivered victory over Harold at Hastings. It is claimed that the Norman fleet included Byzantine-influenced horse transports, ensuring that his army was able to transport its cavalry.[6]

Amphibious capability for land-based powers was also developed in the Islamic world and in East Asia. The Moors were able to invade Spain in 711 and to conquer islands such as Cyprus (649), the Balearic Islands (798), Malta (824), Sicily (827), and Crete (827), as well as to establish coastal bases, notably Bari in Italy (841–871) and Fraxinetum in southern France (890–972). However, in 849, a big Islamic fleet was completely destroyed by a fleet from the cities of Naples, Salerno, Amalfi, Sorrento, and Gaeta, and after that victory, no Islamic settlement was established in the parts of Italy that were not under Byzantium.

In China, for both overseas and river operations, fleets were usually temporary and purpose-built rather than maintained over the long term. Amphibious operations, such as the seaborne invasions of the Korean peninsula in 612 and 660, were rare. There may have been some sort of doctrine, but it is not mentioned in the surviving sources. Certain patterns did repeat. For example, the Sui campaign down the Yangzi River in 589 was very similar to what the Jin dynasty did in 279. This appears to be not a matter of doctrine but of appropriate lessons drawn from history, with geography also recommending some approaches rather than others. However, pretty much anyone attempting to be more than a regional warlord had to span rivers in order to expand outside their locality. Consequently, fortifications by river crossings were important, as were operations to capture them. These entailed amphibious assaults. Joint army and naval operations can certainly be found in China in the tenth century.

As a demonstration of their adaptability, the invading Mongols created an effective river navy in the thirteenth century, after having conquered northern China, to overcome the use of defensive river lines in southern China by the Song empire and thus to complete their conquest. The Mongols were less successful when they launched invasions from Korea against Kyushu, the closest of the Japanese "Home Islands." Khubilai Khan, having established his rule over northern China and his Mongol relatives in their khanates to the west, turned toward his eastern borders. He inherited significant naval resources from the coastal areas of China, and the Mongols had always been good at assimilating the military methods and assets of those they conquered. He therefore decided to attack Japan and subsequently attacked Vietnam and Java. The ships Khubilai Khan had access to were the result of generations of Chinese engineering and development and were possibly the most advanced warships of the medieval period, some with combinations of oars and sail, ideal for amphibious attacks. At the same time, Chinese ships were more riverine than high-seas.

Khubilai sent his first invasion force to Japan in 1274, and part of his strategic design was to cut trade links between Japan and the Song empire of southern China, which was still resisting the Mongols. The attack on Japan was limited in size and consisted of Mongol and Korean troops with Chinese and Korean seamen. The initial attacks were against weakly held islands. The invasion force subsequently arrived at Hakata Bay in northern Kyushu on October 19 and was fiercely resisted. Superior Mongol firepower, both arrows and catapults firing explosive pots, established a beachhead, but due to the severity of the fighting, the Mongols withdrew to their ships to rest and replace their weaponry, especially their arrows. The ships then appear to have been disrupted by a storm and returned to Korea.

However, the Mongols had achieved their strategic aim and gained a great deal of intelligence, which informed their next invasion. This was delayed while Khubilai finished off the Song empire, which crumbled by 1279. He demanded that the Japanese surrender to him, which was predictably refused, and the king of Korea began building another fleet. Korea possessed the resources and knowledge to do this and the manpower to crew the ships.

The second invasion was significantly larger than the first and well organized. Khubilai even established an "Office for the Chastisement of Japan" to oversee the logistical and administrative arrangements for a massive seaborne assault. The ambitious plan called for a Korean-led force with a Mongol army, of nearly one thousand ships and forty thousand troops, to rendezvous with a force of South Chinese ships, the old Song navy, with a further one hundred thousand troops. The buildup was delayed as Khubilai demanded that additional ships be impressed. The forces were to meet and coordinate their attack, but instead the Korean/Mongol force left Pusan in southern Korea on May 2, 1281, and followed the same route as the previous invasion force. This proved to be a bad mistake as the Japanese had prepared a defensive stone wall from which to guard the beach. This proved effective in stalling the attackers, who withdrew to their ships after hard fighting. They seized a neighboring island to act as a base.

The Japanese took the initiative in attacking the Mongol fleet at anchor and achieved considerable success. They also attacked the island base and compelled the invasion fleet to weigh anchor and retreat to Iki Island, across the straits from Hakata Bay. The second Chinese fleet had meanwhile made the 480-mile passage with 3,500 ships and 100,000 men. They avoided Hakata Bay and landed thirty miles to the south. The fleet had been spotted, however, and the Japanese opposed the landing by the second force, causing heavy casualties. Although the invaders established a beachhead, fighting ashore continued for two months. The Japanese used fireships to attack the

Mongol fleet, but it was a typhoon that finally destroyed the invasion force. Marco Polo described the disaster, and modern archeology confirms his account.

The two invasions highlight the logistical difficulty of mounting such massive assaults from the sea, and their vulnerability both to determined opposition at the point of landing and to the vagaries of the weather. These attempts dwarfed anything attempted in the Western world during this period, yet they did not prevent further combined operations.

The failure of the 1281 invasion squandered the massive navy that Khubilai had inherited from the Song and the one created by the Koreans. Khubilai reacted by ordering the construction of more ships, but the effort caused widespread unrest, especially in southern China. The Korean ships, which were simpler but smaller than their Chinese counterparts, seemed to have survived the *kamikaze* wind better than the Chinese. Yuan court records state that many eventually returned to Korea, along with a number of their troops. This provided the fighting core of a new navy, but the cost of the failed invasions of Japan had drained the Mongol finances. Khubilai abandoned his plans for a third invasion of Japan in 1286 and turned his attention to the lucrative trade routes of the South China Sea, and of Vietnam in particular. Money was a key element in such massive combined operations, and he wished to gain control of the rich trading centers of Hanoi and Da Nang.

Khubilai had mounted an amphibious assault on the Champa kingdom, whose capital is present-day Da Nang, in 1281. His Japanese commitments, however, limited his resources, and although the Mongols captured the capital, guerrilla warfare, disease, and, crucially, a lack of reinforcements and supplies due to the operations against Japan led to the disintegration of the invasion force. A much larger invasion, aimed at the northern Dai Viet capital of Hanoi, was mounted in 1286. The Mongols had learned their lessons from the previous campaign in 1281, and the new one was a two-pronged attack. A land army of Mongols advanced through the border hills from Yunnan province, while an amphibious force assaulted Van Don, the main port of the Dai Viet (present-day Haiphong). It was an ambitious operational plan that crucially depended on logistic support, especially rice, from the fleet.

The Dai Viet had learned the lessons of the first Mongol invasion and had adopted guerrilla warfare and scorched earth as pragmatic ways of defeating the invaders. After initial Chinese successes by both arms of the pincer attack, the supply fleet was trapped and destroyed at the battle of Bach Dang. The Mongol fleet was lured into an area of river that had been planted with long, sharpened stakes. As the heavy Mongol ships sailed into the stakes, the tide began to fall, trapping the fleet, which was then destroyed with fire arrows. The remaining Mongols were forced to retreat overland, and very few reached Yunnan. The Dai Viet leader, Tran Hung Dao, was an inspired tactician who wrote a treatise on his tactics for defeating the Mongols. General Vo Nguyen Giap is said to have read the book and used it as the basis of his strategy against the French and Americans in the twentieth century. Tran Hung Dao is still revered as a great hero in Vietnam.

Showing remarkable determination in the face of repeated defeat, Khubilai in 1292 ordered the construction of another fleet and army, to attack the powerful Indonesian king, Kertanagara, who had secured control of the trade routes through the Malacca Straits. By the time the force reached Java the following year, after a month-long sea passage, Kertanagara was dead. His successor persuaded the Mongol commanders to aid him in an internal war of succession, which they did. However, the Javanese then turned on the Mongols, who were forced to make a fighting withdrawal to their ships and to return to China. Although a failure, they brought back a considerable amount of valuable booty and returned with the fleet intact.

The operations mounted by Khubilai were on a scale and level of strategic complexity that dwarfed operations in Europe. Not until Toyotomi Hideyoshi's invasion of Korea in 1592 was anything comparable attempted. The ability of Khubilai to keep generating such forces with the resources he could command was in part due to the high levels of piracy on the Chinese coast and the experienced seamen this produced.

Mongol expeditions reflected the development of a combined capability, although they had no lasting effect. The Japanese themselves used amphibious operations in the Genpei War (1180–1185), if such operations are defined broadly to include any use of boats to transport troops to attack points. Moreover, the Japanese employed fishing boats to conduct guerrilla operations against the Mongol fleet at anchor during the invasion attempts of the late thirteenth century.

European rulers found that combined operations brought success. For example, the Byzantines regained the initiative from the Muslims in the late tenth century. The island of Crete was recaptured in 960–961 after expeditions in 911 and 949 had failed: the Byzantine fleet, which included purpose-built ships for horse transport, was able to transport an expeditionary force and then keep it supplied while the capital was besieged over the winter. The Byzantine navy was essentially treated as a conveyance for the army. At the tactical level, Byzantine combined capability was also significant. Thus, when the troops of the First Crusade besieged Muslim-held Nicaea in Anatolia in 1097, they were unable to prevail until the ships of their Byzantine ally cut supply links across the lake by the city.[7]

The eleventh and twelfth centuries saw extensive combined operations mounted in the Mediterranean. These were focused on the Crusades and the rivalry between the major naval/maritime cities: Pisa, Genoa, Venice, Barcelona, and Marseille. These cities provided the means by which the Crusaders were transported and subsequently supported. They enabled vital backing for major operations, especially during the Third Crusade (1189–1192). A leading participant, Richard I of England, also captured Cyprus from Byzantium in 1191 during a series of brilliant and daring amphibious operations, prior to arriving at Acre. Cyprus, and especially the port of Famagusta, had been crucial as a support base for the Crusader coastal cities that survived the defeat of the Kingdom of Jerusalem's army by Saladin at Hattin in 1187. In 1191, Richard carried out another daring amphibious operation, against Jaffa, which was successful, and he used his fleet to support his army on its march to Arsuf, where his opponent, Saladin, was defeated.

More generally, the Christian powers of Western Europe used combined operations in campaigns against the Muslim powers, although this campaigning essentially involved campaigning on land. In contrast, the efforts by Robert Guiscard to invade the Byzantine dominions across the Adriatic in the early 1080s enjoyed much success but were greatly affected by the presence of a hostile and aggressive Venetian fleet. The Venetians had also aided the Byzantines in their defense of the great coastal fortresses of Calabria, such as Bari, against the Normans. The Venetians, however, were not involved in their defense of Sicily. The Byzantines, having used the Normans as mercenaries in the recapture of Sicily from the Moors, notably during the capture of Syracuse in 1086, then were themselves ejected by the Normans, who had conquered it by 1093.

Crusades launched by Louis IX of France against Egypt in 1249 and Tunis in 1270 led to the landing of forces that were then wracked by disease and, in the first case, defeated in 1250. Ironically, one of the most successful combined operations was the Fourth Crusade against Byzantium Constantinople in 1204, an operation in which, having captured the Adriatic city of Zara the previous year, the Venetian fleet played a major role, demonstrating the expertise and capability of Venice in the execution of complex combined operations. More generally, the Venetian presence in Dalmatia, the Ionian Isles, and the Aegean depended on a capability for combined operations.

Greater Christian maritime effectiveness in the Mediterranean owed much to the development of trading systems centered on the Catalan (later Aragonese) city of Barcelona and the Italian cities of Pisa, Genoa, and, most successfully, Venice.[8] Their fierce rivalry often led to clashes between the fleets and forces of the cities. Their galleys carried archers and crossbowmen intended for battle with opposing ships. A series of island possessions—for example, Corsica for Genoa (after a dispute with Pisa) and the Balearic Islands for Catalonia (from 1229)—and of mainland bases were crucial as adjuncts to their naval capability, while collective memory helped sustain commitment.[9]

The struggle between the Genoese and Venetians for maritime supremacy resulted in four wars, beginning in 1253, which culminated in the War of Chioggia from 1378 to 1381. Galleys had replaced lateen-rigged ships in the

Italian war fleets in the early thirteenth century. Raiding, the capture of ports and islands, and the effective use of galleys over extended distances made these wars essentially a series of combined operations. The culminating battle illustrates this point well. In order to blockade and starve Venice into submission, the Genoese, showing great boldness, seized the island of Chioggia, on the doorstep of the Rialto. This enabled them to support their galleys in a close blockade of the lagoon. They also worked in close cooperation with land forces from Padua, which attacked Venice from the west. The Venetian response was carefully planned and well executed. The three channels linking Chioggia with the Adriatic were all blocked by stone-filled cogs under cover of darkness, while Venetian galleys and troops from the mainland launched a diversionary attack on Brondola, which protected Chioggia from the south. This took place on December 22, the longest night of the year. Despite Venetian success in isolating the Genoese garrison, it was not until June 24 that they finally surrendered.

The campaign illustrates a number of the fundamentals of the later "galley wars" in the Mediterranean. Firstly, it was the first time that gunpowder weapons were extensively used, including a bombard, named *la Trevisana* (it was made in Treviso), which fired a stone ball weighing 205 pounds. Secondly, although Chioggia was cut off, the fortifications of Brondola and Chioggia proved difficult to overcome. Thirdly, the logistics of the campaign were influenced by the remaining Genoese and Venetian fleets, which actively interrupted supplies, including a grain convoy en route from Sicily that was captured by the Genoese. Fourthly, money played an important role in waging war. The Genoese had the financial muscle to continue building and paying for replacement galleys and crucial mercenaries. They also tried to bribe the mercenaries working for Venice. The battle highlighted the symbiotic relationship between guns, fortified ports, galleys, the weather, and money in combined operations in the Mediterranean for the next 250 years.

Having taken over Catalonia, the Aragonese state expanded to encompass Sicily (1282), Sardinia (1322), and Naples (1435). Portugal also built up skill in this area, with the Portuguese seizing Ceuta in Morocco in 1415 in what began a major sequence of Portuguese power projection based on fortified coastal bases.[10]

In the North Sea and Baltic, the maritime legacy of the Vikings was continued by the creation of the Hanseatic League. The league was motivated by the defense of trade between the great north European port cities. This involved frequent conflict, especially with Baltic rulers, with Denmark being particularly expansionist, notably by sea, into Estonia from the thirteenth century. The Hanseatic League made extensive use of mercenaries to provide the fighting power of their fleets, both at sea and ashore. The financial success of the organization meant that they possessed the money necessary to pay for the mercenaries. The cogs of Baltic fleets were able to operate into the surrounding rivers, which provided the Germans of the Hanseatic League and their allies with significant power projection.

During the Hundred Years' War between England and France (1337–1453), Edward III in 1346 and Henry V in 1415 both carried out successful invasions of the French coast. Although both invasions were anticipated by the French, Edward and Henry achieved tactical surprise, such that they were able to unload their troops, horses, matériel, and stores on an open beach without interference. By the time the French had brought their forces up to confront the English armies, the latter were fully established and prepared for battle. Both kings had the advantage of seasoned mariners who knew the tides, winds, and beaches on which they landed. Both also built up the core of their fleets while hiring merchantmen, predominantly from Holland.

The successes in capturing Calais and Harfleur, in 1347 and 1415 respectively, did not make their retention any easier. Both were closely invested after the departure of the kings to England. The survival of both port cities, especially in their first year of occupation, required an effective resupply by sea. In the case of Harfleur, this resulted in a major naval clash in 1416. The French used Genoese carracks, with Genoese crew, as the core of their blockading force. This force was engaged and, after a fiercely fought naval battle, defeated, which ensured Harfleur's survival.

The process of land-based powers co-opting or developing a combined capability in order to fulfill their imperial ambitions was also seen in the fifteenth century outside Christendom. Ming China sent fleets into the Indian Ocean that successfully invaded Sri Lanka in 1411 and reached East Africa in about 1418. More lastingly, the Ottoman Turks did the same in the Mediterranean. They created a fleet to prevent Constantinople from being relieved when they attacked it in 1453 and moved ships overland to the Golden Horn, from which waterway they could bring further pressure on the walls.[11]

Once Constantinople fell, the Turkish fleet was employed to support combined attacks in the Aegean, notably and successfully on Mytilene (1462) and Negroponte (1470) on the islands of Lesbos and Euboea respectively. Large numbers of troops were deployed by sizable fleets. This pattern was also seen with the capture of several of the Ionian Islands to the west of Greece in 1479, notably Cephalonia, followed by the port of Otranto in southern Italy in 1480. That fell to a 12,000-strong force convoyed by a fleet of 28 galleys and 104 light galleys and transport vessels. As a sign of their resources, the Turks were able to take Otranto at the same time that they were besieging Rhodes. An aspect of these combined operations was the movement of heavy siege cannon by sea, although they could not be fired from the sea due to the recoil. As a result, the Venetians were driven from bases in Greece when war resumed in 1499–1503: Lepanto fell in 1499 and Modon and Coron, "the eyes of Venice," in 1500. However, Rhodes proved a tougher target until 1522.[12] The Turks also mounted successful combined operations in the Black Sea, particularly against Amasra (1460), Sinope and Trebizond (1461), and Kaffa (Fodosiya) in Crimea in 1475.

THE RANGE OF COMBINED OPERATIONS

Opposed beach landings were very rare, so the image conveyed in the Russell Crowe version of *Robin Hood* (2010) of a French attack on England is misleading. On a broader reading of amphibious capability, however, maritime troop transport happened all the time, as with the Vikings. To distinguish this from a combined operation is unhelpful as there was no indication of how far most landings would be opposed. Other than simply carrying troops by sea, "beach and pillage" was the most common form of amphibious operation.

The examples already given scarcely exhaust the range of combined operations, but they indicate their significance for many powers. Indeed, the importance of rowed vessels, with the manpower provided by all or part of the crew as well as the additional troops they might be carrying, was such that it is necessary to rethink any separation of naval from land conflict and instead to emphasize a continuance. This was especially the case with canoes. They were shallow in draught and therefore enjoyed an inshore range as well as the ability to beach and be readily carried. Their crews fought both hand to hand and with missile weapons.

Areas where canoes were particularly important, into the nineteenth century, included inland waterway systems, coastal systems, and island systems. Examples of the first included Amazonia; the eastern half of North America as well as its Pacific coastal region; the Caribbean where the Arawaks and Caribs were effective; in Africa, on the rivers Congo, Kwanza, and Niger; in South Asia, the valleys of the Brahmaputra, Irrawaddy, Ganges, and Indus; and, in Eastern Europe, the rivers Dniester, Dnieper, Western Dvina, Vistula, and Volga. Examples of the second included the lagoons of West Africa and, of the third, the Hawaiian archipelago. The key element in such warfare was not conflict between navies for "control of the sea" or of rivers, but rather the use of amphibious operations in order to mount attacks and raids. Moreover, both in order to transport troops and to reduce exposure to bad weather, there was an emphasis on operations across narrow waters rather than seas. Thus, much inshore use of ships was not too different from that on rivers and lakes.

There was generally only limited specialization in river vessels (and their sea equivalents), which helped make them useful for military purposes. Moreover, river vessels were usually lightweight and therefore could be dismantled in order to carry them around areas of shallow or rocky water or between waterways. This porterage, which was particularly important in

Russia and North America, posed issues as did winter ice, spring spate, and summer drought; but the value of waterways for combined operations was readily apparent. Indeed, this value was to prove crucial to transoceanic Western expansion from the fifteenth century.

At the same time, it was not only Western powers who adopted these means. For example, on the Niger River in West Africa, Sonni Ali, ruler of Songhai, used his river fleet to capture the major port of Jenne in 1471. River valleys, such as the Danube and Dniester in east Europe, were, notably for the Turks, a prime means for power projection, not least due to the general availability of water, flat land, and pasturage; this focus could also encourage the use of river vessels. The potential of combined operations is such that any land-based approach to war requires major qualification before it is adopted as the global model.[13]

In turn, in looking at combined operations, it is necessary to appreciate the interplay of natural conditions and ship capabilities. This interplay encouraged the development of well-defined routes along which most voyages were made. In sustaining these routes, ships and their crews, both for war and for trade, required bases as well as the knowledge recorded in charts.[14]

This approach is a long way from considering warfare in terms of the movement of cavalry forces on the Eurasian plains. The latter has dominated much discussion of warfare as a whole, and land warfare in particular, for the millennium from 500 to 1500, but that approach risks underplaying the diversity of such warfare, including of particular types such as combined operations. Indeed, across time, any notion of an "ur" (essential) type of conflict faces this issue. It is more appropriate to note that that analysis might well be true for particular environments due to the constraints they pose. For example, the situation in the Mediterranean, where almost all naval warfare was essentially amphibious because of the limited sea-keeping ability of galleys, was somewhat different from the English Channel, North Sea, and Baltic.

Against that background, the significance of coastal environments bulks large as a factor. So does the idea that particular regions could see conflict between militaries focusing on combined operations and their more land-based rivals. This had a more specific dimension in the case of the importance of river-based capability. The assessment of these issues and their consequences indicates the open-ended nature of military history. Similar issues surround the definition and role of piracy, a wide-ranging activity that overlapped with raiding. Piracy was not only seen in European waters, being, for example, highly significant in Japan.[15]

At any rate, the role of coastal environments or littorals is such that warfare in and about them was of particular significance. Geopolitics, both structural and contingent, played a large role in the respective importance of littoral regions, and notably the extent to which empires were based on them, as with Rome and Byzantium, or whether these regions were in effect tributaries of inland powers, as with the Mongol conquest of China in the thirteenth century. New World cultures, like Russia, were "landlocked" and did not develop any naval tradition. As a further point, if with Rome and Byzantium the focus, nevertheless, was on land, not sea, forces, that owed something to the extent to which all or much of the Mediterranean had been brought under a reasonable degree of control, which encouraged the concentration on the army, which posed less of a technological and organizational demand than the navy. At the same time, such an approach downplays the extent to which cultural factors were significant, notably in the institutional terms of preferences for particular military systems and methods and a lack of imagination, as well as need for the relevant skill and capacity. Thus the factors that affected the use of navies played a major part in determining a reliance on combined operations.

The sea and major rivers were viewed as major highways and essential lines of communication and trade. Their establishment made the movement of combined arms units across long distances both practical and possible. There was, indeed, a continuous trend of combined operations, from the Greek/Persian conflicts; through the Roman/Carthaginian, the Anglo-Saxon raids, and Viking voyages; to the Crusades and early Mediterranean galley wars, although there was no institutional or doctrinal continuity between these episodes.

Chapter Two

The Early Modern Period, 1500–1700

TRANSOCEANIC OPERATIONS

Combined operations became even more significant and conspicuous in the early-modern period because of new types of long-range naval activity with more capable ships and better navigation. The focus here is on Western sail-powered, cannon-carrying warships that reached the Caribbean in 1492 and India in 1498, under Christopher Columbus for Spain and Vasco da Gama for Portugal respectively. These expeditions helped establish a narrative of modernity, or at least globalization, in which transoceanic voyages played a key role, a narrative that, in practice, is highly Eurocentric.

Superficially, such warships might seem to have altered the prospect for combined operations, as they did not need to make physical contact with the land in order to direct damaging fire. In addition, sailing warships tended to have a smaller crew than galleys; this crew was employed more for serving the guns than for storming ashore. In parallel with, or as part of, the discussion of an early-modern European-based "Military Revolution," the transition to sail and cannon can therefore be regarded as the close of a long-standing age of amphibious warfare. A move to a focus on standoff firepower was not too different to the tendencies toward such conflict within Europe and for conflict on both land and sea.

In practice, however, the situation was very different, and not least because the transition to this form of naval strength and activity took longer than might be suggested by talk of a radical technological transformation or, indeed, a revolution.[1] The three ships of Columbus's first voyage were lightly armed and relatively small. In the late fifteenth and the early sixteenth centuries, the cannon on European ships were of relatively small size, although still effective against the Indian, Arab, and Turkish ships encountered in the Indian Ocean. Given the relatively small range of onboard cannon, ships had to come close to the beach to use them effectively, which led to the risk that the ships would run aground and be boarded. Bombardment was effective only against coastal cities with harbors that had a passage for ships to come very close to the shore.

Moreover, alongside the significance of boarding attacks at sea, landing operations remained important. Ships, especially Portuguese ones, were quite able to operate ashore, where the sailors' use of handheld firearms gave them a distinct advantage. In boarding, such firearms were valuable but so also was effectiveness in hand-to-hand combat. Furthermore, separate, although linked, to this issue, the significance of combined operations remained readily apparent with the need for a system of bases. In Asia, these bases supported the Portuguese military and commercial systems. Many of them could only be established as a consequence of amphibious attack.[2] At the same time, technical improvements in ships, as well as in the range of activity before resupply was essential, ensured that a close pattern of coastal bases was not necessary. Although other factors were also involved, this was seen with the Portuguese abandonment of Moroccan bases, notably Safi (1542), Azamour (1542), and Arzila (1549).

Combined attacks achieved many successes for the Portuguese as they expanded their system around African and Asian coastlines, notably against Malacca in modern Malaysia in 1511, but there were also failures, especially at Aden in 1513 and 1517. The operations displayed the importance of combined capability not only in attack but also in defense. For example, in 1517, at Jeddah, a Turkish fleet checked a Portuguese attempt to sail up the Red Sea by taking up a defensive position in the reef-bound harbor under the cover of coastal artillery. This was a vindication of the Mediterranean system of galley warfare against the Portuguese attempt to replicate their success in the Indian Ocean using caravels. More generally, the Portuguese failure in the Red Sea demonstrates the success of one combined capability at the expense of another. Relative distance from bases—with the Egyptians and then, once they had conquered Egypt in 1517, with the Turks operating from the nearby base of Suez—was an important variable in this result, which the Portuguese bases in more-distant East Africa could not match.

In contrast, in 1589, a Turkish fleet under Mir Ali Bey was defeated at Mombasa in East Africa by a Portuguese fleet, in part because the Turkish defensive fire failed to prevent the Portuguese entering the harbor and seizing the beached galleys. Yet the Turkish defeat also owed much to Mir Ali's need to deploy most of his troops and cannon to protect Mombasa on the landward side from a force of Zimba warriors.[3] This serves as a reminder of the value of assessing the effectiveness of combined operations in terms of broader issues of capability and commitment, although that point introduces a variety that poses greater complexity in analysis. Range again was an issue, as the Turks in 1589 were farther from their bases than was the case in the Red Sea. This distance was also linked to a more general lack of sustained political commitment toward Turkish power projection into the Indian Ocean, and particularly so after the 1550s. The Turks preferred galleys that offered tactical mobility and whose short range was not a major problem in operational terms in warfare in the central Mediterranean.

THE MEDITERRANEAN IN THE SIXTEENTH CENTURY

Combined operations were significant in the bitter and lengthy struggle between the Turks and their opponents in the Mediterranean, particularly Spain and Venice, but also Genoa, Tuscany, and the Knights of St. John. Galley conflict in particular depended on fortified ports and anchorages, which often gave the advantage to the defenders.[4] This proved to be the case at Prevesa in 1538, where, on the pattern of Jeddah in 1517, the Turks had withdrawn their galleys onto the beach under cover of their fortress guns, thus creating a difficult basis for their Spanish and Genoese attackers in the battle that followed.[5] Although Venice had lost Modon and Coron, its fortified base at Corfu was successfully defended against the Turks, notably during the siege of 1537 and again in 1716.

Combined operations were on a considerable scale, as with the Turkish capture of Rhodes from the Knights of St. John in 1522.[6] Indeed, any operations on a major scale benefited from being combined due to the need to transport artillery. This was also true for the Turks with the use of rivers, principally the Danube. Rhodes was well fortified and had seen off earlier Turkish attack, but suffered from its closeness to the Turkish coast and from the lack of any prospect of relief. Both the Turks and the Christian powers employed combined operations in the Mediterranean, as with the Turkish capture of Otranto in Italy in 1480 and the Spanish expeditions against Tunis (1535) and Algiers (1541). The attack on Tunis succeeded and won the Emperor Charles V, ruler, as Charles I, of Spain, much prestige. However, the expedition against Algiers was badly damaged by an autumnal storm, which led to the reembarkation of the troops that had been landed. The problems of operating on a coast were amply demonstrated and more particularly for late in the year when such storms were an issue.

The number and scale of combined operations in the Mediterranean in the mid-sixteenth century were impressive, in part because the major powers had plentiful resources. The size of armies that were transported, the distances they were moved, and the speed of transit were all striking and highlighted a degree of competence and capability that was largely due to the experience of the commanders and sailors involved, as well as to the availability of much shipping and the presence of the necessary support infrastructure in a period of economic growth and competition between powerful empires in the shape of Spain and Turkey. Cooperation between the French and Turkish fleets was a significant factor, notably in the 1550s when it enabled France to occupy Corsica in 1553–1554: Genoa, the ruler of Corsica, was an ally of Spain.

In 1559, Philip II of Spain, the son of Charles V, launched an expedition to regain Tripoli (in modern Libya), but delays in assembling the forces meant that the expedition did not sail until late in the winter, and it became storm-bound in Malta for ten weeks. When it eventually sailed for Tripoli, in mid-February 1560, the expedition was driven back by bad weather and instead occupied the low-lying island of Djerba to the west. In turn, a surprise Turkish galley attack defeated the Spaniards, who were in a vulnerable position. The speed of the Turkish reaction reflected on the well-organized nature and professionalism of the fleet, and its transit time to Djerba was impressive.

In 1565, the Turks sent a powerful combined expedition to capture Malta, the new base of the Knights of St. John, who had successively lost Rhodes and Tripoli. Naval strength provided the power-projection capability, but in this case, the Turks were unable to manage combined operations adequately. The land and sea commanders failed to agree on and implement a coordinated and effective command structure and plan. Moreover, having landed, the Turks lost the dynamism of their attack, not least because of the delay arising from the extraordinary heroism of the defenders of St. Elmo, a secondary fortress that commanded important harbor entrances but that faced poorly coordinated attacks. The Knights of St. John had made extensive preparations to receive the invasion, especially ensuring the availability of sufficient gunpowder. The failure of an effective command arrangement for the Turkish force was partially resolved when Dragut arrived, and due to his great experience and the respect in which he was held, he managed to refocus and reenergize the attack on Fort St. Elmo. It was fortunate for the knights that he was killed by a shell splinter the day the fort fell.

With time, the severe fighting and disease demoralized and decimated the Turks, who retreated in the face of an eleven-thousand-strong Spanish relief force from nearby Sicily, which had been deployed in an effective combined operation. At the same time, the vulnerability of such operations to sea conditions was indicated by the delays this one encountered. The difficulty of assembling and dispatching a relief force from Sicily was considerable, with weather a critical element. However, the earlier dispatch of the small relief that landed the day St. Elmo fell was a massive psychological boost to the defenders, encouraging them to persist.[7]

In 1570, Selim II, the new Turkish ruler, launched a combined operation against a closer target, Venetian-ruled Cyprus, which was exposed to such attack from nearby Turkey, as it was to be again in 1974. Indeed, a comparison of the two attacks is instructive as it indicates the changes brought by technology, notably air power and a parachute landing in 1974, but, at the same time, the constant factors offered by geopolitics. In 1570, 116 galleys and 50,000 troops represented a formidable force, one eased by the lack of major Turkish commitments elsewhere. Political factors were to the fore. The new sultan wanted to gain prestige to match that of his father, Suleiman the Magnificent (r. 1520–1566), and thereby to anchor his domestic position, rather as Suleiman had done with his capture of Belgrade (1521) and Rhodes (1522).

There was no defense of the beaches in Cyprus. The heavily outnumbered Venetians were obliged to focus on the defense of the fortified cities: Famagusta, Kyrenia, and Nicosia. This enabled the Turks, as at Malta, to resolve what had originally been a combined operation into a siege conflict in which siege cannon shipped from Turkey played a key role, which prefigured the Turkish attack on Crete in 1644–1669. At the same time, the Turkish fleet covered the invasion of Cyprus and, unlike with distant Malta, ended any prospect of relief.

Nicosia, despite the modernity of its impressive defenses, was far from the sea and lacked any realistic chance of relief. Kyrenia was bluffed into surrendering, although it had a good harbor. Famagusta, on the other hand, was formidably well defended, was well stocked with supplies, and had capable commanders and an excellent port. Venetian attempts to break through the Turkish naval blockade were successful but limited in scale. A major relief was delayed through overconfidence in the strength of the city and problems in assembling the relief force. In the end, Famagusta fell in 1571.

In the aftermath of the fall of Cyprus, the major Christian naval victory at Lepanto (on October 7, 1571) did not bring strategic advantage. It was too late to affect the fighting on Cyprus and was not followed by territorial gains in the eastern Mediterranean: an attempt to retake Modon failed in 1572. In 1573, Don John of Austria, the commander at Lepanto, led a large force of 107 galleys and 30 sailing ships carrying 27,000 troops to Tunis, capturing the city without resistance. In turn, in 1574, Uluj Ali Pasha, who had taken command of the Turkish galleys following Lepanto, carried out an audacious attack on the city with a force of 240 galleys and a fleet carrying 40,000 troops, which recaptured the city and the harbor fortress of La Goletta. The end result in 1574 was the de facto establishment of a maritime frontier between Spanish and Turkish spheres of influence in their respective halves of the Mediterranean.

There had been serious operational issues that affected combined operations, not least the need to transport large numbers of troops. Carrying troops greatly increased galleys' consumption of food and water and therefore affected their range. Another constraint on range was provided by the difficulties galleys faced in confronting rough winter seas, both in maneuvering and in remaining seaworthy. Few harbors and anchorages were able to support and shelter large fleets transporting substantial numbers of troops. This shortage affected operational methods and strategic goals; access to or the seizure of nodal points, such as Valetta in Malta, was crucial. The French port of Toulon was big enough to accommodate the Turkish fleet over the winter of 1543–1544.

ATLANTIC WATERS IN THE SIXTEENTH CENTURY

These factors also affected operational methods and strategic goals elsewhere, although operations in Atlantic waters came to be focused less on galleys than those in the Mediterranean. In both planning and execution, combined operations were significant. This was seen with England and Spain in particular, but also with France. For example, the French deployed an armada of 150 ships and 50,000 men in 1545 that was intended to invade England, although, due in part to disease (which was a frequent problem with troops in confined spaces), no invasion was mounted. The French landed troops on the Isle of Wight, but after skirmishing in the Solent, the force withdrew. The French were more successful in 1547, when a galley force recaptured St. Andrews Castle in Scotland in a well-planned and -executed operation.[8]

In turn, English combined operations against Scotland were carried out in the 1540s in order to establish and support coastal fortresses. Moreover, supporting fire from ships played a role in the English victory in the battle of Pinkie in 1547. Similarly, at Gravelines in 1558, a French army was to be defeated by Anglo-Spanish forces as a result of fire from land and sea, in the latter case, English ships under Captain John Malen. At the battle of the Dunes in 1658, also near Dunkirk, a Spanish army was defeated by Anglo-French forces ashore while its flank was bombarded by English warships, although the fighting on land was the crucial factor.[9]

In 1560, the English fleet played a key role in combined operations in Scotland, leading to the defeat of the French attempt to suppress the Protestant Lords of Congregation, who had rebelled against Mary, queen of Scots, the wife of Francis II of France. The English used both their navy, whose blockade of Edinburgh's port, Leith, was decisive, and also land forces: cut off by English warships, the French army retreated from Fife. The English fleet helped in the land assault on Leith, especially in providing firepower.

In 1562, in support of the Huguenots (French Protestants) in the French Wars of Religion, the English occupied Le Havre de Grace (Newhaven). The occupation was made viable by the support and regular resupply provided by the navy. An attempt to break through to Rouen by several English ships was defeated. When the political situation changed, the English found themselves closely besieged by the French. The navy provided continuous reinforcements until the French managed to close the entrance to the harbor in the town. Disease had decimated the English garrison to such an extent that a surrender was agreed and the garrison evacuated.

In a different geographical and political context, combined operations were also important to Spain's opponents in the Dutch Revolt, particularly with the success of the Sea Beggars, Dutch Protestant rebels, in 1572. They seized the Zeeland towns of Brill and Flushing and thus undermined the Spanish position in the Low Countries. In the fighting then and subsequently, the crews of Dutch ships were landed to take positions, while troops could also be stationed on ships in naval clashes, notably in the Dutch victory at the Battle on the Slaak, or Reimerswaal, in 1574, as a consequence of which the Spanish attempt to resupply their besieged garrison in Middleburg failed. It surrendered the following month.[10] The Spaniards suffered from their loss of access to indigenous shipping as a result of the Sea Beggars.

Combined operations were important in Spain's success in invading Portugal in 1580, particularly in seizing Lisbon, and subsequently, in 1582–1583, in conquering the Azores.[11] The latter was far more ambitious militarily than the 1580 invasion of mainland Portugal and was much more dependent on the naval side: the Portuguese operation, although very well conducted, did not offer any real example. The distance involved with the Azores was considerable, and the amphibious force had to make an opposed landing, as well as fighting off a French fleet. The Spaniards demonstrated a very high level of capability and competence operating in an Atlantic environment, rather than in the less demanding conditions in the Mediterranean. A significant element of the landing force was made up of galleys, and for them to tackle the Atlantic was a mark of the confidence of the galley commanders. Spanish galleys tried to intervene in Dutch waters in 1596 but were intercepted and destroyed by the English, although they did manage to land and burn the port of Mousehole in Cornwall.

Operations were also attempted on a very different scale: that of the Spanish Armada of 1588, an attempt to overcome England and thus end English support for the Dutch cause. Had the Spanish Armada been successful, it would have seen the coordination of two different plans: one for an amphibious invasion of England from Spain by the Duke of Medina-Sidonia's fleet, and the other for a crossing from the Spanish Netherlands (Belgium) by the Duke of Parma's Army of Flanders. The final plan was for the armada to proceed up the English Channel and then cover Parma's landing, but the details of how the two elements were to cooperate had not been adequately worked out. Confronting difficulties in communications but also in sorting out ambiguities, Philip II underestimated the problems facing Parma, who could not keep his troops sitting in their invasion barges for extended periods and required a significant period of time to load them. Philip, who lacked Charles V's personal experience of combined operations, worked on the assumption that the time would be available, once the armada had destroyed the English fleet guarding the Channel and also the Dutch ships that were blockading his embarkation ports. The vulnerability of Parma's open barges to attack by Dutch *flybotes* in the shallow waters around the ports of Ostend and Sluys was never appreciated by Philip.

In the event, this was a combined operation that did not work. The Spanish fleet fought its way along the English Channel, retaining its cohesion and strength in the face of persistent English attacks and anchoring off the French port of Calais. It found there, however, that, although Parma had been able to assemble the transport vessels necessary to embark his army for England, they could not come out until after the English and Dutch blockading squadrons had been defeated. That still offered opportunities for cooperation, but the Spanish fleet was disrupted by English attack and driven off into the North Sea. It then sought to sail back to Spain around Scotland and Ireland but was badly pummeled by storms in the process. Thus, although the armada had been intended to be a combined operation, it ended up being a purely naval one, in large part as a result of the Dutch blockade of the coast occupied by Parma.

THE FAR EAST IN THE SIXTEENTH CENTURY

Those in Europe were not the largest combined operations of the century. Those were seen in the Far East, as Toyotomi Hideyoshi, a leading Japanese general, first united Japan and then attacked Korea, in order to put pressure on China. His combined operations in Japan involved both successful strategic moves, notably Hideyoshi's invasion of Kyushu, the southernmost Home Island, in 1587, as well as the ability to overcome water in tactical situations. Thus, Hideyoshi's success in sieges, especially against the Hojo faction in eastern Honshu in 1590, owed much to the use of entrenchments to divert the water defenses offered by lakes and rivers. These entrenchments threatened fortresses with flooding or with the loss of the protection provided by water features, on which many in part relied.

In 1592, Hideyoshi launched about 168,000 men in an initially successful invasion of Korea. Korea's decision to fight the Japanese, instead of giving them free passage to attack their goal, China, was crucial and helped ensure that the war involved large-scale combined operations. The combined operations of their Chinese and Korean opponents thwarted the Japanese, notably by hitting the supply routes of the latter on land and at sea. China made a major commitment, on land and sea, to oppose Japan in Korea, as well as strengthening coastal defenses against possible Japanese attack. Another Japanese invasion attempt of Korea in 1597–1598 similarly failed.[12] These attempts did not involve fighting on invasion beaches. Instead, sieges were important, both to establish control and to support logistics. The latter was more significant due to the large number of troops involved.

THE SEVENTEENTH CENTURY

The characteristics of combined operations in the sixteenth century unsurprisingly were repeated in the seventeenth, a period of the same technology and socioeconomic systems, although with one major alteration—a geopolitical one. In the sixteenth century, the transoceanic Western presence had been dominated by Spain and Portugal, allies for most of the century and, after Philip II's conquest in 1580, under one ruler from 1580 until 1640. In contrast, in the seventeenth century, there was a multipolar system. The Dutch, France, and England developed major transoceanic empires and became both increasingly concerned to protect and expand them and able to deploy force to do so. This was very much a matter of combined operations, both between warships and troops and between metropolitan and provincial forces. The range was not global, as the Dutch, France, and England were not Pacific powers, but was transatlantic and extended into the Indian Ocean.

There was no comparison in Asia. The major event there, the Manchu conquest of Ming China in the 1640s–1650s, was a land struggle, as were the conflicts in India, both within the Mughal dynasty and between it and its opponents. Japan ceased its expansionism, and the Turks, although also invading Crete, focused heavily on land struggles with Persia (Iran) and Austria and, to a lesser extent, with Poland and Russia. There were combined operations by non-Western powers, notably focusing on Formosa (Taiwan) and also the maritime campaigns of the Omani Arabs, but they were far smaller in scale than the land campaigns of major non-Western powers.

Western transoceanic operations ranged from Formosa, the Moluccas, Sumatra, Malaya, and Sri Lanka to West Africa and the Americas. In part, this range reflected the wealth derived from colonies and the export of their products. Only high-value goods, such as bullion and tropical cash crops (e.g., sugar, coffee, and indigo), were worth transporting long distances, but it was these very goods that offered the wealth that made the entrepreneurial aspect of conflict profitable. For combined operations, the key opportunity was provided by the dependence of this trading system on ports, and by the very vulnerability of these ports to amphibious attack.

Such operations were a theme throughout the century as control was contested over bases such as Malacca (Malaysia), Colombo (Sri Lanka), Luanda (Angola), Bahia (Brazil), Pernambuco (Brazil), New York, and Québec. The usual pattern was that of the arrival of a naval squadron carrying troops and the surrender of the outnumbered and outgunned garrison, with troops landed to impose and maintain the new order, as with the Dutch capture of Bahia in 1624, its recapture in 1625, the Dutch capture of Pernambuco in 1630, and the English capture of Dutch-ruled New York (then New Amsterdam) in 1664. This pattern was more common than that of a contested landing, whether on a beach or in the port, although the latter could occur.

In technological terms, there was no change in combined operations during the century, and there was no development in doctrine. However, considerable experience was acquired. This was the case both in particular zones of frequent conflict, notably the slaving stations of West Africa and the (linked) sugar plantations of the West Indies and northern Brazil, and with reference to prominent rivalries, especially that which led to repeated and often successful Dutch attacks on Portuguese colonies in the 1630s and 1640s.

Both the potential and the limitations of combined operations were amply displayed. As far as the former was concerned, results were repeatedly delivered, and many of these results lasted for over a century. This was particularly the case with Dutch gains from the Portuguese in Malaya and Sri Lanka and with English gains from the Dutch in North America, especially New York. Malacca fell to the Dutch in 1605 and, more lastingly, 1641. The Dutch drove out the Spaniards from Taiwan, which was a lasting defeat as far as Spain was concerned. The Spaniards had established bases in 1626–1629 and claimed the island in 1627. In 1642, a Dutch force of 591 men took San Salvador, the main Spanish base on Taiwan, which had a garrison of only 115 Spaniards and 155 Filipinos, being an outlier of the Spanish colony on the Philippines, itself an outlier of the Spanish colony of Mexico. When such small forces were involved, there was a premium on experience, morale, and command that was at once bold and skillful. The positioning of cannon on commanding positions helped the Dutch.[13]

Numerous gains were not sustained. This was notably so with the Dutch total failure to hold their conquests from Portugal in Brazil and Angola and that despite a major effort to conquer the former. Repeatedly, on a long-standing pattern that reflected wider strategic factors, cooperation with local elements was important in helping determine success or failure,[14] but so also was the extraneous factor of the range of alternative commitments. Thus, for France, there were far greater political and military concerns in Europe. Given these factors, it is not surprising that it frequently proved difficult to sustain initial successes.

Combined operations generally enjoyed the initiative in transoceanic operations, but the situation thereafter, once troops had landed, was often very different, as for the Dutch in Brazil. This was not the sole reason for failure. Although the English Western Design of 1654–1655 succeeded against Jamaica, where the Spanish presence was limited, it failed against its original target, the key colony of Hispaniola: launched with high hopes, the expeditionary force was poorly organized and seriously affected by disease. The availability and reliability of logistics was also a major problem for trans-oceanic expeditions. Smaller islands were easier to capture, as when the French took Tobago from the Dutch in 1677. These islands lacked the defense in depth provided by a significant hinterland and the general need, therefore, to operate for longer in a hostile environment.[15]

The English gained increased experience in combined operations in the West Indies and North America as well as benefiting from the development of colonies in both regions. These could provide manpower with some immunity to the diseases there as well as logistics and support. This experience was important to success, although it did not necessarily bring victory and not least because of the multiple frictions between conception and execution. In May 1690, an expedition of eight ships and seven hundred men under Sir William Phips sent by the Court of Massachusetts successfully captured an unprepared and poorly defended Port Royal, the main French base in Acadia, later Nova Scotia. The fort was burned down.

That July, however, an expedition of 32 New England ships and 2,200 troops, again under Phips, failed to drive the French from the St. Lawrence. A diversionary attack overland against Montréal under Colonel Winthrop did not advance beyond Lake George, allowing the French to concentrate on defending Québec, which Phips unsuccessfully bombarded. He had failed to coordinate land and sea operations and suffered from adverse winds, a shortage of ammunition, and smallpox. With Québec clearly too formidable for Phips's force, it reembarked and returned to Boston. As was to be seen until it was last tried (in this case by the Americans) in 1814, the overland attack on Canada regularly faced major difficulties, not least of communications by means of improvised trails and logistics. These factors combined to lead to a highly problematic time environment, difficulties that helped explain the decision to try amphibious assaults while also making coordination between these and overland advances difficult.

In 1691, the English attacked Guadeloupe, a French Caribbean island. Troops were successfully landed, but the strength of the fortifications (which crucially held out), the arrival of a French squadron, and disease among the English troops and sailors led to the abandonment of the expedition. It had been plagued by poor relations between the two commanders and was followed by bitter recriminations. In 1693, a force was landed on Martinique, another French Caribbean island, but it failed to capture the French positions, in part due to the very different factors of yellow fever and poor leadership. In 1695, serious differences between the army and naval commanders and the impact of disease again hit English operations, notably in attacking French-ruled Saint-Domingue (Haiti).

The operations in the West Indies and North America did not determine the outcome of the 1689–1697 war between England and France, which instead was settled in Europe. Indeed, conflict in the West Indies bore many of the characteristics of buccaneering or at least privateering. At the same time, England and France were able to launch major attacks in the West Indies, although they found it much more difficult to sustain operations in the face of opposition and of the major ecological and logistical problems of campaigning there. These attacks were intended to lead to permanent gains, those that could be retained or exchanged in the subsequent peace treaty, as in the case of the Anglo-French contest over bases in Hudson Bay, bases from which the fur trade in Canada could be organized.

EUROPE IN THE SEVENTEENTH CENTURY

Combined operations remained significant in Europe. They were particularly important in the Baltic and Mediterranean but also in Atlantic waters, notably the British Isles, while there was a significant role on rivers, especially the Danube. The main bases of the Turks' Danube flotilla were Belgrade and Hassan Pachà Palanka. The flotilla operated freely until 1716 when the Austrians were able to launch their first effective one.

The largest-scale combined operation was the Turkish conquest of the Venetian-ruled island of Crete. Launched in 1645 with 348 ships and 51,000 soldiers, this involved combined operations on both sides, as each supplied their own forces and sought to block supplies to those of their opponents, including by raids into ports. Unlike the relatively rapid Turkish success in conquering Cyprus in 1570–1571, the operation resolved itself into a long and seemingly intractable siege of the Venetian fortress of Candia, one greatly complicated by Venetian attacks on Turkish supply routes across the Aegean. Candia finally fell in 1669 after the Venetians failed to sustain the garrison. The "War of Candia" included hundreds of naval and combined operations, including, on behalf of Venice, by the French.[16] The Dardanelles were blockaded many times by the Venetians and their allies (the Papacy, Malta, and Tuscany). Many small islands in the eastern Mediterranean were lost and retaken. Moreover, especially in 1645–1647, the Venetian conflict with the Turks in Dalmatia (modern Croatia) involved a wide use of amphibious actions.

In the subsequent War of the Holy League (1684–1699), the Venetians also launched combined operations, as in attacks on the Aegean island of Euboea in 1689 and on Crete in 1692, both unsuccessful, and, successfully, in the Gulf of Messenia in the Peloponnese in 1685 and on the Aegean island of Chios in 1694. Galley-borne forces demonstrated their continued viability. From the war, Venice acquired the entire Peloponnese in the 1699 peace treaty, although the Turks conquered it anew in 1715, and rapidly so in an impressive campaign.

The Turks also faced conflict in the Black Sea, where they confronted pressure from Cossacks based on the Don and Dnieper Rivers in Ukraine to the north of the sea. Prominent instances of Cossack pressure included raids on Sinope in northern Turkey in 1614 and on Yeniköy on the Bosporus in 1623[17] and the occupation of Azov, the key fortress on the Sea of Azov, from 1637 to 1641. In response, the Turkish fleet engaged in both defensive patrols and mounted expeditions. The Cossack *chaikas*, with their flat bottoms and no keels, had a shallower draft than the Turkish galleys and were therefore difficult to pursue, as the Turkish Black Sea fleet discovered in 1615 when it ran aground while in pursuit. In turn, in search of a form of combined operations that could thwart those of others, and as an instance of the action-reaction cycle of military capability, the Turks developed flat-bottomed rowing boats of their own from the 1630s and used them with success against the Cossacks in the Strait of Kerch, to the east of Crimea, in 1639.

Crimea was to be a long-standing target of combined operations, notably in 1854–1856 and 1941–1944, although, with the exception of the Anglo-French attack in the Crimean War of 1854–1856, invasions of Crimea generally focused on land operations. This was the case in Russian assaults, notably in 1738 and 1771, and in the German invasion of 1941 and the Soviet one in 1944.

Combined operations in the Mediterranean were not restricted to the Turks and their opponents. The ability to ferry reinforcements between Barcelona, Tuscany, and Naples was important to Spanish power in Italy. In turn, the French, opposing Spain, repeatedly intervened in Italy, with combined operations providing a range and flexibility denied overland ones over the Alps. More distant targets, such as Naples in 1647–1648, could readily be engaged by France, and there was not the same firm bar to operations caused by Alpine winter snow (in a manner that contrasted with that facing Hannibal during the Second Punic War). In 1646, the French, based in Marseille, captured from Spain Porto Longone on the island of Elba and Piombino, important bases for naval movements along the Italian coast near Tuscany.

Further afield, French intervention in support of a rebellion against Spanish rule in 1674 in the city of Messina in Sicily led to the deployment of more than eleven thousand troops and to a number of naval battles in Sicilian waters in 1675–1676. These battles involved Dutch, French, and Spanish squadrons that sought to affect the operations on land. The French squadron outgunned the Spaniards in 1675 and therefore raised the Spanish siege of Messina that year, only for the Dutch, in response, to send a fleet.[18] Blockading by sea a fortress that was being besieged was a key way to help ensure its fall, not only by cutting off supplies but also by demonstrating the strength of the attacking power. Combined operations were also seen in the next war, that of the League of Augsburg (the Nine Years' War of 1688–1697).

Naval clashes in the Baltic were an aspect of combined operations. They were linked to expeditions and to challenges to maritime routes, notably those between Sweden and its possessions on the eastern and southern shores of the Baltic, routes repeatedly attacked by the Danes. These possessions stemmed in large part from the success of Gustavus Adolphus's campaigns. At Riga, the major city in Polish-ruled Livonia, in 1621, Gustavus mounted a complicated siege supported from the sea, with much fire support from warships. The Poles were defeated. As a result of a similar victory at Narva in Estonia in 1581, the Swedes drove the Russians from the Baltic for over a century. Gustavus's intervention in Germany was initially dependent on a large-scale combined operation in 1630 that transferred his army to Germany.[19] Subsequently, in 1632 at the Lech River, Gustavus mounted a successful river crossing that defeated the opposing Austrian army.

In 1676, supported by the Dutch, the Danes attacked the Swedes in a combined operation on and off Scania (southern Sweden). In 1700, a surprise Swedish amphibious landing under the young Charles XII on the island of Zealand (which contains Copenhagen) drove Denmark to peace. In 1715, a Danish-Prussian landing of 17,500 troops on the island of Rügen cut off the Swedish garrison at Stralsund (in modern Germany) from hope of relief. It surrendered soon after.

On the Atlantic coast, combined operations played a major role in successful royal efforts to defeat the Huguenot (French Protestant) rebels and, in particular, seize their major stronghold, the port of La Rochelle. Blockade was a key element, and one that linked the seizure of positions on land, notably on offshore islands, and the establishment of naval superiority. A large-scale but mismanaged English relief attempt was defeated in 1627, and La Rochelle was starved into surrender the following year, a success that required the royal forces to engage in combined operations because of the geographical situation of La Rochelle.[20] This was the key military campaign against the Huguenots and one that was important to the consolidation of the position of Cardinal Richelieu as the leading minister of Louis XIII.

In the British Isles in the late 1630s, 1640s, and 1650s, conflict on land was crucial, but there was a combined component. In 1639, James, Third Marquis of Hamilton, operating on behalf of Charles I in eastern Scotland, seized local shipping as he moved south but was thwarted by the limitations of support for the king.[21] In 1642–1646, during the First Civil War, combined operations were involved both in mounting and raising sieges (for example, by the Royalists of Parliamentarian-held Plymouth, Lyme Regis, Hull, and positions in Pembrokeshire, all of which were supported by the Parliamentary navy) and in deploying troops along the coasts and across the sea, notably by both sides between England and Ireland. The Cromwellian invasions of Ireland and Scotland and occupation of the Channel Islands in 1649–1651 were dependent on maritime power projection and logistical support.[22] Thus, in 1649, Cromwell landed at Dublin with twelve thousand veterans, and in 1651, he used his command of the sea to outflank the Scots at Stirling and capture Perth. The navy protected his supply routes.

Combined operations were also significant for large-scale invasion attempts of the British Isles. In 1688, the English navy, although large and undefeated, failed, as a result of contrary winds and divided leadership with differing political views, to block the invasion of England by the Dutch under William of Orange, who became William III of England by overthrowing James II. As a result of this failure, there was no naval battle in what was one of the most successful combined operations of the century. The wind was important for its influence both upon the navigation of ships, ensuring that William landed in Torbay and not, as originally intended, Yorkshire, and also with sea conditions in the landing zone.

In contrast, in 1689, French intervention in Ireland on behalf of James II, who was supported by the Irish Catholics, and, in 1692, preparations for a French invasion of England led to battles respectively at Bantry Bay and Barfleur. In the former case, a French covering squadron drove off an English attempt to stop the landing of a French force in Ireland.[23] This force had to be defeated in conflict ashore in 1690, at the battle of the Boyne, as also, after another French landing in Ireland at a smaller scale, in 1798 when the French surrendered to a far larger British force. In contrast, in 1692, the defeat of the French covering squadron meant that there was no invasion of England.

Combined operations were of varied significance and type in the campaigning in and about Ireland. This was dramatized on July 28, 1689, when the city of Londonderry, then under siege by supporters of James II, was relieved by the fleet after the boom across Lough Foyle blocking the harbor had been broken. In August 1689, the port of Carrickfergus surrendered to William's troops after a two-day bombardment by warships and shore batteries. The following year, an expedition of William's forces under John Churchill, Earl of Marlborough, captured Cork and Kinsale, the major ports on the south coast, which made French reinforcement of the Irish from the Breton ports more difficult and enhanced English naval capability. In September 1691, the last Irish Catholic stronghold, Limerick, fell to William's forces: its siege had been supported by a naval squadron at the mouth of the River Shannon that blocked the prospect of French reinforcements.[24]

There were also relevant institutional developments in Europe. In Spain, the Marine Corps was established in 1537. For the standing navy created in the 1580s, Marine infantry were organized in *tercios*, with identical structures to those of the *tercios* of the army in Spain. With *tercios*, in reality administrative bodies, each including companies divided among ships,[25] the company at sea was the key battle formation. Portugal followed in 1618, France in 1622, and the Dutch in 1655.

In England, the Marines, in the shape of a "Marine" regiment, developed during the reign of Charles II (1660–1685) and were a response both to the value of combined operations apparent during the previous civil wars and interregnum period and to the particular issues posed by Charles's need to create forces in a developing crisis with the Dutch Republic. Charles wanted a force of seagoing soldiers for such a conflict, and a body known as the Admiral's Regiment, and under the command of his brother, James, Duke of York, the Lord High Admiral (later James II), was formed in 1664. It became known from 1672 as the "Marine" regiment and took part in the Second (1665–1666) and Third (1672–1674) Anglo-Dutch Wars. It was also used for overseas tasks in the Low Countries and in the English colony of Tangier, in 1678 and 1680 respectively. Disbanded in 1689, when the military system was overhauled as part of the Glorious Revolution and the men were drafted into the Coldstream Guards, the Marines were reestablished under William III (r. 1689–1702) in 1690, in order to give force to his amphibious campaigns. They served with the fleet until 1699, when they were transferred to the army.

For Denmark (which also ruled Norway), the navy could enlist marines, but there was no standard organization until a Marine regiment was established in Norway (ruled by the king of Denmark) in 1671. The first Marine regiment in Denmark was established in 1680. It was part of the navy but was transferred to the army in 1682. During the Great Northern War (1700–1721), the Marine duty was performed by troops from the infantry and another specialized Marine regiment was not established until 1798. Savoy-Piedmont participated in the battle of Lepanto in 1571, but a Marine battalion was not then established until 1717, four years after the acquisition of Sicily gave the state a more pronounced, albeit short-term, maritime role.

NON-WESTERN POWERS IN THE SEVENTEENTH CENTURY

The combined operation that excites most attention outside Europe was the Chinese conquest of Dutch positions in Taiwan. In 1661, Taiwan was invaded by Zheng Chenggong, known to Europeans as Coxinga. With the profits of piracy and trade, he developed a large fleet based in the southeastern Chinese province of Fujian and amassed a substantial army of more than fifty thousand troops. In 1656–1658, thanks to combined operations, he regained some of the coastline of southern China from the Manchu for the Ming claimant to the empire, only to be driven back in 1659. Deprived of his mainland bases, Zheng turned his attention to Taiwan and, with a force of twenty-five thousand men and three hundred junks, captured the Dutch bases in 1662. In turn, the Manchu used a newly constructed navy to force Taiwan into surrender in 1683, a process aided by serious division among Zheng's successors.[26]

In the Indian Ocean, the principal non-Western force able to deploy naval power across a considerable range and to mount combined operations was the Omani Arabs. Under Sultan Ibn Saif al-Ya'rubi, they captured the Portuguese base of Muscat in 1650 and, on the basis of the ships they seized there and the hybrid culture they took over, the Omanis created a formidable navy with well-gunned warships that enabled them to mount combined operations and amphibious assaults as well as to attack trade. The Omanis pressed the Portuguese hard, attacking their bases in India-Bombay (Mumbai) in 1661–1662, Diu in 1668 and 1676, and Bassein in 1674, and in East Africa, especially Mombasa.[27]

The key element of combined operations was the extent to which there was a determination to seize fortified positions as well as to raid settlements. The commitment involved in the former could be far greater, as seen in East Africa. In 1661, the Omanis sacked Mombasa but avoided the Portuguese fortress there, Fort Jesus, and, in 1670, pillaged the Portuguese base of Mozambique, only to be repulsed by the fortress garrison. Fort Jesus in Mombasa finally fell in 1698, but the siege had lasted since 1696 and the Omanis had no siege artillery. The Portuguese, instead, were weakened by beriberi and other diseases that killed most of the garrison. This was combined operations with a vengeance, or, more realistically, beyond the proper scope of the term. Men and microbes might in effect cooperate to deadly effect, but in practical terms, bar poisoning wells, there was little that could be done to ensure such an outcome.

In India, the Mughals had ships with brass and iron guns lashed on the decks. The big ships carried infantry, siege equipment, and cavalry and landed them along the coastline. The Mughals practiced this kind of warfare against the Portuguese; against pirates, notably with the capture of Sondīp Island and Chatgāon in 1665–1666; against the kingdom of Arakan in coastal Burma; against the Ahom in modern Bangladesh; and, in cooperation with the Siddis of Janjira, against the Marathas on the west coast of India. The Mughals also had light rowing boats for movement in the shallow estuaries.[28]

The struggle between Christendom and Islam extended to the Atlantic, both in operations against islands, such as the attack by an Algerine fleet on Lanzarote in the Canary Islands in 1618, and on the coast of Morocco. Thus, in 1614, La Mamora was captured by the Spaniards after an attack by troops on its land defenses at the same time as a naval assault.

CONCLUSION

The developing world of print politics, which became important in Europe notably from the seventeenth century, enables us to glimpse combined operations in the perspective of contemporary discussion, which is a perspective that remains important to the present. This development was particularly apparent in England (from 1707 Britain), as the pace, intensity, and public character of politics all increased following the Glorious Revolution of 1688–1689, which was itself the product of such an operation. The establishment of a system of annual parliaments and triennial elections combined in 1689–1695 with the lapse of many controls over the press, notably prepublication censorship, and the development of political parties, the Whigs and Tories.

These parties, especially the Tories, defined distinctive views on foreign policy and military strategy. During both the Nine Years' War (1687–1697) and the War of the Spanish Succession (1702–1713), the Tories fully contributed to the promotion of combined army-navy operations, otherwise known as "descents," along the French coastline as diversionary attacks to alleviate the stress upon the Allies' military situation in the "Cockpit" of Europe, the Low Countries, and also such operations in North America and the West Indies in an attempt to seize French and Spanish colonies there.[29] Thus, Tory foreign policy was engaged and expressed during wartime by a mixed and nuanced grand strategy that sought military progress both on land and at sea through the catalyst of amphibious action. This was a broad understanding of combined operations, one that saw them not only as a combination of means but also as a force-enabler for both.[30]

Such public discussion, which in Britain proved long-standing,[31] was rare on the global scale, but that does not mean that combined operations elsewhere lacked a grounding in policy analysis and strategic insight or an expression in a form of doctrine. Nevertheless, the publicity surrounding British combined operations, as well as Britain having the largest navy in the world from its supplanting of France in the early 1690s, mean that Britain has to be the center of scholarly attention from that period. This is not a case of Eurocentricity or Westerncentricity (both persistent problems in military history), as no other power engaged in combined operations on anything like this scale or with any comparable results. The British were also to be fortunate in their opponents, as France in particular proved to have a vulnerable empire, in part due to its having a much smaller population than that of Spain. Combined operations existed in both defense and attack, and England's, then (from 1707) Britain's, naval predominance left French imperial positions seriously exposed to attack.[32]

At the same time, an emphasis on such operations risks overplaying their relative significance to contemporaries. Most states, whether in Europe or

Asia and even more in Africa, pursued conflict overland, whether against foreign rivals or domestic discontent. Moreover, the social prestige of military service rested in most European, Asian, and North African societies on the cavalry and certainly on the army. This emphasis created normative assumptions about behavior. There were different ones in maritime societies, notably Venice, but as far as armies were concerned, the focus on the cavalry had an impact, albeit an intangible one, on combined operations. If a cavalry culture could adapt to greater infantry firepower and related organizational and tactical changes, as widely happened in the sixteenth century, that did not mean that it did so to the extent of necessarily favoring combined operations involving a navy.

On the one hand, Charles V's willingness to take part in the expeditions to Tunis in 1535 and Algiers in 1541 was instructive, but, on the other, most monarchs did not take a comparable role. Philip II had fought in battle on land but not at sea, and the same was true of French and Turkish counterparts. Suleiman the Magnificent was at the siege of Rhodes in 1522, but he did not play a subsequent role at sea. He was too old for the Malta expedition in 1565, but his presence could well have made a decisive difference. The lack of "ownership" of such operations by the traditional ruling caste possibly helped underline their interest to urban groups and notably in the developing public sphere.

Chapter Three

The Eighteenth Century, 1700–1775

The eighteenth century saw British combined operations become a key force in global history. They changed the face of the world by ensuring that Britain became the most dynamic and successful of the European oceanic powers. Equally, the failure of this British capacity was crucial to the military success of the American Revolution (1775–1783). This chapter focuses on England (from 1707, Britain) and its opponents before turning to look at developments elsewhere, from the Baltic to Hawaii. Alongside this approach, it is important, as always, to note the suffering and casualties involved in such operations, not least in order to avoid any triumphalism. For example, on June 8, 1758, Richard Humphrys of the 28th Regiment of the British army (a unit that had taken part in the aborted expedition to Louisbourg in 1757) recorded of the successful attack on this major French base in 1758:

> About three in the morning the men of war began to play against their batteries and breastworks, and the troops being in their boats two hours before day. . . . About six the signal was made to land, when the whole set off with the greatest eagerness and a terrible fire began on both sides, that nothing was seen or heard for one hour but the thundering of cannon and flashes of lightning, where the never daunted spirits of British soldiers landed and forced their way through the batteries and breastworks, as soon as the enemy found that we had landed and that they could not make any farther resistance, they gave way and began to retreat in great disorder leaving us to take possession of all their works. The attack on the right behaved gallantly and forced their way through the rocks, but unfortunately as one of the boats was making for the shore a wave took her and she overset, being loaded with grenadiers.[1]

All bar one drowned, but the British were able to land and to exploit the landing.

BRITAIN LAUNCHES FORTH

The War of the Spanish Succession, in which Britain participated from 1702 to 1713, created a range of opportunities for combined operations that was greater than that in the previous Nine Years' War (1689–1697). In part, this was because the fate of the Spanish empire, the largest and most far-flung in the world, was at stake. The two claimants to the succession each drew on formidable alliance systems, and these included the leading naval powers, all of whom were European. This empire encompassed not only Spain and Spanish America but also Mediterranean possessions that could only be attacked by sea. This was the case with Sicily, Sardinia, and the Balearic Islands, while cities on landmasses, for example Barcelona and Naples, were also highly vulnerable to attack by sea, which helped to ensure the efforts made to fortify them.

The significance of combined operations was increased by Britain playing a major role in the alliance and being determined to use its naval mastery in order to help direct the war effort and to gain subsequent territorial and other advantages. This determination reflected domestic political drives as well as strategic goals, alliance diplomacy, and military opportunity. As Britain was at war with France, as well as trying to seize the Spanish empire for its ally, the Austrian archduke Charles as Charles III of Spain (and make gains for itself), the opportunities for action were unprecedented. These were further enhanced because Britain also had to protect its own maritime empire, and the best way to do so was to launch attacks on opposing bases.

Naval action alone could not secure these advantages because of its dependence on wind and current, the need for bases in order to prepare expeditions and support naval operations,[2] and the inherently transient nature of blockades. Instead, it was necessary to capture the bases of other powers in order to limit their options, a task that involved a very different capability to that of naval action alone. Such attacks were another aspect of blockade. It was better to seize a fully prepared transoceanic base from a rival than to create a new one with all the costs entailed and the uncertainties as to whether an appropriate site had been chosen.

At the same time, there was need for less military support in attacking most transoceanic French targets than if proceeding with combined operations against French bases on the European landmass. In the latter case, although it took time, especially in the case of Brittany, France could readily deploy many troops to counter landings. Attacks on coastal positions in Spain offered an in-between target, as the prospect of the defenders rapidly deploying a matching or greater defensive force was much less than in France, where the army was much larger and the topography more suitable for responding to attacks on the coastal periphery. In contrast, in the Americas, Spanish colonies, notably Mexico, tended to be more populous than those of France and, partly for that reason, the colonies had greater strategic depth. As with other forms of military activity, the prospect of success owed much to the nature of the likely opposition, a point that was (and is) always pertinent for combined operations and amphibious assaults.

From 1703, when Portugal became an English ally, there was the possibility of a land base for attacks on Spain in the shape of neighboring Portugal. However, the logistical issues posed by operating in and from Portugal were acute, as were those of terrain and summer heat. Instead, it was far easier to consider operating from the sea. This was especially so as the English were generally less concerned with advancing into the hostile Castilian interior from Portugal than with establishing a presence on Spain's Mediterranean coast where support for the British claimant was strongest, notably in Catalonia. More generally, shifting alliance structures offered possibilities for, as well as impediments to, English combined operations. Alongside England's naval strength and the modest size of its army, this factor spurred combined operations.

Combined operations were mounted from the beginning of the war in 1702. In September, a mismanaged amphibious English attack on Cadiz failed. The repetition of such places in the narrative reflects the significance of attacks on major naval bases and important coastal cities. In this case, England deployed a large fleet as well as fourteen thousand troops, but the naval and army commanders differed. It was particularly unclear how best to treat the Spaniards: England was intervening in a disputed succession there.

Yet, the following month, combined operations were important to success at the expense of the Spanish treasure fleet. Crucially, as had not been the case at Cadiz, the Spanish reliance on safe ports was shown to be flawed. An Anglo-Dutch amphibious force successfully attacked the Spaniards at Vigo. The treasure fleet from the New World was protected by a floating boom and strong batteries. However, the southern battery was captured by an amphibious force, the boom was broken by the *Torbay* under heavy fire on October 12, 1702, and the following engagement was decisively won by the Anglo-Dutch fleet. Paul Methuen, the English envoy in Lisbon, reported:

> Our action at Vigo has been so great a blow to the French and Spaniards, that if ever they recover of it, it will be but very late; and the ill consequences of it in Spain, where it has put all things out of order, and into the greatest confusion, discover themselves every day more and more.[3]

The triumph was celebrated in England in songs such as "The Vigo Victory," songs that helped establish norms for expecting and interpreting future success. Such norms were generally highly misleading as they focused on martial resolution as the key to success and ran down the fighting caliber of opponents.

The range of combined operations was greatly increased by the attempt to establish Archduke Charles. John Chetwynd, the English envoy in Turin, commented in 1704 about the plan to send an English fleet to the Mediterranean: "Unless there are 10,000 soldiers aboard the fleet it will not have that respect paid to it which it deserves."[4] English amphibious forces captured poorly manned Gibraltar in 1704; Barcelona in 1705; Alicante, Majorca, and Ibiza in 1706; and Minorca and Sardinia in 1708, although a combined operation, mounted by the British navy and the Austrian army, failed against Toulon in 1707. Moreover, this was not the limit of combined operations. Naval strength ensured that positions once gained could be protected, as with Gibraltar in 1704 and 1705, finally thwarting French naval moves and a French siege, and the same with Barcelona in 1706. The effort involved was considerable. For example, the supplies necessary for British squadrons were formidable,[5] but the challenge was met and the fleet was the largest in the world.

When the War of the Spanish Succession broke out in 1702, six new regiments of Marines were raised for the English fleet. These Marine regiments took part in the capture and holding of Gibraltar in 1704 against French and Spanish attack for eight months, a magnificent combined operation undertaken with the Dutch. The successful defense was due to the inability of the Spanish and French fleets to blockade the port and the success of the English navy in keeping the garrison supported and resupplied. The whole Gibraltar episode encapsulated the nature of combined operations, including the vital role of ports for the maintenance of power projection and the equally crucial role of naval forces in keeping the garrisons of ports resupplied and reinforced where necessary. Equally, the task of besiegers required the assistance of naval forces to blockade and isolate garrisons. The Corps of Marines was not established on a permanent basis until 1755 and became "Royal" in 1802.

At the same time, the war in Spain demonstrated the limitations of combined operations as well as of invasion from Portugal. It proved far easier to intervene on the coastal littoral of Spain than to control the interior. The projection of amphibious force within the interior was highly dependent on a number of variables, but for it to be far and successful, local reinforcement and support, or at least acceptance, was crucial.[6] Madrid was occupied by Allied forces briefly in 1706 and 1710, but Castilian loyalty to the French candidate for the Spanish throne, Philip V, and Louis XIV's support to his grandson proved too strong. Allied forces in the interior were defeated.

Moreover, the British found that France itself proved a difficult target for combined operations, a situation that looked toward subsequent wars. There were bold plans as the British moved to the offensive. Thus, in July 1708, Joseph Addison, an undersecretary of state, wrote to a British diplomat:

> Our expedition is ready to embark and only wants a wind, so that we expect the alarm in France will be universal if the Duke of Savoy and Elector of Hanover can make an irruption at the same time that the Duke of Marlborough's detachment is ravaging Picardy and as our expedition is moving along the sea coast.[7]

This was not to be. Marlborough tried many times, from 1708, to convince Prince Eugene, his Austrian counterpart, and the Dutch, who provided a major part of the Allied forces in the region, to mount coastal landings, especially at Dunkirk, in order to create a beachhead for a march on Paris. These plans were always rejected by Eugene and the Dutch. Thus, although the Whigs supported the plans, the land-minded opposition of both Austria and the Dutch proved crucial. Moreover, plans to intervene on the Languedoc coast of France on behalf of a Protestant rising in the Cévennes mountains in the interior proved largely abortive, and landings in 1707 and 1710 certainly did not sway the situation on behalf of the Camisards, the rebelling Protestants. The second led to the temporary capture of the port of Sète before reembarkation in the face of a buildup of French forces.[8]

In contrast, in 1707, there was a highly successful combined operation against Toulon with the total elimination of France's Mediterranean fleet thanks to the Anglo-Dutch naval bombardment, which was combined with a siege by Austrian and Piedmontese forces. The siege was stopped when it appeared clear that the city would not fall speedily and, instead, could resist until the arrival of overwhelming French forces. The Anglo-Dutch fleet played a key role in supporting the siege, providing cannon, supplies, and medical care. The Toulon campaign indicated both the growing importance of combined operations and the extent to which the key issue was not the seizure of territory but the achievement of particular strategic goals. Full success was achieved in destroying the fleet.[9] It is a mistake to judge the campaign in terms of seizing Toulon and exploiting it as a beachhead for further penetration.

There were fundamental problems facing any major combined operation designed to establish a long-term presence, notably the size of the French forces and the need to deploy thousands of troops to face them and others to secure the supply lines. The 1707 campaign showed that the French militia, although weak against regular troops in the open field, could be effective against convoys and small standing garrisons scattered along the main supply routes.

British forces also mounted combined attacks in the New World. For example, the island of St. Kitts in the West Indies was captured in 1702. In Florida, however, an attempt to capture St. Augustine, the major Spanish base, failed that year. Spanish warships from Cuba relieved the garrison, indicating the importance to operations on land of the situation at sea. Relief was more likely to come by sea when there was no strategic depth on land. Looked at differently, the maritime dimension as an aspect of the strategic depth made it hard to control the situation, as it was difficult to turn being locally predominant into any aspect of command of the sea. There was also a major systemic problem, one captured in 1703 by William Blathwayt, the English secretary at war, when he wrote to George Stepney, a diplomat:

> Our attempt upon Guadeloupe under the command of Captain Codrington has been so far unsuccessful that after plundering and spoiling the greatest part of the island we were forced to retire to our own islands by the fresh succours the French had received from Martinique. This they say has been chiefly occasioned by the disagreement of the sea commander with our land general which has been the bane of all expeditions from that against Hispaniola in Cromwell's time [1654–1655] downwards to this last instance but the influence of the Admiralty will always prevail to make it so.[10]

This systemic problem of land-sea command cooperation, a problem also seen with other powers, was greater than that between the army and the (independent) ordnance or artillery service. In addition, there were the problems of friction. Most notably, in 1711, a British attempt was mounted on Québec. However, it failed in large part due to the consequences of poor navigation in the St. Lawrence. The experience in combined operations that was to be displayed by Britain in the mid-eighteenth century was not to be gained without earlier failure, as well as setbacks at the time. It took a lot of experimentation and experience to reach the point where Britain could obtain the successes it was to have in the early 1760s.

The attack on Québec in 1711 was the culmination of a series of combined operations. In particular, New Englanders were happier mounting amphibious attacks than engaging in frontier warfare. The latter was a harsher course where they had to face Native Americans, the rigors of the terrain, and their opponents' effective transport system, which was based on birchwood canoes. The technology employed in frontier warfare was within the grasp of New Englanders, but there was a lack of adaptation to the environment. In contrast, in 1704, a 550-strong amphibious Massachusetts force attacked Castine but decided that Port Royal, the leading French base in Acadia (Nova Scotia), was too formidable an objective. When the latter was attacked in 1707 by a New England army, the assault miscarried badly. That failure increased pressure for a different form of combined operations, that of regulars and militia. However, as a crucial instance of the significance of context, that use was delayed by the demands of the European theater, which consistently received higher priority, while, more specifically, individual personalities and events played a key role.[11] In 1710, 400 British Marines joined with 1,500 colonial militia to capture Port Royal: the French garrison was only about one hundred strong. Instead of burning down the settlement and then leaving with their loot, the captors left a garrison in Port Royal.[12]

In 1711, a force of 5,300 troops in 31 transports escorted by 14 ships of the line, the largest expedition hitherto sent to North America by any power, was designed to improve Britain's position in negotiations with France and to vindicate the "blue-water" policies strongly advocated by the Tories, not least by distracting attention from the Duke of Marlborough's successful campaigns on the Continent: a focus on Marlborough was backed by the Whigs, who supported military cooperation with Britain's allies, notably the Dutch and Austria. Preparations, however, were hasty in 1711, generally a serious mistake in combined operations, and the British government relied too much upon their overoptimistic assumptions of logistical support from New England. Nevertheless, difficult relations between the New Englanders and the British commanders did not prevent the assembly of a large force at Boston, including more than one thousand militia. The loss, due to a nighttime error in navigation, of eight transport ships and nearly nine hundred men on rocks near Ile aux Oeufs in the St. Lawrence estuary led to the abandonment of the expedition. This ensured that the landward prong of the advance, one of 2,300 men from Albany on Montréal, gave up. The loss of nine hundred troops was a large number for such expeditions.

Failure in 1711, however, has to be set alongside the British willingness to make a major commitment. This reflected both an understanding of the significance of transatlantic centers and a willingness to deploy substantial army and naval forces.[13] At the same time, Britain was then greatly affected by the press of alternative commitments for both troops and warships,[14] a situation that was repeatedly seen and that needs to be borne in mind when evaluating operations.

In 1719, the international situation was very different, as Britain was allied with France and at war with Spain. The British followed the pattern set in the War of the Spanish Succession by launching a combined operation against the background of naval predominance. An expedition under Lieutenant-General Richard Temple, Viscount Cobham, was ordered to attack the Spanish Atlantic port of Corunna, Spain's base for any invasion of Britain. Thus, on the long-standing pattern, the combined operation launched by Britain was an amphibious assault designed as a form of forward defense. Judging Corunna too strong, Cobham instead attacked and captured the port of Vigo without opposition, destroying the shipping and military stores there. From Vigo, British troops captured nearby Pontevedra, destroying the arsenal, barracks, and stores. Two hundred twenty cannon were brought back to Britain as stores.[15]

British amphibious power was significant in the forward defense that bore fruition as this planned attack, but it was a French army, operating overland, that invaded the Basque country in 1719 and captured Fuenterrabia and San

Sebastian. The British army was simply too small for the task. It could play a role in combined operations, but the peacetime army was too small for effective and strategically significant campaigning inland on the Continent. This was a situation repeatedly seen in English/British operations, for example, those of the sixteenth century.

In 1726–1727, Britain and Spain waged a limited and undeclared war. The main components were an unsuccessful Spanish siege of Gibraltar and a British blockade of Porto Bello, a key port on the isthmus of Panama for the shipment of bullion from the New World to Spain. The conflict did not escalate, but there was much speculation about combined operations had it done so. These included the case of Spain's ally Austria, with Austrian interest in an invasion of Britain and British interest in action against the Austrian Netherlands (Belgium), and the threat of attack on Spanish Italy, notably Naples and Sicily. Concern about a possible Spanish attack led the British government to press for a French invasion of northwestern Spain in order to overrun likely invasion bases.[16]

Britain went to war with Spain again in 1739, the War of Jenkin's Ear, this time both powers alone. This war began with a dramatic combined operation that encouraged already ambitious views of what Britain could achieve by such means,[17] and thus could apparently obtain without the need to compromise its goals and efforts through alliances. Despite the problems that had repeatedly faced colonial expeditions by Britain (and others), support for them continued in Britain. This was partly made possible by the tendency to attribute the reason for failures to specific persons or several simple reasons, such as secrecy and the timing of departure. As a result, support for expeditions remained strong.[18]

In 1739, Vice-Admiral Edward Vernon, a bold and self-confident officer, with six ships of the line, attacked Porto Bello, which was defended by three fortresses, although the fortresses were neither well built nor well sited. The British warships were becalmed alongside the first but, with a heavy fire, silenced the fort before landing sailors and Marines who, climbing through the embrasures, took the surrender of the position. The other forts and the town then surrendered.

Despite the strong euphoria in Britain at a success that wiped out alleged past national humiliation, this operation indicated the limitation of such attacks: Vernon destroyed the fortifications, as he was in no position to retain them. In 1741, the situation appeared to change with the arrival in the West Indies of a British army, which was launched against Cartagena on the Caribbean coast of modern Colombia. Siege warfare in the tropics, notably if conducted in a formal manner, was never easy, but supporting fortresses were captured in March, and the fall of the city appeared imminent. However, an assault on the hill fort that dominated it failed. After disagreements about the best way to launch another attack in the face of heavy losses through disease, the troops reembarked in April.

This unexpected failure led to the bitter recriminations that are so often instructive for contemporary attitudes. Vernon blamed the army commander, Brigadier-General Thomas Wentworth, for moving too slowly to attack the city. However, Vernon's volatile nature created problems for combined operations when, totally misjudging the strength of the Spanish position and the determination of the well-led defenders, he refused to land his seamen. This lessened the manpower available and contributed to failure.[19]

Subsequent British operations in the Caribbean during this war suffered from the impact of failure at Cartagena and the consequent loss of impetus, morale, and confidence, although that did not make defeat inevitable. The next major target in 1741 was Santiago, a port in southeastern Cuba and one from which British colonies, notably Jamaica, could be threatened. Troops were landed, but they did not reach their goal and instead, as generally in the tropics, suffered heavily from disease before being reembarked. Vernon's decision to land the troops at Guantanamo Bay, more than eighty miles from Santiago, had foolishly exposed them to a long and dangerous advance through woody terrain ideal for Spanish guerrilla action.

Disease was the best defense for the Spaniards, but it was supplemented by the building of new fortifications, for example, those ordered in December 1741 for the Central American coast. These were to be supported by the construction of new warships. In opposition, as with other combined operations, the British also sought to draw on local support, notably of the Native Americans on the Caribbean coast, the so-called Mosquito Indians, who were well attuned to fighting on the coast, not least to moving by canoe. This represented a very different form of combined operations to that of the European forces, but it was one that was highly successful because it was matched to environmental considerations and, in particular, highly mobile.

A planned British attack on Panama also failed, in large part due to an inability to direct the dynamic of operations. Despite the agreed plan to land an outflanking force that would prevent the Porto Bello garrison from reinforcing Panama, Vernon adopted a course that allowed the garrison, in retreating, to do so. The Council of War then decided not to attack Panama, a caution encouraged by heavy losses due to disease. The army remained on Jamaica, doing little, until ordered back to Britain in late 1742, by which time it was clear that Britain would move to operations against France on the Continent as part of the War of the Austrian Succession in which France and Spain were allied. Indeed, fighting involving Britain and France began in Germany in 1743.

Combined operations, however, did not stop. Instead, the emphasis was on local forces, both in North America and in the West Indies. In the former, where the climate was better and disease less of an issue, the French fortified the port of Louisbourg on Cape Breton, and its warships challenged the British position in Acadia/Nova Scotia and also threatened New England interests in fishing, trade, and territorial expansion. As a result, the government of Massachusetts organized a force of three thousand militia, who sailed for Louisbourg in 1745. This force was transported by New England ships and supported by the small Leeward Islands squadron under Commodore Peter Warren.

Louisbourg was the best-fortified position in New France, one newly created on the Vauban plan. However, it was designed to resist attack from the sea and was most vulnerable by land, and the morale of the garrison was low. In April 1745, Warren blockaded the harbor, and the New England militia was able to land safely in Gabarus Bay. The attackers bombarded the land defenses, although inexperience led to casualties among the artillerymen, while Warren's blockade reduced the food available to the defenders. With the walls breached, and Warren able to force his way into the harbor, the governor capitulated in June. The Massachusetts militia had acted like European regulars.

In the Caribbean, a squadron sent to act against the Spanish settlements on the Caracas coast (Venezuela) in 1743 lacked the element of surprise and was beaten off when it attacked La Guayra and Porto Cabello. In 1748, a combined expedition, of troops from Jamaica and a naval squadron, captured Port Louis in French-ruled Saint-Domingue (modern Haiti), but a boom across the passage to the harbor led to the abandonment of the attack on Santiago in Cuba. As a result of the peace signed in 1748, Britain's wartime gains were all restored.

Combined operations were also important in Europe during this war. As in the War of the Spanish Succession, plans in 1744 for a major landing on the French coast in support of an invasion from the Austrian Netherlands (Belgium) proved fruitless, but there was far more activity in the Mediterranean. Now, however, the focus was not Spain, where Britain in this conflict lacked the entrées provided in the War of the Spanish Succession by alliance with Portugal and by civil war in Spain, but rather Italy. In 1742, a squadron entered the Mediterranean ordered to support Britain's new ally, Charles Emmanuel III, king of Sardinia, the ruler of Savoy-Piedmont. As a result, the Spanish army destined for Italy marched via southern France rather than crossing the Mediterranean. The British fleet then landed 1,800 Marines who helped Sardinian troops thwart the Spanish threat to Nice, then part of the Sardinian dominions. Charles VII of Naples, a son of Philip V of Spain, had sent his army north to help the Spaniards, but, in August 1742, a British squadron entered Naples harbor and threatened to bombard the city and land Marines unless Charles recalled his troops, which he did. This had a consequence for the war in northern Italy.

In 1743, the British fleet landed cannon and Marines in an unsuccessful attempt to protect Nice and, in 1744, provided supplies to the Austrian army operating south of Rome while also preventing France and Spain from sending troops by sea to Italy. In 1745, Genoa entered the war on the Franco-Spanish side, but in 1746, with British naval support, the Austrians and Sardinians conquered Genoa, liberated Nice, and invaded southern France. British warships also transported Sardinian troops to back a Corsican rebellion against Genoese rule and, when Genoa drove out its Austrian garrison, helped blockade the city.

Also in 1745–1746, the British government benefited greatly from naval support in its operations against Jacobite insurgents in Scotland. This was largely a matter of shipping British troops back from the Continent and of preventing French support from reaching the Jacobites, but there was also consideration of combined operations behind Jacobite lines, for example, the seizure of the ports of Aberdeen or Montrose.[20] In the event, troops were not landed at Montrose until after the Jacobites had evacuated the city. After victory at Culloden, combined landings were used in the "pacification" of the Highlands and islands.

In the French and Indian War (1754–1763), the British again benefited from combined operations, while also developing an institutional support in the shape of the Marines, which the Admiralty placed on a permanent footing in 1755.[21] The most successful attacks on the French in Canada were those in which naval power was used. These began with attacks in 1755 on the French positions in Cape Breton Island that threatened Nova Scotia: attacks mounted by a naval force combined with regulars and New England militia. In contrast, in inland operations, the British force that advanced on Fort Duquesne in 1755 was heavily defeated. In 1757, after the invasion scare of 1756 was surmounted, the British returned to the attack in Cape Breton, sending a large fleet to Halifax. It was designed for an expedition against first Louisbourg and then Québec.[22] However, poor weather and then the presence of a French squadron deterred the British commanders from attacking. This served as a reminder of the need to be clearly more potent at sea.

In contrast, in 1758, there was a successful attack on Louisbourg by a large and well-prepared force including 23 warships, 19 smaller ships, 150 transports, and 14,000 troops. Impressively detailed preparations included the formation of a joint staff to plan the landing and, more importantly, joint training at Halifax and a system of control for the landing boats. The net effect was a cohesive force. As in 1745, this attack concentrated on the landward defenses of the fortress. The siege and bombardment, in which the army and navy cooperated, not least with the provision of sailors to help haul the cannon and dig trenches, were effective. British cannon breached the walls, while British warships penetrated the harbor. The defeated French, who had not shown such army-navy cooperation, surrendered.[23]

In turn, Louisbourg served as a base later in 1758 as British combined forces captured Ile Saint-Jean (now Prince Edward Island) and raided the French fishing stations on the Gaspé Peninsula. On the other hand, the major British overland attack that year, that against Fort Carillon (later renamed Fort Ticonderoga) on the Lake Champlain axis into Canada, was a costly failure.

As a result of these contrasting outcomes, the British in 1759 concentrated on the St. Lawrence where combined operations could be mounted. Benefiting from reliable pilots and nearby harbor facilities at Halifax, both of which had been lacking in 1690 and 1711, the navy conveyed a force of 8,600 men under James Wolfe to nearby Québec. Quartermaster-general of the Rochefort expedition in 1757, of which he had criticized a drive among the land and sea commanders, Wolfe had played a major role at Louisbourg in 1758, notably in the landing.

The subsequent details of his 1759 campaign show the value of combined operations. Wolfe arrived near Québec on June 26, but the natural strength of the position, French fortifications, and the skillful character of the French dispositions thwarted him for more than two months. Initial moves failed, notably the repulse at Montmorency of Wolfe's approach on Québec. Winter neared, with all the problems it posed not just to logistics and operating, but to very survivability. (The same factor confronted the British in the Falklands War in 1982.) Wolfe risked a bold move. James Cook had thoroughly surveyed the St. Lawrence, and British warships had passed beyond Québec from July 18 onward and made upriver raids. The army was to follow and landed to the west of the city in the early hours of September 13. Some two hundred light infantry scaled the cliffs and successfully attacked a French camp of one hundred men. The remainder of the British force, fewer than 4,500 men, then landed and advanced to the Plains of Abraham to the southwest of the city, where it defeated the French army.

Québec's surrender ended neither the conflict nor the importance of combined operations. Indeed, British dependence on the latter was shown by the French riposte the following spring. This benefited from the closure of the St. Lawrence by ice, which deprived the garrison of both naval support and supplies. In turn, the opening of the St. Lawrence later in the spring of 1760 enabled a British squadron to arrive, destroy the French ships in the St. Lawrence, and bring reinforcements. The French raised the siege, and the British then advanced on Montréal, where the French forces in Canada surrendered. The 1760 campaign saw British forces operating both along the St. Lawrence and on the Lake Champlain axis, in each case with success.

Combined operations were also very important for the British elsewhere. This was especially true of the West Indies but was also the case in India and West Africa. There were failures. In 1759, an invasion of Martinique failed. This was not a failure on the landing beaches, where, more generally, naval mobility gave the British a major advantage. At Martinique, the British troops landed successfully, but, thereafter, the defending French militia proved adept in fighting in a dispersed fashion and in taking advantage of natural cover. The British commander, Major-General Peregrine Hopson, felt that he had inadequate forces to besiege the citadel at Fort Royal, the main French base, and to maintain his lines of communication to the landing base.

Guadeloupe was a second best that year, but one that demonstrated the importance of combined capability. The French position at Basseterre was heavily bombarded by Commodore John Moore's warships, and after the defending batteries had been silenced, troops were able to land and occupy the town. Driven into the mountains, the French soon surrendered.[24]

In 1761, a similar combination brought the capture of Dominica. On January 16, 1762, a force twice as large as that in 1759 landed on Martinique. Supported by sailors and Marines from the fleet, the troops cleared the fortified hills behind Fort Royal, built a battery on Mount Garne from which the fort could be bombarded, and cut it off from its hinterland. With no hope of relief, the French surrendered less than three weeks after the landing, and the fall of Fort Royal was followed by the surrender of the island on February 4. The islands of St. Lucia, Grenada, and St. Vincent were also captured from the French that year.

In 1762, when the war broadened out to include Spain on the side of France, British operations were launched against the Spanish bases of Havana and Manila. In each case, the navy provided crucial firepower and manpower to assist the army and, in doing so, maintained the dynamic of the campaign. A British force of twelve thousand troops, covered by twenty-two ships of the line, a major concentration, landed east of Havana on June 7, 1762. Operations were concentrated against the still-impressive Fort Moro, which commanded the channel from the sea to the harbor and was protected by a very deep landward ditch. On July 1, the British batteries opened fire, supported by three warships, but damage from Spanish cannon forced the latter to abandon the bombardment. The summer passed with the troops in siegeworks, which were hindered by the bare and exposed rock in front of the fortress, and in artillery duels. A third of the British force was lost to malaria and yellow fever, but the Spanish batteries were silenced by heavier British fire.[25] On July 30, the British exploded two mines on either side of the ditch, creating an earth ramp across it and a breach in the wall that was stormed successfully, enabling them to capture the fort. From there, artillery could dominate the city, and it and the Spanish ships in the harbor surrendered on August 13.[26]

Accumulated experience played a role. For example, William Howe, the adjutant general in this campaign, had served in the attacks on Louisbourg (1758), Québec (1759), and Belle Isle (1761). He was to go on to take command in North America in 1776–1778. The fall of Havana in the first campaigning season against Spain demonstrated an amazing degree of sophistication and skill based on such experience, both individual and institutional.

The expedition against distant Manila was on a smaller scale and more daring, but Manila lacked the defenses of Havana: the fortifications were weak, the garrison small, and attack on what was a remote base was not anticipated by the Spaniards. The project was mounted from Madras (Chennai) in India, where its commander, Colonel William Draper, complained that the small numbers he had been allocated "will sufficiently evince the impossibility of my acting against the place with the formalities of a siege. My hopes are placed in the effects of a bombardment or *coup de main*." Draper could only dispose of a single battalion of regulars, which, with additional sepoys, pioneers, and French deserters, provided a force of only 1,700 men. Fortunately, cooperation with the naval squadron, of eight ships of the line and two East Indiamen under Rear-Admiral Samuel Cornish, was very good. The admiral landed about one thousand sailors and Marines to help the attack.

Arriving in Manila Bay on September 23, 1762, and landing on the 25th, Draper captured Manila on October 6 after a vigorous advance that contrasted with the purposeful but slower operations against Havana. He had to move fast because of the breaking of the monsoon and its impact on the land and, in particular, on surface waters. This was a serious problem, as was the opposition from Filipino irregulars. However, Captain Richard Kempenfelt's capture of the well-equipped naval dockyard of Cavite enabled repairs to the warships, while, after the artillery mastered the defenses, Manila was stormed.[27]

It is instructive to contrast the 1762 capture of Manila with those in 1898, 1942, and 1945 by the United States, Japan, and the United States respectively. Technology was a key variable, but so also was the relationship between the dynamic of the attack and the determination of the defense. In 1762, 1898, and 1942, this relationship favored the attackers, but in 1945, the Japanese defense was determined and not disoriented, as well as having a stronger force vis-à-vis the attacker than the earlier episodes. This led, in 1945, to a difficult, lengthy, and costly capture, in part due to unimaginative American tactics. Such comparisons may appear far-fetched and ahistorical as they range across long periods of time. However, it is precisely the attempt to do so that provides insights, not only into development across time, the key element in military history, but also with regard to capabilities. Aside from other consequences in terms of increasing firepower and reducing the impact of disease and food spoilage, technological changes enhanced speed, although not for the Americans in and around Manila in 1945.

Nevertheless, for both sides, attacker and defender, it was not until the airborne dimension was brought in that it was possible for the crisis of the contested coast to be replaced by a broader landing zone, which offered the attacker a quantum leap forward in terms of opportunities and potential success. Prior to that, it is continuity, rather than change, that is most apparent. Another crucial problem was posed by the degree to which the attacker had not only the initiative but also the element of surprise. A lack of intelligence stemming from the limitations of reconnaissance was a continual problem for defenders.[28]

The captures of Havana and Manila in 1762 were major blows against the Spanish overseas empire, blows made more significant because they were not matched by Spanish gains at the expense of Britain. At the same time, there was a significant defensive combined operation in the shape of the deployment of an army to help protect Portugal from Spanish invasion. This task was successfully accomplished, thus denying Spain a possible negotiating tool in the eventual peace treaty. England/Britain's interest in combined operations in Portugal went back to the English role in the capture of Lisbon from the Moors in 1147 and had been important in the fourteenth, sixteenth, and seventeenth centuries, as it also was to be in the nineteenth. As the key element was the defense of Portugal from invasion, power projection was frequently important not so much in landing troops but rather in protecting and supporting those already landed and operating into and in the interior. This protection in large part was a matter of safeguarding supply and trade routes.

The British were also involved in combined operations on the French coast. This was seen as a second front that would divert French forces from the war with Britain's ally, Frederick the Great of Prussia, who went to war with France in 1756. He himself was more concerned to see British troops in Germany. However, the failure of a poorly organized attack on the French Atlantic port of Lorient in 1746 during the previous conflict—in part because it was not pushed home, but also because of issues of distance, time, and terrain[29]—did not prevent a repeat of the strategy. In 1757, William Pitt the Elder, one of the two secretaries of state, supported the idea of an attack on the French Atlantic port of Rochefort. This was seen as a way to employ forces (army and naval) that had to be retained in or near Britain for defensive purposes, as a way to resist pressure to send troops to Germany and yet reduce French pressure there, and as a demonstration that, in joining the ministry, Pitt had not thereby abandoned traditional "patriot" views of hostility to Continental interventionism. Rochefort was also part of the structure of the French Atlantic system and could therefore be presented as a target that helped British operations in North America.

Nevertheless, after the British reached the port's approaches on September 21, 1757, a combination of poor intelligence, inadequate cooperation between army and naval commanders, and indifferent and hesitant generalship led to a failure to attack the port. The combination of accurate information and decisive action, both essential to successful combined operations, especially if benefit was to be taken of surprise before larger opposing forces were deployed, was missing.

The consequences of this failure reflected the politicization of combined operations, including the problems, for Britain, of fighting a war in the glare of newspaper publicity, a situation that was to be seen on other occasions, notably the invasion of Walcheren in 1809 during the Napoleonic Wars. Public disquiet in 1757 led to the establishment of a Commission of Enquiry into the conduct of the generals and to the unsuccessful court-martial of the army commander, Sir John Mordaunt. Pitt played an active role in the last, appearing in order to criticize the generals. In contrast, William, Duke of Cumberland, whose influence Pitt held responsible for failure at Rochefort, espoused their cause.[30] Thus, the issue became part of the political battle between Cumberland and Pitt. The surviving son of George II, Cumberland was the key figure in army patronage.

In 1758, a plan for an attack on the French port of St. Malo was initially abandoned due to the apparent difficulty of the task. Instead, another port, Cherbourg, was successfully attacked on August 8, and its fortifications were destroyed. The force then reembarked. Without a second step of "inland" attack, any landing is more likely to be a raid. At the northern end of the Cotentin Peninsula, Cherbourg was more exposed to attack and less supported by nearby French forces than St. Malo. The following month, a force landed for an attempt on St. Malo had to reembark at St. Cast, with the loss of 750 men, in the face of a larger French army.[31]

Belle Isle, an island off the Breton coast, was captured in 1761 and held until the peace in 1763.[32] The British naval victory at Quiberon Bay in 1759 meant that the island was cut off from reinforcements. A second successful landing, achieved by climbing steep cliffs, which were not defended, led to a siege of the French fortress, which was strongly contested. Only after a successful breach was made, and knowing that there was no possibility of reinforcement, did the French surrender. This puts the feasibility of landings on the French mainland in perspective.

Even if successful, however, the military, strategic, and political effects of such operations were limited and were certainly far less than anticipated by supporters of the policy. A fundamental strategic imbalance affected combined operations. Whereas Britain could be threatened by invasion with serious consequences, France was far less vulnerable, thanks in part to the greater size of its armed forces. John, Fourth Duke of Bedford, observed to George III's favorite, John, Third Earl of Bute:

> Mr Pitt tells you, that by the conquest of Belleisle, you are enabled to spread the alarm so thoroughly over the whole coast of France which is on the Atlantic Ocean, so that the people will not be able to sleep quietly in their beds. But

> can we do more? Upon the continent of France, after they have had so long a time to guard against us in the material places, such as Bordeaux, Rochefort, Brest, Lorient and St Malo, I fear not, especially as it will be impossible to spare any more troops from hence or Ireland, without leaving your own coasts liable to be insulted, even by a handful of men. What then in our situation can be expected from our efforts during this summer from Belleisle? Why possibly the taking another island, or burning a few miserable villages on the continent.[33]

By 1763, the British had developed considerable capability and experience in combined operations and had repeatedly won success.[34] There was also a development in doctrine, notably with Lieutenant-Colonel (later Colonel) Thomas More Molyneux's 1759 book *Conjunct Expeditions; Or, Expeditions that have been carried on jointly by the Fleet and the Army, with a Commentary on a Littoral War*, which was a response by an army officer to the failure at Rochefort. Molyneux covered "operations that have been jointly transacted by the Fleet and Army," in short "this amphibious kind of warfare." He went back to the invasion by Julius Caesar as part of his discussion of seventy such expeditions involving England, a discussion that was alive to problems but more generally positive.[35] A different form of experience was offered by the posthumous publication in 1768 of James Wolfe's *Instructions to Young Officers*, which covered many aspects of the practicalities of joint operations. British vulnerability to invasion had helped push them to be aggressive and innovative, and having fewer troops than France helped spur them in the direction of these operations.

The British also developed ships designed for combined assaults on coastal targets. Bomb ships, such as HMS *Carcass*, launched in 1759 and on which Nelson served in 1773, were flat-bottomed and very stable. They contained artillery used to bombard coastal installations. These ships were not capable of precise targeted attacks but were useful in softening up an enemy's towns, fortifications, and will.

Landing craft were also developed. The attacks on the French coast in 1758 had highlighted a number of lessons. The need to land the troops in sufficient numbers, and as a coherent unit that could be quickly deployed, was appreciated. To do this, a uniform method of getting the troops to shore was required, which would ensure that the boats all reached the shore at the same time. The standard ships' boats were inadequate for large troop landings. On April 7, 1758, the Admiralty approved the design of a "flat bottomed boat, or landing craft." Only nineteen days later, the Navy Board witnessed demonstrations of the new craft and immediately ordered twenty to be built. They were ready at Portsmouth at the end of May and were employed during the landing at Cancale, west of St. Malo, in June. The version eventually brought into full service carried thirty-two Marines and sixteen rowers, with a petty officer or midshipman in charge and a small two-pounder cannon in the bow. The boats were stacked for stowage on board, and all of the benches and other items could be slotted into place before launch. The design held good for many years.

Whereas Elizabethan combined operations in Scotland, Portugal, France, and the Low Countries in the late sixteenth century had been greatly affected, in both planning and implementation, by the need to cooperate with allies, this was not a significant issue in the 1750s despite pressure from Frederick the Great. British success ensured that such operations remained a significant aspect of the public's understanding of distinctive British military power. It remains to turn to other states to see whether that approach was well grounded.

OTHER EUROPEAN POWERS

Britain very much dominated combined operations, both in capability and action, but it was not the only Western power involved in them. The moves of the others can be classified under two categories, first operations in European waters and then further afield, so long as that does not serve to detract attention from the degree to which there was therefore a range of capabilities for individual states.

Attention would generally focus on France, the second-ranking naval power and Britain's principal opponent. Thus, the French attacked British islands in the West Indies and British-held Minorca in the Mediterranean, the latter successfully so in 1756. They were less successful in 1734, when an attempt to relieve the city of Danzig (Gdansk) from Russian siege was defeated on land by stronger Russian forces, or in 1746, when an attempt to regain Louisbourg was thwarted by storms and disease. The French also deployed forces against non-Western opponents, as on the coast of Yemen.

The case of Russia is also instructive in indicating the range of opponents that Western powers could face. For Russia, these included Western opponents, notably Sweden, the Turks, and the local opponents of Russian expansionism in the Aleutian Islands and Alaska. In each case, Russia developed an impressive combined capability. This was especially so in the Baltic. There, an emphasis on the use of galleys, with the capacity they offered for transporting troops, that in part looked back to the Don River flotillas of the Russians, notably in the 1690s, was combined with the proximity of Russian bases, notably St. Petersburg; the direct interest of the Russian court, which was based there; and the vulnerability of Sweden and its territory Finland. The Russian navy was in practice an amphibious force from the start.

The Russians made an effective use of their galley fleet toward the end of the Great Northern War (1700–1721) when they ravished the Swedish coast in 1719, 1720, and 1721, landing naval infantry and burning down all the cities, iron mills, and major castles along the coast north of Norköping. They even threatened the capital, Stockholm, although the raid against Stockholm was stopped at the battle of Stäket in August 1719. The Russian raids were designed to undermine the Swedish economy and to increase the Swedish willingness to negotiate, and they succeeded in doing so. Much of the crew and the officers were recruited in the Venetian Empire among Slav-speaking Balkan peoples and thus drew on the existing expertise in galley warfare.

In 1742, the British envoy in Russia, Sir Cyril Wych, reported that there were 130 galleys in St. Petersburg, both Russia's capital and its chief naval base, in "constant good order," each with three cannon and able to carry two hundred troops, and that "with these they can make great and sudden . . . irruptions."[36] In 1753, there were rumors of an Anglo-Russian negotiation to transport Russian troops to Holstein by sea as part of a wide-ranging assault on Prussia. The naval side was more important than the creation of a distinct force of naval infantry or Marines, although the *Morskaia pekhota* (naval infantry or marines), about one thousand strong, was established by Peter the Great in 1705.

In response to Russian capability, Sweden enhanced the separate amphibious fleet they had had since the sixteenth century as a consequence of the general geographical conditions in the Baltic, creating in effect what became a special archipelago fleet, largely (but not only) in order to defend roadless Finland more efficiently. This force, known as the "Fleet of the Army" from 1756, was supplied with effective ships by the Scottish engineer af Chapman. The sole significant victory Sweden won during its war with Prussia in 1757–1762 was through the "Fleet of the Army" in an amphibious operation in the Stettiner Haf in Pomerania. The Danes had a long-established amphibious capability and used it during the Great Northern War, for example, in the capture of the island of Heligoland in 1714 and in a successful attack in 1719 on the island of Marstrand, which led to the destruction of the Swedish warships there.

The Russians also made extensive use of shallow-draft ships elsewhere. In 1737, one thousand boats were allegedly employed to transport forty thousand troops across the Sea of Azov, so that Crimea could be invaded during a Russo-Turkish war. In 1790, a Russian flotilla played a role in the successful siege of the Turkish fortress of Izmail on the Danube. With deep-draught ships, the Russians deployed in the Aegean in 1770, also landing troops, for example, in the Peloponnese. These did not have a significant impact, in part because of the inherent difficulty of the task and the limited landing forces, but also because the mission was secondary to an attempt to blockade the Dardanelles. Another Russian squadron blockaded and bombarded Beirut in 1773, extorting money in return for lifting the bombardment and occupying the city until the rest of the tribute was paid in 1774.[37]

Spain was a major player in combined operations, although without a particular doctrine or specific preparations in terms of distinctive boats. Its role brought together a powerful tradition; infrastructure, notably the Mediterranean galley base at Cartagena and North African bases, especially Ceuta and Melilla; and Spain's continued determination to play a major role in the western Mediterranean, both in Italy and in North Africa. Thus, successful major expeditions were launched against Sardinia in 1717 and Sicily in 1718 with thirty-six thousand troops landed in the latter case, and in 1734–1735, Naples and Sicily were conquered. In 1732, Oran in modern Algeria, which had been lost in 1708 during the War of the Spanish Succession, was recaptured. Algiers, however, proved more difficult, and two attempts to capture it failed.[38]

Spain also launched combined operations in Atlantic waters, although less successfully. In 1719, the main Spanish invasion attempt on Britain was thwarted by the weather, although a subsidiary invasion attempt reached Scotland, only to be defeated. In 1735 and 1762, British naval strength ensured that Spanish pressure on Portugal was exerted overland. In 1779, a joint Franco-Spanish invasion attempt against Britain, which reflected the conviction that such attempts could be valuable, fell victim to delays and disease. In contrast, Austria and Prussia relied on forces operating overland, as did France in Europe, although not against Britain.

There were French invasion attempts of Britain in 1708, 1744, 1745–1746, 1759, and 1779. These attempts indicated the problems of staging combined operations and also the need to put them in political contexts. The French decision to risk an invasion in 1744 was a measure of their determination to prevent Britain from blocking their Continental schemes. Defeated at Dettingen in Germany by a British army in 1743 and facing the danger of the loss of Bavaria, its major German ally, the French government decided on a knockout blow. This decision owed much to the discrediting of French ministers who had advocated a concentration of effort on campaigning in Germany and the rise instead of the secretaries of state who viewed the Jacobite option, that of the exiled Stuarts, with more favor.[39] Impressed by reports of Jacobite popularity in Britain, Louis XV decided on invasion. Dependent on favorable winds and tides, amphibious operations were notoriously difficult, and the French had little experience of them. Despite this, they were reasonably confident, hoping that their Brest fleet would be able to gain control of the Channel and enable an expeditionary force to sail from Dunkirk to the Essex coast.

Delays in preparation, however, proved fatal, for British warships, off Brest for reasons of observation, reported the French fleet, first as ready to sail and then as sailing. In response, the British took preparations. The French fleet was able to pass the British fleet assembling at Portsmouth, but the weather then gained the upper hand, scattering the Brest fleet and destroying many of the transport vessels prepared at Dunkirk. The expedition was abandoned but encouraged the British to focus on blocking future attempts, which they did successfully in 1745–1746 and 1759, in the latter case defeating the French covering fleet at Quiberon Bay.

NON-WESTERN FORCES

Outside Europe, there were, as in previous centuries, combined operations. For example, in modern Indonesia, the Buginese state of Bone mounted major raids by sea, and in the 1720s and 1730s, a Bugi pirate of royal descent, Arung Singkang, conquered part of east Borneo. As before, amphibious assaults were more important than battles between fleets, and a focus on combined operations meant that there was scant need for deep-sea capability. The crews of non-Western boats frequently fought with projectile weapons, which, in the eighteenth century, increasingly meant muskets instead of bows or javelins. A small number of canoes also carried cannon. In the 1780s, a free Black from Brazil introduced brass swivel guns in the canoe fleets of the coastal lagoons of West Africa. Due to their shallow draft and maneuverability, these fleets were more effective in inshore waters than the deeper-draft Western warships.

The use of sizable combined forces to pursue operational, indeed strategic, goals was seen in many conflicts. One with a lasting effect was the unification of the Hawaiian archipelago. Kamehameha used guns and cannon to help win dominance of the island of Hawaii in 1791 and of the islands of Maui and Oahu in 1795, with the key engagements occurring on land. In 1796, however, difficult waters and disease ended his plans to invade the island of Kauai.

Combined capability was also important in inland waterways, notably in North America and West Africa, providing vital operational and tactical mobility.[40] This was less the case in East Asia, as the Chinese wars with the Zunghars were entirely waged on land, principally in Xinkiang, Mongolia, and Tibet. However, in 1769, the Chinese forces preparing for the invasion of Burma sought to take advantage of the waterways there. Several thousand sailors were deployed as part of the Chinese force, while hundreds of boats were built locally.[41] In the event, they were not significant in the unsuccessful overland invasion, and the boats were burned before the Chinese withdrew. Further from the Chinese frontier, the rivers of Burma encouraged the powers there to develop and use combined capability, as with the capture of the cities of Syriam (1756) and Pegu (1757) by ‘Alaungpaya, a rebel who seized power. Lower Burma was particularly vulnerable to waterborne forces. The Burmese invasions of Siam (Thailand) focused on operations mounted overland, but there was an important maritime dimension, notably in 1785 when alongside an advance overland another force proceeded by sea from Tavoy to Phuket Island.

Combined operations lacked prestige in China, as was demonstrated by the use of Green Standard troops for the navy rather than the elite Manchu bannermen. Cause and effect can be confused, and Chinese combined capability for this period has not been well studied. Patrol craft were reasonably effective in maintaining order on China's extensive rivers, but less so in defending coastal waters against pirates, who were a long-standing problem, especially from the sixteenth to the nineteenth centuries.[42]

In the Islamic world, Nadir Shah of Persia was able to mount combined operations in Oman, deploying forces of several thousand troops across the gulf, although, in 1739–1740, an attempt to move by land and sea from Fars to Sind failed. Moreover, a lack of commitment by Nadir, comparable to that he showed for the army, helped lead to eventual failure.[43] Under Sultan Selim III of Turkey (r. 1789–1806), a corps of one thousand Marine fusiliers was created for the navy. Organized into two regiments, the men were trained for service on land and at sea and were capable of handling artillery and sail.

CONCLUSIONS

The British Royal Navy developed a very sophisticated doctrine of combined operations, one based on considerable experience.[44] Practicalities as well as policy, however, were at issue. Combined operations were greatly affected by bad weather and also by the possibility of such weather. There was a lack of weather-forecasting equipment. Charles, Third Duke of Marlborough, the commander of a British expedition, wrote from the Channel off Cherbourg in June 1758:

> We had been excessively unlucky as I was prevented three days ago from landing on the coast of Normandy by a gale of wind. . . . Last night I had everything ready to attack the forts of this place, just before we stepped into the boats the wind blew so excessive hard that we were forced to desist, and have had great difficulty in preventing some of the transports from being blown on shore.[45]

Three years later, Major-General Studholme Hodgson, the commander of the land forces in the Belle Isle expedition, reported at one stage: "We could get nothing landed yesterday, it blew so excessively hard."[46] At the same time, weather was scarcely the only limitation. In 1758, Holdernesse explained the failure of hopes of taking St. Malo, noting that Marlborough

> found that the place could not be carried without a regular siege; that roads must have been made in a most impracticable country for the artillery; and consequently that the undertaking would have taken up too much time, as the enemy would have been able to assemble a superior corps . . . and as the transport vessels could lie no nearer than Cancale, His Grace might have run the risk of having his retreat cut off; which induced him to reimbark the troops.[47]

The period up to 1815 was the last before capabilities were changed by steam power. Instead, capability under sail was amply demonstrated in all forms of combined operations and amphibious assaults. That remark suggests that technology was the basic driver of circumstances and change. While true to an extent, that interpretation underplays the role of politics in setting the context within which operations were mounted and their success determined in political terms. It is primarily for that reason that the period from the outbreak of the American Revolution in 1775, a period also without steam-driven warships, is separated out for attention in the next chapter.

Chapter Four

The American Revolution and the French Revolutionary and Napoleonic Wars, 1775–1815

The years from 1775 to 1815 represented an apogee in the pre-steam-power age of combined operations. British naval power and amphibious capability were called on for much of the period. In this, there were new versions of the already established distinction between operational success and strategic limitations. Combined operations enabled Britain to project its power but could not bring lasting success on land. The British were able to mount operations in what became the United States, but not to determine the outcome of war there, either in 1775–1783 or in 1812–1815, in the former case in part due to French, Spanish, and Dutch naval participation in war with Britain from 1778, 1779, and 1780 respectively.

In 1778–1783 and 1793–1815, the British were able to seize French and allied colonies and to mount attacks on French and allied coasts. Moreover, drawing on the legacy of Pitt the Elder, with the Peninsular War in Portugal and Spain from 1808, these attacks had already become central to the British idea of a distinctive type of war focused on avoiding conflict with the main opposing army but wearing down Britain's opponent through combined operations in secondary theaters. This concept became more significant from the 1790s, but the defeat of Napoleon, first in 1814 and then in 1815, was settled on land in the main theater and had the British army of Arthur Wellesley, First Duke of Wellington, been defeated at Waterloo in 1815, then advancing Austrian and Russian armies would probably have ensured victory. Thus, the ambiguous nature of sea power was fully revealed. It could protect crucial trade routes and deliver an important verdict against opposing fleets and therefore limit the risk of invasion and attacks on colonies. Nevertheless, as an offensive force, sea power had many problems, even when considering it in terms of combined operations focusing on amphibious landings.

THE AMERICAN REVOLUTION

The idea of bringing revolution to the Americas was not new. Indeed, the British had devoted episodic thought to it when considering action against Spain in Latin America during the eighteenth century. Thus, on February 17, 1750, *Old England*, a leading London opposition newspaper, suggested, at a time of peace with Spain, that

> the insurrection, which from its resolution deserves the name of rebellion, now in Peru, is an inviting circumstance to tempt us to fit out a fleet for the Caracas to assist a people that appear so ripe for a revolt, to set up themselves independent of the Crown of Spain.

In the event, such hopes proved fruitless, and it was to be French intervention on behalf of American rebels that proved a decisive instance of combined operations, most clearly so at Yorktown in 1781. In the first instance, however, the American Revolution provided a key demonstration of British capability in combined operations. This capability, indeed, ensured that the war continued. Initially, the British were driven from the Thirteen Colonies. This process was completed by the close of March 1776, when, under the threat to the British anchorage posed by the deployment of American cannon, they withdrew from Boston. In addition, the Americans were able to mount a successful invasion of Canada, capturing Montréal and beginning a siege of Québec.

However, in turn, the British, in 1776, used not only their mastery of the sea but also their ability to move and land troops in order to relieve Québec from siege, drive the Americans from Canada, and mount a large-scale invasion of the New York area. In this period, there was not a classic hinterland because most settlement was close to the coast. However, prior to that, a combined expedition against Charleston failed in part because naval gunfire could not overcome coastal positions.[1]

In the New York campaign, the nearest Britain came to victory during the war, the British, having landed unopposed on Staten Island, made an unopposed landing at Gravesend Bay, Long Island on August 22. Naval strength gave the British commander the ability to choose where he should launch amphibious attacks. As always, the prospect for combined operations was enhanced not only by the circumstances but also by the response of the other side. In particular, New York was impossible to hold with the forces George Washington had facing the power of the Royal Navy, which quickly proved that it could sail and land troops at will. Rather than concentrating his forces,

Washington placed them all over the harbor area, each section too small to do anything other than attempt to hinder a landing.

Once heavily defeated on Long Island, the American position on Manhattan, another island, was exposed to the threat of an amphibious British flanking attack. However, the bold proposal for a landing in the south Bronx, followed by an advance to cut off Washington's escape route from New York, was rejected by the cautious British commanders, who never made full use of the combined capability. Instead, there was a tendency to land amphibious forces in front or at the flank of American positions rather than behind them. On September 14, 1776, four thousand British troops landed at Kips Bay, halfway up eastern Manhattan near the site of the modern United Nations building. Captain William Leslie, a British army officer, reported:

> We landed under cover of the shipping, without opposition, although the Rebels might have made a very great defence as they had high grounds, woods, and strong breastworks to cover them, but they scoured off in thousands when the ships began to fire; indeed they are so outgeneralled that it is impossible for them to know where to prepare for defence.[2]

The American defenders, mostly Connecticut militia, fled in panic; but, far from being cut off, the American troops still in lower Manhattan were able to retreat up the west side of the island.

As success for the British snowballed, notably with the capture of Fort Washington at the northern end of the island, they moved on to invade New Jersey. The Americans then seized or destroyed all the boats on the Delaware River to prevent their opponents pressing on further toward Philadelphia, the capital of the Revolution, but that desperate step did not appear a decisive stop to combined operations for it was assumed that the British would press on when the river froze or when rafts or pontoons could be built. Moreover, General Sir Henry Clinton proposed sending the fleet carrying the necessary number of troops up the river. Instead, it was Washington who, near the close of the year, showed the ability to confront water obstacles, with a difficult night crossing of the icy Delaware River as a prelude to the defeat of the surprised garrison at Trenton.

In 1777, instead of resuming the overland advance on Philadelphia, General Sir William Howe decided to move by sea. However, the problems he encountered underlined the potential difficulties of combined operations and, in particular, the problems of trying to fit them into a time frame, problems that made both logistics and realistic planning difficult. Having been delayed by contrary winds, a factor that a sailing navy, as opposed to a rowing or rowing/sailing navy, could not counter, the fleet sailed from New York on July 23 but was becalmed on the 24th and 25th and affected by fog and thunder on the 28th. The Virginia Capes were not weathered until August 17.

The British troops finally landed at modern Elkton on August 25 without any opposition but having lost the initiative.[3] Washington was able to deploy in a blocking position behind Brandywine Creek to protect Philadelphia, although he was to be defeated there on September 11; Howe entered Philadelphia five days later. Later in the campaign, British warships supported troops in capturing Forts Mifflin and Mercer, which blocked the advance along the Delaware River to Philadelphia, but only after an attack on the first had been defeated, on October 22, with heavy casualties due to fire from the fort and its supporting ships.

The delays involved in this campaign did not cause the failure of the separate British campaign in the Hudson Valley, where an army advancing south from Canada was forced to surrender at Saratoga, but they contributed to making any cooperation between the spheres of British operations unviable. Those in the Hudson included what have been seen as a series of classic British amphibious landings, which, advancing north from New York, successfully captured the fortifications on the Hudson Highlands.[4]

The assumption that combined operations should be mounted could be found repeatedly in British planning. In the instructions on January 23, 1779, to Clinton, then the British commander, Lord George Germain, the secretary of state for the colonies, a former general who had not, however, served in North America, wrote:

> It is intended that two corps of about 4,000 each assisted by a naval force should also be employed upon the sea coasts of the revolted provinces, the one to act on the side of New England and New Hampshire, and the other in the Chesapeake Bay and by entering the rivers and inlets wherever it was found practicable, seize or destroy their shipping and shores and deprive them of every means of fitting out privateers or carrying on foreign commerce.[5]

In the event, there were insufficient troops, but a successful attack on the Chesapeake in May 1779 inflicted extensive damage, including on the shipyard at Gosport.[6] Washington responded by pressing for the removal of stores from coasts and navigable rivers, a comment on American vulnerability to British combined operations and the presence of a deep hinterland. In July, there were similar British attacks on the Connecticut coast at Norwalk, New Haven, and Fairfield, raids that the Americans could not thwart and that threatened their morale. At the close of 1778, a British combined force under Lieutenant-Colonel Archibald Campbell, who had served under Wolfe at the capture of Québec, seized Savannah, having outfought the poorly led defenders in winter weather that was well suited for this operation.

In 1780, combined operations proved important in enabling British forces to capture Charleston, the most important city in the South and one that they had failed to take in 1776 and 1779. The British fleet cleared Sandy Hook off New York on December 26, 1779, and mostly reached Tybee Island off

Savannah on January 30, 1780. However, the voyage also illustrated the drawback of such operations because, on December 28, a terrible storm struck the fleet off Cape Hatteras. Much of it was dispersed, one transport ship ending up off distant Cornwall, while most of the horses and much of the supplies, especially ordnance stores and entrenching tools, were lost. John Hayes, an army physician, suffered "full forty days beating the boisterous ocean."[7] As a result, the fleet did not anchor off North Edisto Inlet, thirty miles south of Charleston and the original destination, but instead went to Savannah for recuperation, repair, and better weather.

This delay, which underlines the precarious nature of amphibious operations in the age of sail, indicates the mismatch between claims that combined operations could have been more effectively managed by moving forces between America and the West Indies in order to achieve seasonally propitious annual campaigns in both and, on the other hand, the reality of a range of significant frictional factors. The fleet sailed again on February 10, 1780, and the troops were disembarked on Simmons Island on North Edisto Inlet. The British then closed in on Charleston, in a series of moves in which combined capability played a role. This was especially so of the crossing of the Ashley River at Drayton's Landing, twelve miles above Charleston on March 29. On April 8, seven warships forced their way past American fortifications on the north side of Charleston harbor, providing both firepower and a morale boost. A Hessian quartermaster recorded: "We could see nothing of the ships except the flashes of their guns because of the smoke. The majesty of this sight can hardly be described."[8] In subsequent moves, cutting-out parties of Marines and seamen took part in seizing American works. Heavily bombarded, the city, with 5,500 Continental soldiers, militia, and armed citizens, finally surrendered on May 12, the largest surrender of an American force during the war and to a "foreign" enemy until Bataan in the Philippines to the Japanese in 1942.

As so often happens, this dramatic instance of the success of combined operations owed much to the choices made by the defense. The unimpressive American commander, Benjamin Lincoln, was unwilling until too late and then unable to withdraw from Charleston, a position the retention of which was necessary for political and logistical reasons, but where he was at a serious disadvantage: surrounded and constantly hammered by a British force supported by naval firepower and supplies. The failure to defend outlying forts was serious, not least in affecting the time context within which the dynamic of a combined attack, or indeed any siege, could be lost, as the British had discovered at Cartagena in 1741 and nearly done so at Havana in 1762. This failure enabled the British to concentrate their army and navy against Charleston. Moreover, the defense was irresolute, unimaginative, and, on the whole, lacking the determined fighting spirit that the Americans displayed on so many occasions during the war.

This was not the close of British combined operations. An expedition under Benedict Arnold left New York on December 20, 1780, and, having been disrupted by a winter storm, reached Hampton Roads on December 30. Moving up the James River, the British landed at Westover on January 4, 1781, entering Richmond next day. They displayed a nimbleness and dynamic that the Union's Army of the Potomac under George McClellan was notably to lack in 1862: his far larger force was cumbersome but was also poorly handled.

Having destroyed much of the town and nearby supply bases, the British left on January 6, 1781, retiring, largely unopposed, to Portsmouth, where they established a base. The vulnerability of the Chesapeake to British combined operations had been amply demonstrated. On the 6th, Frederich Wilhelm Steuben informed Thomas Jefferson, the governor of Virginia, that he had "not heard of a single gun being fired at them either on their march from Westover or during their stay at Richmond."[9] However, in a classic instance of a common problem with such operations, Arnold felt that he needed reinforcements if he was to hold Portsmouth against a likely attack. Mounted from Charleston, another British operation took the port of Wilmington, North Carolina, without resistance, on January 28, 1781.

In the last stages of the war, it was, however, the combined operations of Britain's opponents that increasingly took a dominant role. The entry of France, the second-largest naval power, into the war in 1778 transformed the situation at sea, and this created possibilities for combined operations aimed against the British. The most significant were mounted by the French, who were joined in 1779 by Spain, another leading naval power, and in 1780 by the Dutch.

At the same time, looking back to earlier British (and therefore also British colonial) operations against French and Spanish colonies and, in part, to a popular understanding of tactics based on the Royal Navy's experience, the Americans developed a capacity for amphibious assaults, beginning with a raid on New Providence Island in March 1776. Whaleboats became one means to conduct such operations.[10] The Americans launched a major combined operation in 1779. In June, a British force from Nova Scotia established a post at Castine, on Penobscot Bay, on the coast of what was then Massachusetts and is now Maine. This post was designed to deny the Americans both a naval base from which they might threaten Halifax, Nova Scotia, the key British naval base in Canada, and timber supplies from the area. The General Court of Massachusetts, acting unilaterally without congressional assent or assistance, decided on a swift response, and a force of one thousand militia under Brigadier-General Solomon Lovell, supported by a fleet under Commodore Dudley Saltonstall, reached the bay on July 24. American attempts the next day to force the entrance of Castine Harbor and to land nearby failed. The Americans landed on the 28th, but although they outnumbered the British force, whose fort was very weak, they did not press their advantage and instead began slow siege operations. Meanwhile, Lovell and Saltonstall sought to shift the burden of the attack onto each other.

However, a British squadron arrived on August 13, and rather than fighting, the American force fled with serious losses to its shipping.[11] Castine was held by the British for the remainder of the war. The American debacle, which effectively knocked Massachusetts out of the war financially and for which Saltonstall was court-martialed and summarily dismissed from the service, indicated that the Americans lacked the combined capability enjoyed by the more experienced British and that temporary control of the sea did not have to bring decisive results.

These were not the sole failures for combined operations in 1779. Delays caused by the need to coordinate French and Spanish forces, and their effect in exacerbating disease in the invasion force waiting on board ship, put paid to an attempt to invade Britain. Inadequate supplies and poor leadership were part of the equation.[12]

The same year, a combined Franco-American attempt on Savannah safely concentrated forces there in mid-September, but bad weather and a lack of preparations delayed the siege. For example, the French cannon were not mounted on traveling carriages. After bombardment had failed to lead to a British surrender, the French admiral, Charles-Hector, Comte d'Estaing, insisted on storming the position, which would mean that his ships would have a secure base or could leave, even though the French army officers were opposed, as was the American commander, Benjamin Lincoln. The attack, mounted on October 9, was repulsed with heavy losses.[13] As with Newport in 1778, where the American land commander and his French naval counterpart did not see eye to eye,[14] a situation complicated by language problems, the combined operation worked in creating the opportunity but not in enabling it to be effectively implemented.

Much greater success was achieved in 1781. In May, Pensacola, the major British base in West Florida (the panhandle of modern Florida and coastal Alabama and Mississippi), fell to a far larger Spanish force. The significance of combined capability in defense was underlined when the British commander attributed his defeat "to the notorious omission or neglect, in affording Pensacola a sufficient naval protection and aid."[15]

More generally, the British army that year fell victim to a naval strategy that could not ensure a close blockade of French ports and therefore the retention of French warships in European waters. François, Comte de Grasse, was able to leave Brest, France's major Atlantic naval base, for Martinique with twenty ships of the line in March 1781, just as d'Estaing had been able to leave the Mediterranean in 1778.

In August 1781, encouraged by Spanish support,[16] de Grasse and three thousand French troops sailed from Saint-Domingue (Haiti) for the Chesapeake. This move provided the Americans and French who had concentrated troops there with crucial naval superiority. British commanders were aware of the significance of the issue, but they lost control of the naval equation. As a result, French troops were able to land in the Chesapeake, while, with the British navy failing at the battle of the Virginia Capes on September 5, the most consequential victory in French naval history, there was no relief for Yorktown when the British force was besieged there. Its surrender fatally undermined political and public support for the war in Britain and thus ensured American success even though neither New York nor Charleston subsequently fell to American attacks. Indeed, the strength of British naval and land forces was such that, despite American efforts in 1782, these defensive positions could not be recovered until the British chose to evacuate them as part of the peace.

Combined operations were also mounted elsewhere during this war, notably in the West Indies, Central America, West Africa, the Indian Ocean, and the Mediterranean. In each case, cooperation between land and sea forces emerged as a key element, and due to the pace of activity, experience increased. For example, the successful British siege of Pondicherry, the major French base in India, in 1781 owed much to support from Sir Edward Vernon's squadron. On the pattern of successful combined operations, it both blockaded Pondicherry and landed Marines and sailors to help the siege. Repeatedly, this cooperation was a key tactical advantage, although it created major issues for coordination. Many of the British army and naval commanders had relevant personal experience from recent years, while the value of accumulated knowledge was reflected by the publication in 1780 of a second edition of James Wolfe's *Instructions to Young Officers*.

THE FRENCH REVOLUTIONARY AND NAPOLEONIC WARS

This experience proved useful in the French Revolutionary War in which Britain joined in 1793. That experience, however, did not necessarily mean success. Indeed, there was a series of British failures, including at Toulon (1793), at Ostend (1798), in Holland (1799), and at Belle Isle, Ferrol, and Cadiz in 1800. The reasons for failure throw much light on the difficulties attending joint operations. At Toulon, a British fleet supported local Royalists, but Napoleon used artillery to make the harbor untenable by the fleet, as Washington had done at Boston in March 1776, obliging the British warships to leave. In 1798, a raid was mounted on Ostend in order to destroy the lock gates of the Bruges canal and make it harder for the French to use the canal system for invasion preparations. This anticipated what the British were to do when the Germans held the area in 1918 in order to block submarine operations. In 1798, 1,300 troops disembarked and cut the sluices at Ostend, but a strong wind prevented the ships from coming in to allow the troops to re-embark, French reinforcements arrived, and the British were forced to surrender. Evacuation was/is always a key element in combined operations.

These failures were matched by successes for British combined operations, including the capture, in 1798, of Minorca, a target that was important due to its potential as a naval base. However, neither successes nor failures were of key significance for the war. Instead, the other powers of the coalition against France were defeated on land, and Austria crucially made peace with France in 1797, leaving Britain isolated.

The War of the Second Coalition played out in similar fashion, although, again, Britain made a major attempt with combined operations. The most important in Europe was an attack on the Low Countries in 1799, designed in cooperation with a Russian force. Launched against the northern coast of Holland, this attack was intended to seize the Dutch fleet, a key element in the naval balance, but also to encourage an uprising against the pro-French Batavian Republic and in favor of the pro-British exiled House of Orange. The expedition was mismanaged. More to the point—for many expeditions were mismanaged—it was unsuccessful. The goal was unclear and the necessary planning had not been carried out: too little was known about the terrain, the opposing forces, and the attitude of the population, and much of the available information was inaccurate. Moreover, the French were expecting an attack.

At first, the expedition went well, creating new hopes. The British force under Sir Ralph Abercromby landed safely south of Den Helder on August 27, and a French counterattack was driven back, in part thanks to covering fire from the British fleet. The capture of Den Helder, and thirteen disabled Dutch warships, opened the Texel Passage to the Royal Navy. A squadron sailed into the Zuider Zee, where a mutiny led to the surrender of the rest of the Dutch fleet. Abercromby, however, rested inactive for three weeks while he waited for Frederick, Duke of York, the British commander, and the Russian force, and the expedition lost the vital dynamic of success. In addition, troops were not provided to support the idea of a combined operation against Amsterdam or the eastern shore of the Zuider Zee where the navy had captured several towns. From September 19 until October 6, the Anglo-Russian forces fought the French, but the latter blocked them. Affected by poor weather, supply issues, and sick troops, York, on October 17, signed the Convention of Alkmaar under which they were able to evacuate in return for handing over their French prisoners. The failure was greeted with much criticism in Britain and is remembered in terms of the satirical popular song "The Grand Old Duke of York," although other bases for the song have been advanced.[17]

The Royal Navy, however, played a major role in forcing the French out of southern Italy. The French had entered Naples in January 1799, the court escaped to Palermo, and Anglo-Neapolitan forces burned the Neapolitan fleet to prevent the French seizing it. However, in February 1799, a Sicilian irregular loyalist force on behalf of the king of Naples landed in Calabria, the southernmost part of the mainland, and started reconquering the kingdom of Naples. In addition, a thirty-two thousand Russo-Turkish expeditionary force with forty men-of-war captured Corfu and then arrived on the Adriatic coast of Italy. It landed in lower Apulia and marched north, capturing the cities of Taranto and Foggia, before moving west and capturing Ariano, Avellino, and Nola. At the same time, an Anglo-Sicilian force threatened Naples. On April 15, 1799, five hundred (Sicilian) Neapolitan regular loyalists were landed from British ships together with British forces, seizing Castellammare di Stabia and its naval arsenal. A second Anglo-Sicilian force landed south of Naples at Salerno (where the Allies were to land in 1943) and approached Naples, seizing en route the towns of Vietri, Cava, Citara, Pagani, and Nocera. Although the French troops reacted well against the attackers, subsequent Anglo-Sicilian seizures of the islands of Ischia and Procida in early May completed the blockade, and Naples was captured on June 13. Subsequently, Allied forces, including a British naval blockade of Genoa, cleared Italy of the French in 1799.

In 1800, attempted British landings at Belle Isle, Ferrol, and Cadiz all failed, and Charles, Marquess Cornwallis, described the army as the laughingstock of Europe. Failures meant that Britain's diplomatic weight in the Second Coalition against France was lessened. With more understanding, Henry Dundas, the secretary of state for war, replied to Major-General Thomas Maitland's explanation of why he had decided not to attack Belle Isle: "It was certainly judicious in you under all circumstances not to expose the troops under your command, by attempting a landing in the face of a superior force, possessing in addition to the natural strength of their position, a strong fortress to support their operations."[18] Less sympathetic, Vice-Admiral William Young wrote to his wife from Vigo Bay on August 30:

> We arrived here yesterday from Ferrol Bay, where the troops landed, and made a kind of attempt on Ferrol, where several sail of Spanish men of war lay; but the General did not think it advisable to make a formidable attack on it—therefore after being on shore about 24 hours the troops embarked again, with a trifling loss—I confess myself, as well as the naval gentlemen in general, are at a loss to account for landing the troops at all, unless a more formidable attack was made—and I cannot conceive the reason of our lying here. . . . I am heartily tired of such ridiculous expeditions.

The following month, Young commented on the problems of combined operations, writing from Tetuan Bay in Morocco:

> We may truly be considered as a wandering army, at the mercy of the winds and waves—for we left Gibraltar merely on account of the anchorage there being unsafe, for a large fleet, in case of a Westerly gale, and if we should meet with a Levant, or easterly, wind here we must then weigh from this, and push out of the Streights.[19]

Departure from the Mediterranean would lessen the diplomatic and strategic value of British combined capability.

At the same time, the British were more successful in combined operations in the West Indies in the 1790s, despite very heavy manpower losses due to disease and major problems caused by a shortage of shipping and by storms. Army-navy cooperation was better than in previous conflicts, notably between Lieutenant-General Sir Charles Grey and Major-General Sir Ralph Abercromby on the one hand and Rear-Admirals Sir John Jervis, Sir Hugh Christian, and Henry Harvey on the other. Similarly, combined operations were highly successful against the Dutch in Cape Town, Sri Lanka, and the East Indies.

The French conquest of Egypt in 1798 created a new issue. Their army there appeared both a threat to the overland route to India and a vulnerable target against which the British could use the advantages of their amphibious power. Appointed commander in chief in the Mediterranean, Abercromby carefully trained his troops in 1800–1801 so that they should be able to face the French veterans in battle. As part of this, he focused on a crucial aspect of British operations, the assault landing. Abercromby held landing exercises on the Anatolian coast of Turkey, also in the Mediterranean, developing effective cooperation with the navy. Abercromby had learned from the confusion of the 1799 landing on the Dutch coast. As so often with combined operations, for example in the Second World War, there was a learning curve.

The results were seen on March 8, 1801, when the British successfully landed in Aboukir Bay in the face of French opposition. A contested landing was never an easy operation, but Abercromby's well-trained men were up to the challenge: training and tactics were applied in battlefield conditions and with success. Hudson Lowe, major-commandant of the Corsican Rangers, a force of Corsican émigrés that took part in the landing, wrote to his father:

> The fleet arrived in Aboukir Bay on the 1st but contrary winds prevented our disembarkation until the 8th. The French availed themselves of this interval to strengthen their position on the coast, collected about 3,000 men to oppose our landing and lined the whole coast with their artillery. About 2 o'clock in the morning the first division of the army were in the boats and after rowing five hours came within gun shot of the coast when the enemy opened the hottest fire upon us, at first of shell and round shot and, as we approached nearer, of grape shot and musketry. Several boats were sunk, many persons killed, and in one boat alone 22 persons killed or wounded by musketry before the boat took ground, but nothing could withstand the ardent spirit and impetuosity of our

> troops who forced their landing in spite of every opposition immediately attacked the enemy whom they completely repulsed after an action of about half an army.[20]

This began a campaign that brought the surrender of the French force in Egypt.[21]

The forces involved were generally in some discomfort. In December 1801, after serving in Egypt, John Hill of the Royal Welsh Fusiliers wrote to his mother from Gibraltar:

> From the time the Regiment left Plymouth [in 1800] until it came into this garrison, the soldiers never pulled off their cloathes day or night, except to bathe or put on a clean shirt, all the time of the campaign they were forced to sleep in their accoutrements. It was the case with the officers in the field—but on shipboard private soldiers suffer ten times as much almost, as before an enemy.

The letter referred to another problem with combined operations in the Age of Sail: "The gale that drove Sir Ralph Abercrombie's army out of the Mediterranean previous to our going up to Malta was fatal to my poor brother."[22]

Peace with France in 1802, the Peace of Amiens, proved short-lived, and war was renewed in 1803. Having largely been returned under the peace, the European colonial world of France and its allies had to be conquered anew, while warships were also deployed to blockade the French forces trying to suppress the Haitian Revolution. However, the British forces available on overseas stations were greater than those in 1793, and naval superiority permitted offensive operations. This was a matter of naval superiority in European as well as local waters. Captain William Cumby, a naval officer, wrote of British operations in the West Indies:

> The unremitting perseverance with which the vessels maintained the stations assigned to them, through all the variety of weather incident to the season, on a steep and dangerous shore, where no anchorage was to be obtained, as well as to the vigilance and alacrity of those officers and men who were employed in the night guard-boats, by whose united exertions the enemy's accustomed supply by sea was entirely cut off, and the surrender of the city greatly accelerated.[23]

The navy also provided crucial cannon to support sieges. Cannon technology was advanced enough (from iron casting and gunnery training) to provide effective cannon for this purpose. Blockades encouraged French garrisons to surrender, thus acting as a valuable prelude to a British invasion. This was also the case with the Indian Ocean, notably with the capture in 1810 from the French of Mauritius, long a British goal.

The British were less successful in Spanish-ruled South America. Buenos Aires was captured by about 1,200 troops under Brigadier-General William Carr Beresford and a squadron under Commodore Sir Hugh Popham in 1806. This was an unauthorized expedition that took advantage of the presence of sizable British forces across the South Atlantic in newly captured Cape Town in South Africa. The troops landed near the city on June 25, and after a weak resistance, Buenos Aires surrendered on July 2. Unrealistic hopes of opening South America to British trade and of spreading British power by means of expeditions to Chile, Mexico, and the Philippines took fire in Britain.[24] However, in the meantime, the small garrison was forced to surrender on August 12 in the face of a major popular rising. The garrison was then taken prisoner and the Royal Navy left to blockade the coast. Combined operations had failed.

The British government reinforced failure, a frequent fate of combined operations (for example, Gallipoli in 1915), by sending a force to recapture the city and free Beresford's troops. The first British force to arrive, 4,800 men under Brigadier-General Sir Samuel Auchmuty, successfully stormed the city of Montevideo, on the northern coast of the Plate estuary, in February 1807, although it suffered 350 casualties. Auchmuty, who felt he had insufficient forces to attack Buenos Aires, was superseded by Lieutenant-General John Whitelocke, who brought fresh reinforcements. A garrison was left in Montevideo, and on June 28–29, 1807, about eight thousand men landed thirty miles from Buenos Aires. Although delayed by swampy terrain, Whitelocke attacked the city on the morning of July 5. It was strongly defended, with the numerous garrison actively supported by the population in the barricaded streets. Whitelocke had been inaccurately informed that the inhabitants would be friendly. The attacking columns failed to provide mutual support in what was a poorly coordinated attack, and the sluggish Whitelocke lost control of the operation. Some of the British units were cut off and then surrendered. Having suffered three thousand casualties, Whitelocke on July 6 accepted Spanish proposals for an exchange of prisoners and the British evacuation of the Plate estuary, including Montevideo. This failure led to much criticism in Britain, and Whitelocke was court-martialed and cashiered.[25]

This was one of the more serious failures of combined warfare in the period. It has generally received little attention because there was nothing heroic about the defeat or the general and because it did not lead to the loss of a long-held possession. Whitelocke's failure, however, was an important indicator of the limitations of combined operations. Although in command of a substantial force, enjoying good naval support, and not facing an ecosystem as hostile as that in the Caribbean, Whitelocke was confronted by a hostile population that did not want to exchange Spanish control for that of another group of foreigners, as well as one that was Protestant. This factor was crucial to the battle on July 5, 1807, but even had Whitelocke won that engagement, he would have faced a sullen population and been obliged to use large numbers of troops to extend and maintain control, which had been the French situation in Egypt in 1798–1801. Unlike the French, however, the British, thanks to their naval situation, would not have had to fear a hostile foreign intervention.

Conversely, the British position in the River Plate estuary was vulnerable because it was very different to the situation for British attackers in the French transoceanic empire. In the latter case, there was no large, hostile population and the defenders were gravely weakened by the consequences of British naval power.

Popham, however, remained a great believer in the need to take action in order to deny France bases. He used this argument in November 1807 when justifying the seizure of Madeira and of Santa Catarina Island off the coast of Brazil. In turn, Popham saw geopolitics in terms of combined operations capability when he warned that "if he [Napoleon] gets Lisbon, Ireland will be his object."[26] Although this view was frequently expressed by British commanders and politicians concerned with the situation in France, Spain, and Portugal, this was not in practice Napoleon's major intention. Instead, Portugal was regarded as a key element in closing Europe to British trade.

In Europe more than in the European transoceanic world, British combined operations were very dependent on the overall diplomatic and military situation. In particular, France's ability to force the Dutch and Spain into alliance left Britain isolated among Atlantic naval powers, while the danger of invasion from France increased markedly. As a result, there was a major increase in home defense. This involved raising militia and other volunteer units as well as a process of building. This was not restricted to fortresses. Indeed the construction, from 1792, of barracks to house the expanded forces, in place of the traditional reliance on billeting them in inns (taverns), was important. Fortifications included the major Berry Head fortifications built between 1794 and 1804 to the east of Brixham, where William of Orange had landed in 1688, and a large number of Martello Towers, modeled on a tower attacked in Corsica, built along the south coast from 1804: seventy-four were built in Kent and Surrey alone. These fortifications were to be an aspect of what was intended as a total war in which, as one prominent minister urged in 1796, "every inch of ground, every field may to a degree be disputed, even by inferior numbers."[27] Thus, the principle of fortification, as an aid to defense, was to be expanded to cover everywhere.

Construction, repair, and maintenance were all important, for British fortifications had their weaknesses. When, in 1797, a French expedition approached Fishguard Harbor, the garrison in the fort there was desperately short of ammunition. In 1787, Charles O'Hara, a major-general on the staff at Gibraltar, complained of "defenceless works, unserviceable artillery, exhausted stores, weak garrison etc. etc. all of which is most true to a scandalous degree."[28]

In turn, winning allies and doing well at sea encouraged British power projection. The outbreak of the War of the Third Coalition against France in 1805, and victory over a Franco-Spanish fleet at Trafalgar that year, encouraged plans for the movement of a British army to northern Germany: twenty-five thousand troops were deployed by late January 1806 and the North Sea port of Bremen was occupied, which provided the basis for British operations into Germany. However, Napoleon's rapid victories, over first Austria (battles of Ulm and Austerlitz in 1805) and then Prussia (Jena in 1806), as well as the slower pace of British preparations and the delays caused by storms in the North Sea, ensured that the strategic situation collapsed before the British could contribute. Napoleon's concentration of his forces had brought him the crucial success.

The British also launched more successful attacks. In 1807, John Oldershaw Hewes wrote to his father from the fleet that was part of the combined attack on Copenhagen:

> On the 31st [August] the enemy hove a shell in the Charles tender and she blew up and wounded nineteen men belonging to us besides took off one of our Lieutenant's legs, broke his collar bone, cut him very bad on the head and almost knocked one of his eyes out. . . . It killed a young man about my own age, my most particular acquaintance, a masters mate, and killed two sailors besides what belonged to the vessel. On the 1st of September I went on shore with 15 sailors to make a battery close under the enemy's walls. We were obliged to go when it was dark as they should not see us or else they would have certainly have shot us. We could hear them talking and playing a fiddle. It rained excessively all night and I was almost perished with wet and cold. We left it as soon as it began to get light in the morning. On the 2nd our two batteries began bombarding the town . . . the greatest part is burnt down.[29]

British troops that had landed nearby defeated the Danes in battle. The Danes were forced to surrender their fleet. This was a major strategic achievement, a humiliation for the Danes that still rankles.

Operations continued in the Mediterranean. The British had landed a force in the Bay of Naples on November 21, 1805, in order, in cooperation with a Russian expeditionary force, to protect the kingdom of Naples against French attack. However, after Napoleon's victory over Austro-Russian forces at Austerlitz in central Europe, the French advanced in strength and the Anglo-Russian units withdrew: the British to Sicily, a strategic island base where they were protected by the British navy and could be a threat to mainland Italy. Subsequently, a British force landed in Calabria in mainland Italy where, at Maida, an attacking French army was stopped by the heavy fire of the British infantry. The British then returned to Sicily, having had an important morale boost, although there was to be criticism for a failure to exploit the victory sufficiently.[30] This criticism captured the difficulties of determining what was a reasonable outcome. Exploitation risked leaving British troops operating into the interior and becoming exposed to responses by superior opposing forces as happened to Sir John Moore in Spain in 1808–1809 with serious consequences. The issue of exploitation was always critical. In Europe, when the objective extended beyond a coastal purpose, the whole nature of the campaign shifted and the ability to support an army from the sea was a skill that took a long time to develop.

The dependence of combined operations on the general strategic situation, again a theme also to be seen in the Second World War, was readily apparent, as a British force sent to Swedish Pomerania withdrew in the face of the 1807 Tilsit agreement between France and Russia, while, in 1808, the Swedes rejected the offer of a force sent to help them resist Russia and to conquer Norway from France's ally Denmark. Another weakness was the need for a continuous naval presence. This was true in both attack and defense. Thus, the key defensive element of the navy in combined operations was seen in 1808 when British-held Capri fell to French attack, an outcome the British commander blamed on a lack of adequate naval assistance. Such assistance could deter attack or leave it exposed.

In 1809, there was a much larger-scale British combined operation. The strategic goals were clear: the destruction of the dockyards at Antwerp and a powerful diversion to help the Austrians in the War of the Fourth Coalition with France. Forty-four thousand troops, a very large force for the period, were deployed, but the planning was inadequate and the weather hostile. Landing on the island of Walcheren (where there was to be another contested landing in 1944), the British force was poorly led and decimated by disease, especially malaria, while the French responded rapidly, blocking the British advance. Besieged on August 1, Flushing, the main port on Walcheren, fell on the 16th, but by then the French had greatly reinforced Antwerp. On August 27, a council of war decided to abandon the expedition, but the withdrawal was very slow, permitting sickness to spread. The last troops did not embark until December 9; the French did not need to drive them away. This operation, like that against Copenhagen in 1807, reflected the importance of naval considerations in the strategic rationale for British combined operations: it was crucial to disrupt Napoleon's attempts, after naval defeat at Trafalgar in 1805, to preserve, assemble, and develop his naval power, attempts in which Antwerp played a key role.

Although the British naval blockade of the major naval base of Toulon was important, British combined operations in the Mediterranean were of less strategic significance. The islands of Ischia and Procida in the Bay of Naples were captured in June 1809. This was an effective use of the British army and navy forces designed to protect Sicily, but it did not contribute materially to the defeat of Napoleon, and the islands were evacuated in the face of a possible French naval attack.

Conversely, the major British commitment was in Iberia, where Britain deployed troops from 1808, with the Peninsular War becoming the key model for subsequent discussion of British "indirect warfare." This deployment was not always successful, and there were conspicuous failures to inflict lasting damage. This was the case with the Anglo-Sicilian amphibious force sent from Sicily to the east coast of Spain in 1812, and in 1813 when this force hastily abandoned the audacious siege of Tarragona on the advance of a French force. There was also the problem of locating operations in one area in terms of wider commitments. Robert, Second Viscount Melville, the First Lord of the Admiralty, informed Sir Home Popham, the area naval commander, in 1812 that more ships and men could not be spared for operations in northern Spain:

> In addition to the American hostilities [War of 1812], which require to be met as they were likely to be of much longer duration than some people suppose, we have had such demands from the Baltic and the Mediterranean as will completely drain us of all our disposable means, and still leave us deficient in many important points.[31]

The Baltic referred to convoying trade, the Mediterranean to blockading Toulon and supporting amphibious landings. Popham himself pressed for more determination and energy: "It is too rigid an adherence in many instances to the departmental forms which have clogged half the expeditions which have sailed from England."[32]

Nevertheless, the availability of naval support was highly important to successful operations on land in Portugal and Spain. Cooperation was good from the initial stages in 1808.[33] The British benefited from this being an Atlantic rather than a Mediterranean commitment, and thus from there being far shorter maritime routes for deployment and supplies and therefore less dependence on winds. Linked to this, it was easier to treat the Home Fleet as a resource also able to support the British presence in Iberia than if the focus for the latter had been on the Mediterranean.

Spanish amphibious attacks were a particular feature of their operations against French forces in 1810 and 1811. On a number of occasions, substantial expeditions were dispatched to various spots on the coast of Andalusia and then moved inland in order to attack the French. On the coast of both Catalonia and the Basque provinces, there were also frequent commando-style raids by small forces of regular troops, with a British squadron under Popham joining in 1812.

In 1815, Napoleon was defeated on land, but British combined operations contributed to the sense that he had lost control of the situation. This was seen not only with the blockade particularly of France's Atlantic ports, a blockade that ultimately led to Napoleon's surrender as he could not flee to the United States, but with amphibious attacks, notably on Marseilles and Toulon. Others were successfully launched against Guadeloupe and Martinique, which fell rapidly, indicating, in part, the extent of British accumulated skill.

THE BALTIC

Combined operations were seen in the Baltic, notably with the Russo-Swedish wars of 1788–1790 and 1808–1809. In the first case, the powerful diversion offered by the Turkish attack on Russia in 1787 appeared to provide Gustavus III of Sweden with an opportunity to use his new fleet—of gunboats designed for amphibious operations and of "archipelago frigates" armed with swivel guns—to attack Catherine II of Russia. However, it proved very difficult to direct and coordinate land, amphibious, and naval operations. As a result, in 1789, Gustavus failed to obtain success, although, in 1790, the Swedish navy won a major battle at Ruotsinsalmi in the Gulf of Finland, a victory best known under its contemporary Swedish name, Svensksund.[34]

Galleys and combined operations also played an important role during the Russo-Swedish War of 1808–1809. The surrender of the fortress of Sveaborg doomed the defense of Finland for the Swedes as it meant surrendering their galley fleet to the Russians, which made a counteroffensive impossible. The Russian crossing of the frozen Gulf of Bothnia to attack the Swedish mainland in 1809 did not involve naval assistance. The Swedes eventually rebuilt their galley fleet and attempted a landing operation at Ratan behind Russian lines in northern Sweden in August 1809 (the last combat on Swedish soil), but command-and-control problems with a divided army and navy helped lead to failure when they were exploited by a fast-moving Russian force on land. The galley fleet, as well as the fleet of the line, was also important during the successful Swedish conquest of Norway in 1814.

THE WAR OF 1812

The conflict between Britain and the United States from 1812 to 1815 was highly significant for the last stage of pre-steam combined operations as it displayed both their strengths and their limitations. Moreover, these were displayed for the leading naval state, Britain. Each side had considerable combined capability. It was highly important for operations against and in defense of Canada, which was part of the British Empire. This was due not only to the vulnerability of lakeside targets, such as York (Toronto), to attack, but also to the possibilities offered by the lakes for rapid communications and the movement of artillery, certainly when compared to the lakeside. Thus, for the Americans, the development of combined operational capability proved important to success on Lake Erie in 1813,[35] a success that very much moved the tempo of operations against British forces. Conversely, poor cooperation between army and navy commanders undermined American operations around Lake Ontario that year.

Combined capability was also significant due to the vulnerability of the United States to attack from the Atlantic. There was a fundamental strategic asymmetry as, due in part to the British blockade of American ports, the United States lacked the ability to cut British supply routes to Canada, let alone to mount amphibious attacks on oceanic Canada, particularly Nova Scotia, which was exposed to such attack. In contrast, the Americans had no control over whether British raids would escalate into large-scale amphibious attacks. When they occurred, the Americans lacked adequately integrated defenses. Such attacks were seen as a way to defend Canada. Indeed, in 1808, Archibald Robertson, a British army engineer whose advice had been sought, reported:

> In the case of an American war taking place, I do not doubt but that a flying squadron with some troops in transport, threatening either the Chesapeake or Delaware Rivers might alarm and impede any intended movement of the enemy against Canada, without (on our part) any particular attempt to land in any place, but only threatening particular points thought of consequence by the enemy and after attracting their attention to one point shift the ground and threaten some other.[36]

Combined operations faced more problems than such a proposal might suggest, but such power was a key aspect of the British way of war and the sole means feasible in conflict with the United States. The British sent a squadron into the Chesapeake in 1813 in order to stop it becoming a base for naval and privateering activity, as well as to divert American forces from attacking on the Canadian frontier and to mount raids that would emphasize American vulnerability and lessen support for the war. The latter was a political and thus strategic point. The intention was to encourage backing for the Federalists, who, as later with the Democrats in the North in the American Civil War, sought peace (in both cases with Britain but, in the latter case, more particularly with the South). Prior to 1814, the British policy had had mixed success. American naval and privateering activity had been hit, but the raids failed to sap American support for the war or to stop attacks on Canada.[37]

However, in 1814, the end of the war in Europe enabled the British to send more troops and warships to North America. These troops had frequently had experience in combined operations. Thus, Captain Peter Bowlby, who was sent to the Chesapeake in 1814, had served in the 1809 Walcheren expedition and in the Peninsular War.[38] He went on to the Caribbean having taken part in foraging in Maryland:

> Parties went on shore from every ship for the purpose of foraging. They took all the livestock they could find, leaving the price on the table, the inhabitants having fled into the woods on our approach. Sir Peter Parker commanding the *Menelaus* accompanied one of these parties; a shot from the woods struck him in the thigh cutting an artery, and before they could get him on board he had bled to death.[39]

He wrote upon approaching New Orleans: "The boats of the fleet proceed up the Lake [Pontchantrain] to attack the American gunboats which they succeeded in capturing, and these prizes were afterwards useful in conveying the troops 80 miles up the Lake."[40] Major Joseph Hutchison of the 7th Regiment of Foot, who had also served in the Peninsular War, sailed to the Caribbean for the New Orleans expedition. His journal captured the uncertainty of such combined operations for the troops involved. Having been detained by contrary winds for nearly three weeks in Plymouth in October 1814, he sailed "for nobody knew where. . . . After knocking about the Atlantic for two months we reached the West India Islands." Disembarking off Louisiana, twenty soldiers died in a capsize.[41]

As in 1775, the bulk of American population, industry, and purchasing power were concentrated on and close to the Atlantic coast, which increased vulnerability to British combined operations. Nevertheless, as an important limitation to the latter, the defense had depth as a result of "country" space in the form of a bigger and more densely populated hinterland. The population increased, from about 2,500,000 in 1776 to 7,666,314 in 1812. This depth proved valuable in operations around the Chesapeake in 1814. The Americans had the opportunity to withdraw from vulnerable Washington without losing their capacity to maintain their forces.

The British failure to take Fort McHenry outside Baltimore in 1814, and their more serious defeat near New Orleans in 1815, the last battle in the war, can leave an impression of the tactical and operational limitations of combined operations, let alone the uncertain strategic and political consequences that repeatedly require emphasis. There were certainly systemic tactical and operational problems. Naval fire support could be weaker than its land counterpart as guns fired from the land did so from a stable platform, while ships were large targets and fired with the roll of the ship against small targets. However, although forts may have housed larger-caliber guns, this artillery was not maneuverable, unlike cannon on ships. At the same time, there were some other variables. Ships could bring a greater weight of fire, in terms of number of guns and speed of firing, than most coastal batteries, although effectiveness depended on getting close enough.

Secondly, the assault craft were flat-bottomed boats powered by naval oarsmen and by a small auxiliary sail, a system that made it difficult to move rapidly. In addition, inshore navigation was a problem, while it was particularly hard to land horses. Moreover, horses who have been long at sea present a number of problems once they return to shore, notably loss of muscle due to a lack of exercise and problems with balance. This naturally limits their value in the initial stages of an amphibious operation or after landing in a port. The landing of cannon was also a slow process and could be dangerous.[42]

The processes of approach to shore and disembarkation were often slow and difficult. Moreover, once troops were ashore, they lost the advantage of maritime mobility and instead were frequently vulnerable to attack. Due to the difficulties of transporting cavalry, amphibious forces had a lopsided force structure, one that was similar to the later relative immobility of airborne troops once landed. Indeed, Major-General Robert Ross, who commanded the British troops landed in the Chesapeake in 1814, wrote of the "serious disadvantage being experienced from the want of cavalry."[43] The lack of cavalry was one of the important problems when exploiting a landing inland. At the same time, the British sought to improve their capability by using dedicated fire-support ships in the form of rocket ships. These supplemented the "bomb ships" containing large-bore mortars that the French had used against Algiers in 1682 and the British against French ports.

Yet, there was also a degree of fear. It was unclear what the Americans could do to stop such British attacks. In October 1814, the Senate was told by James Monroe, the secretary of war, that New York City was at risk from such attack, and he pressed for an expansion of the regular army to defend the Atlantic coast, a costly and unwelcome prospect. In 1815, the British failed heavily at New Orleans, but they then went on to threaten Mobile and to plan attacks on Savannah and Charleston. It is unclear what would have happened had these attacks been mounted. They could certainly have been destructive, but it would have been difficult to retain any gains in the face of troops deploying from the hinterland.

For America and Britain, the period of warfare between them therefore closed with a demonstration of the significance of combined operations. It was not surprising that the American strategic focus in the coming decades was on providing state-of-the-art fortifications to protect coastal cities from British attack in any further war.[44] Investment in such fortifications indeed offers an indication of concern, then and at other times, about combined operations. The costly "Third System" of coastal forts was developed by the Board of Engineers created in 1816. This system became apparently more necessary with rising population density on the American littoral and with the American failure to sustain their post-1815 naval plans. Forts protected New Orleans, especially Jackson and Macomb, founded in 1822 and 1827 respectively, and New York, notably Fort Hamilton, established in 1831. The protection of the North Carolina coast, with the foundation of Fort Macon on an offshore island in 1834, was clearly designed against European attack, although the key fear that year was of France. This system grew with American expansionism. Fort Brooke was established in Florida in 1824 and the Presidio of San Francisco in 1847, to protect from possible British attack. In total, $41 million was spent on fortifications, a substantial proportion of federal expenditure.

In turn, the British upgraded the citadel in Québec after the War of 1814 and the defenses of Bermuda in the late 1840s. There was no sense that the limitations of combined operations meant that they were without value, both military and political. This assumption was strengthened by Britain being not only the world's leading naval power, but also the wealthiest state and one willing, as well as able, to use such means.

OTHER POWERS

Combined operations were also seen elsewhere in Europe during the period. The results of individual campaigns revealed the importance of a range of tactical and operational factors including leadership and climate. This was clearly seen in 1775 when Charles III of Spain launched a major offensive against Algiers. On June 27, an army of about twenty-one thousand men embarked at Cartagena on Spain's Mediterranean coast and set sail in a convoy of 6 ships of the line, 12 frigates, 26 other naval vessels, and about 350 transports. Having been delayed by bad weather, the landings were not staged until July 8 because the Conde de O'Reilly could not make up his mind exactly where to attack. The landings were characterized by great confusion, and the Spaniards were pinned down on the beaches by heavy fire from Moorish coastal artillery while their artillery was delayed by the coastal sand. By midafternoon, the Spaniards had suffered 2,400 casualties for no gains, and O'Reilly ordered reembarkation. In the course of this operation, complete panic ensued with the loss of nine cannon and possibly three thousand prisoners. In 1784, a line of Algerian warships prevented the Spaniards from coming ashore.

In 1798, it was the intervention of the British navy that undermined the French expedition to Egypt, rather as the British had done with the Spanish expedition to Sicily in 1718. The French also conquered the Ionian Islands, landed forces in Wales (1797) and Ireland (1798), and prepared a large-scale invasion of England for 1805. However, British naval strength limited their options and in 1805 blocked their plan. The forces landed in Wales and Ireland were defeated, that in Ireland by Cornwallis.

In contrast, British naval support was a key background to Russian participation in expeditions to Holland (1799) and Swedish Pomerania (1805). Aside from against France and against Sweden in 1808–1809, the Russians made other moves on their own. In 1807, they landed a force near the Turkish fortress of Anapa, capturing it, only to abandon it and launch another successful operation against Anapa in 1810. An attempt on Trebizond failed. Against Persia, the Russians launched a minor combined operation at Baku in 1805.

The range of combined operations, including amphibious assaults, can be expanded, not least to emphasize those in Hawaii. There were repeated issues, not least translating tactical success to strategic results. Partly as a result, such operations were most successful against islands rather than against coastlines that had significant hinterlands.

Chapter Five

The Nineteenth Century, 1815–1914

The situation was transformed during the nineteenth century due to the impact of steam power. Indeed, Robert Fulton's *Demologus*, a steam-powered floating battery, was constructed in the War of 1812 for the defense of New York Harbor against the British, even though it was completed only in 1815, too late for war service. Steam power was subsequently to have a major impact on combined operations during the century, although the understanding of this impact, and of how best to foster and counter it, varied. These operations were closely related to Western expansionism on a global scale, but were also seen with non-Western powers, notably Japan, which acquired its first steamship in 1855 with help from the Dutch and built its first steam warship in 1861.

At the same time as the application of steam was a key element in capability and usage, the primacy of strategic factors has to be considered. For example, combined operations played only a limited or no real role in some major struggles, especially the German Wars of Unification in 1864–1871, a series of conflicts that helped set the pattern for planning for war in Europe up until the outbreak of the First World War in 1914. Moreover, although they were attempted in the American Civil War (1861–1865), combined operations were less significant to Union victory than the punishing campaigning on land in the East in 1864–1865 and were more important as naval support from rivers than as coastal landings. As for other periods, a balance is required between an awareness of the significance and potential of combined operations and, on the other hand, an understanding of continued limitations, both technologically and with regard to impact.

STEAM

Sir George Cockburn, an experienced British admiral, was in no doubt of the impact of steam. He wrote in 1845, while First Naval Lord of the Admiralty, "From the period when the first large seagoing steam vessel was successfully completed, it became evident to everybody that a facility never before existing, must be afforded thereby for sudden invasion of this country."[1] The steam engine lessened the problems posed by the need to rely on a large crew and its requirements for food, water, and sanitation, notably so in the case of galleys.

The initial impact of steam on naval activity, both at sea and on rivers, had been with relatively modest warships, and early steamships faced many operating difficulties. However, in the 1840s, the screw propeller, placed at the stern, offered a better alternative to the paddle wheel, by making it possible to carry a full broadside armament. Alongside the greater mobility offered by screw steamers, this made their tactical advantages clear. Although the process was not fully complete until late in the century, steam power replaced dependence on the wind, making journey times more predictable and quicker and planning more practicable, which was significant both operationally and tactically. This increased significance could have a strategic effect.

In addition, steam power increased the maneuverability of ships. This capability made it easier to sound inshore and hazardous waters, to attack opposing fleets in anchorages, and to bring troops close inshore. The last was also greatly encouraged by the major improvement in the availability of accurate charts about coastal waters. This availability reflected active charting, notably by the British navy and in particular from the 1820s.

To thwart such inshore operations, it appeared necessary to have effective naval defense. In 1856, General Sir John Burgoyne, the British inspector-general of fortifications, who had served on expeditionary forces, including to Malta (1800), Egypt (1807), the Peninsula (1808–1813), the United States (1814–1815), and the Crimea (1854–1855), wrote:

> The progress in the state of gunnery and steam navigation renders it necessary to reconsider from time to time the principles of attack and defence of coast and harbours. Whatever improvements may be made in land batteries, their entire adequacy for the purpose of defence cannot be certain against the rapidity of steamers, and the facility of their manoeuvring power . . . but they may be powerful in combination with . . . the floating batteries with their sides coated with thick iron plates.[2]

BRITAIN

Improvements both enhanced and challenged the position of the leading naval power, which throughout the period was Britain. Indeed, these factors helped explain why the British were fearful of a French invasion. In 1844, François, Prince of Joinville, the son of King Louis Philippe and a key French admiral, published *De l'état des forces navales de la France*, in which he presented steamships as a means by which France could challenge Britain. In Parliament, Henry, Third Viscount Palmerston, the prime minister, raised the prospect of a "steam bridge" from France and pressed the construction of coastal fortifications as a means to thwart any French amphibious assault. These were duly built in the early 1860s.

Meanwhile, the British had used their own combined operations in order to enforce their views outside Europe. Intimidation and more lethal action were both employed. This was seen in 1840 when Britain intervened to assist the Turkish Empire against the expansionism of Mehmet Ali of Egypt, who had defeated the Turks and occupied Egypt and Syria. British pressure included the blockading of the Egyptian fleet in Alexandria, the successful bombardment of Acre (in modern Israel), and the use of warships and Marines to storm Sidon (in modern Lebanon) and to help the Turks defeat the Egyptians. Mehmet agreed to evacuate Syria. At Acre, Admiral Sir Robert Stopford used the steamer *Phoenix* as a temporary flagship. This was a lightly armed ship but one appropriate, thanks to its mobility, for command and control, rather like a modern helicopter. In the attack on Sidon, the steamships involved led.

Similarly, troops and warships in combination brought Britain victory over the Chinese in 1842, a victory that included an advance up the Yangzi River against the Chinese capital, Nanjing. British forces had already captured Guangzhou (1841) and Shanghai (1842).[3]

Combined operations had a capacity to affect the situation far distant from the sea. This was seen when the British attacked Persia in 1856–1857. They staged successful landings in 1857, notably at Bushire, seizing Persian positions and intimidating Persia into evacuating Herat in Afghanistan. Thus, naval power secured a political settlement far from the sea: Britain was concerned about the impact of Persian expansion on Afghanistan's ability to act as a buffer for India against Russian expansionism in Central Asia.

This combination was of greater importance as the British directed energy to colonial expansion. Even when the operations were largely conducted in the interior, as with Ethiopia in 1868 and Asante in 1874, it was necessary to transport the British forces to the relevant coast (on the Red Sea and the Atlantic coast of West Africa respectively) and then to land them. This was also seen in the British conquest of Egypt in 1882 as the bombardment of Alexandria's defenses was a crucial prelude to the landing of fifteen thousand troops and to their subsequent successful operations in the interior. Hospital ships and the ship-based desalination of drinking water were also significant in this campaign.

Egypt represented a key element of combined operations in the shape of the strategic capability it brought for such moves. Securing Britain's position on the route to India via the Suez Canal, the construction of which was finished in 1869, both became a commitment and a means to envisage new commitments and to support them. The Suez Canal changed the geopolitical situation in a revolutionary way. The combined nature of the British deterrent was displayed in 1878, in response to a war scare with the Russians over their advances in the Balkans at the expense of the Turks. This crisis led to the reinforcement of British forces in the Mediterranean, with Indian-based units swiftly moved via the Suez Canal to Malta, from which British troops were sent to Cyprus, and the dispatch of a British fleet to Constantinople through the Dardanelles. This was a route the British failed, in the face of firm Turkish opposition, to follow successfully in 1915.

IMPERIAL COMBINED OPERATIONS

Britain was far from alone, although the scale of its activity very much varied. Other Western states also pursued transoceanic interests, including expansionism, and used combined operations and amphibious assaults to those ends. Indeed, France proved particularly active in North and West Africa and in Indochina and Mexico. The French made much use of riverboats, steamers, and Marines. Spain was active in West Africa, the Philippines, and Morocco and intervened in the Dominican Republic in 1862–1865. Late entrants to imperial expansion came in the shape of Germany, Italy, and Japan. Japan was not the sole non-Western state at issue. Earlier, Mehmet Ali of Egypt had tipped the balance in Greece in 1824 against the insurgents opposing Turkish rule by dispatching a potent combined force, and in turn, that force played a major role until its fleet was defeated by an Anglo-French-Russian fleet off Cape Navarino in 1827.

Alongside expansionism, there were also counterinsurgency and antipiracy expeditions, as for Spain in Cuba and the Philippines. The early introduction of steam power by Spain in the 1840s was due to the need for fast troop transport and amphibious warfare. Steamers got preference over other types of ship because the army was interested in the strategic mobility that they provided. By 1898, the Spanish navy in Cuba and the Philippines had a sizable number of ships, but they were specially designed for colonial and amphibious operations. As a result, there was no proper battle fleet to confront the American navy.

THE UNITED STATES

The United States is classically understood as a late entrant to Western imperial expansion but, in practice, American imperial expansion, and the use to that end of combined operations and amphibious assaults, can be seen from the colonial period. The colonists had largely pursued such expansion overland, although the southern colonies had employed combined operations against the Spaniards in Florida and had taken part in British operations against the Spanish Caribbean. New England employed similar operations against French Canada.

As an independent state from 1776, the United States pressed ahead with expansionism, although in the shadow of British naval power, the key means was overland. This contrasted with the preindependence period, with expansionism into Spanish Florida now overland and the invasions of Canada similarly mounted away from the ocean. Ideological factors were also significant to American policy. Although the Declaration of Independence (1776) included statements of theoretically global applicability, in practice there was scant attempt to export the American Revolution, other than to contiguous areas that could be annexed. There were more specific reasons Spain was the ally of the Americans during the American Revolution. Then, during its weakness in 1793–1815, Spain was to a degree protected by the risk of angering France and/or Britain, each variously an ally of Spain and each of which subsequently supported a side in the Spanish civil war from 1808 to 1814. As a result, there was little prospect of America benefiting significantly from the vulnerability of Spanish America during the French Revolutionary and Napoleonic Wars, as opposed to making gains at the expense of Spain's colony Florida. In addition, Haiti could not have been conquered as an American colony not only due to the local situation but also because of the British attitude. Moreover, the weakness of the American navy and the limited experience in mounting combined operations counted against that technique, although it was employed on a small scale in the Mediterranean in the 1800s against the Barbary States of North Africa.

During the Latin American revolutions against rule by Spain (and in Brazil by Portugal), there again were not really opportunities for the United States. Britain supported the cause of the newly independent states, while France was sympathetic to Spain. This left few opportunities for the United States, not least as it still had only modest strength for combined operations. These opportunities were further lessened by the Spanish retention of Cuba and Puerto Rico, as the United States did not want war with Spain. In 1898, when the United States did fight Spain, the latter was isolated and with a weak economy, while the United States was stronger.

The Americans did acquire experience in combined operations and amphibious assaults in the 1820s, as there was extensive activity against pirates and slavers in the Caribbean, with operations offshore and onshore: in Cuba, Puerto Rico, Santo Domingo, and the Yucatan.[4] Such activity was important to the training of officers and crew. A marked degree of assertiveness was shown, which, indeed, is one of the frequent characteristics of combined operations. In 1824, Captain David Porter, commander of the West Indies Squadron, landed armed sailors on Cuba, spiked Spanish cannon, and threatened to destroy the port of Foxardo unless local authorities apologized for arresting one of his lieutenants, who had made representations on behalf of an American merchant.[5]

In the 1830s and 1840s, the use of the navy to protect American trade and interests continued. Marines were used in particular for these purposes. They were landed at Buenos Aires in Argentina in 1833 and at Callao and Lima in Peru in 1835–1836 to protect these interests during insurrections. This protection, as well as that against attacks on American interests, also led to the landing of forces on Fiji in 1840; Drummond Island and Samoa, both in 1841; and at Guangzhou (Canton) in China in 1843. Also in 1843, sailors and Marines from four American warships landed on the Ivory Coast in West Africa to discourage the slave trade and to act against those who had attacked American shipping.[6]

Mexico presented a far more serious challenge and one that would involve combined operations. In late 1846, when war was declared, American forces under Zachary Taylor, operating from Texas across the Rio Grande into northern Mexico, captured the provincial capitals of Monterrey and Saltillo. The last, however, is about 550 miles from Mexico City. These distances were part of Mexico's natural defenses and underlined the marginal character of operations in Mexico's northern provinces as far as Mexico's center of power was concerned. British-ruled Canada was far more vulnerable to American attack. Moreover, American successes in 1846 did not lead the Mexicans to negotiate peace.

As a result, reliance was placed on combined operations. The bold stroke of a strike at the Mexican center was deemed necessary by President James Polk and Winfield Scott, the commanding general of the American army and a talented strategic thinker and actor. Already, on November 14, 1846, the American navy had captured the port of Tampico on the Gulf of Mexico, and this provided a base for the attack, further south, on Vera Cruz, Mexico's major port and the gateway to Mexico City, which is inland. To support this expedition, troops were transferred from Taylor's army, which, for Polk, had the beneficial consequences of weakening a Whig who was likely to be the presidential candidate in 1848. Repeatedly, the strategic choices involved in combined operations should not be separated from political issues, both domestic and international.

In an impressive instance of interservice combination, Scott landed nine thousand troops near Vera Cruz on March 9, 1847, meeting no resistance.

This reflected a force-projection capability that had not been there for the United States in the War of 1812. However, this capability was in part dependent on British neutrality.[7] Given this neutrality, the United States at sea was in practice in a position akin to that of Britain in the War of 1812. As then for the United States, American amphibious capability served to make the entire Mexican littoral feel threatened. It could be overawed, blockaded, interdicted, and bombarded. American forces landed along the gulf across a broad front.[8]

Benefiting from the limited Mexican response along the coast, Scott pressed on to capture Vera Cruz on March 29 after a short siege supported by a naval bombardment. As so often with combined operations, speed was of the essence. A lengthy siege would have been fatal, as it would have exposed the Americans to high casualties, as the British had suffered from yellow fever outside Havana in 1762. Furthermore, if Vera Cruz had held out for any length of time, then Scott might have had to divide his forces between the siege and watching for any relief attempt. Scott then moved inland, finally, after a number of victories, storming the Mexican capital on September 14.

A very different form of combined operations was involved in California. Already, in 1842, warships under Commodore Thomas ap Catesby Jones, the commander of the Pacific Squadron, who had been ordered to protect American interests in California and who erroneously believed that war had begun with Mexico, briefly seized Monterey and San Diego. In 1846, when war really had been declared, the navy acted in support of American settlers in California, occupying Monterey, San Francisco, San Diego, Santa Barbara, and Los Angeles. The squadron commander, Robert Stockton, appointed himself governor of California.

There was not really a "brown-water" or riverine dimension to the Mexican war, but the Americans were ready to use such operations as with the army-navy cooperation in the Florida Everglades in 1839 during the Second Seminole War against the Native American population.[9]

The Mexican War was followed by the stepping up of the landing of forces to protect American interests: in Buenos Aires in 1852–1853; Nicaragua in 1853; Shanghai in 1854, 1855, and 1859; Uruguay and Fiji in 1855 and 1858; and Guangzhou and Panama, then in Colombia, in 1856. In 1871, two warships and a small Marine force attacked Korea in revenge for the burning, five years earlier, of an armed merchant schooner, the *General Sherman*, that had sought to open up Korea to American trade, although without deploying the force Commodore Matthew Perry had used to intimidate Japan into doing so in 1853–1854. In 1871, about 650 Koreans were killed, but the American use of force, especially superior firepower, yielded them no benefit and their force sailed off.[10]

The range of American combined operations was impressive but did not match that of Britain. Again, this serves as a reminder of the need to locate such operations in a broad context. The United States not only lacked the drive for overseas colonies but also, in part as a result, did not have the necessary military infrastructure. There was no equivalent to the vital adjunct to transoceanic naval power in this period: the local forces, officered by Europeans, deployed most successfully by Britain, notably in South Asia. The United States also lacked the bases and traditions of interest in particular areas, while the Napoleonic warfare that had left Britain with possessions around the world was not matched for America. Despite its marked capability, industrially and geographically, for combined operations, the United States was really a continental power at this stage.

THE AMERICAN CIVIL WAR

This had consequences in the Civil War (1861–1865). Like the contemporary civil wars in China and Mexico with which it deserves comparison, this was essentially a land struggle within the context, notably for the United States, of the all-important access to the trade offered by the open oceans. Attempts by the Union (Northern) side to use combined operations were important to the course of the war but not ultimately decisive. The primary effect of Union amphibious attacks was to reinforce the blockade, although Brigadier-General Benjamin Butler's clever amphibious movement in the Chesapeake in April 1861, which bypassed a sabotaged section of railroad track and secessionist-inclined Baltimore, had important strategic and political consequences. His troops were virtually the first to reach Washington.

Union combined operations were the case both on the coasts and on rivers, notably those of the far-flung Mississippi basin. The Union forces rapidly became adept in the latter, and the combination of the "brown-water navy" with army units was repeatedly effective. Indeed, in tactical and operational terms, this use was frequently more so than that of railways, as in western Tennessee in February 1862 and in the capture of Vicksburg in July 1863. David Dixon Porter both created a shipyard at Cairo, Illinois, where a river fleet was built, and led the Mississippi Squadron effectively during the Vicksburg campaign. The Union exploited its inland naval supremacy in the Mississippi basin, particularly to sustain logistics and to maintain the dynamic of campaigning, whereas the Confederacy (South) was unable to counter this.[11] By controlling the Mississippi, the Union strangled the essential overseas trade in cotton and forced the Confederacy to fight a two-front war in the Western Theater. Combined operations were critical in opening up that theater and in advancing in it. The success of the Union in this theater helped make the successful Union campaign of 1864–1865 in Virginia possible.

However, such cooperation between army and navy was harder to apply in the case of combined operations along the coast. Moreover, there was a need in these for the Union to respond to the ability, or at least attempts, of Confederate forces to build up opposing strength. This need and ability matched the situation elsewhere. In 1854, Sir James Graham, the First Lord of the British Admiralty, wrote to Fitzroy, Lord Raglan, then the master-general of the ordnance, about plans to defend the port of Hull and Humberside from amphibious attacks: "I quite concur in the opinion that the permanent presence of a large military force at Hull is not requisite: that inland concentration, with rapid means of distribution by railroad, is the right system."[12] At that point, Russia was the principal threat to Britain.

For the Union in the Civil War, it could be possible to land in the South, itself a formidable logistical task, but not always to move inland. Thus, Port Royal in South Carolina was seized in a surprise attack on November 7, 1861, but the Union forces that were landed failed to press on overland to attack Charleston to the north or Savannah to the south. This contrast limited the effectiveness of combined operations. The most recent interpretation argues that failure was not likely for structural or institutional reasons, but was "anchored in the confluence of personality, military paradigm, and strategic choice." The dismissal of Scott in November 1861, and the abandonment of his design and of the effective integration of expeditionary operations within the larger context of Union grand strategy, are seen as mistakes and as helping commit the Union to a war of attrition in Virginia that delayed Confederate defeat as it only became successful in the winter of 1864–1865.[13] George B. McClellan, who had succeeded Scott as general in chief of the army, advanced on Richmond along the James River in May 1862 after a landing to the east of the city. This advance could have been a decisive blow, one that provided a specific strategic purpose to combined operations. However, Robert E. Lee succeeded in blocking McClellan's cautious advance in the Seven Days Battles and went on to regain the initiative by advancing northward. Thereafter, the Union forces focused on the direct overland approach to Richmond, which also had the effect of blocking any such Confederate moves north toward Washington.

Looked at differently, it was the very pressure that could be brought to bear by Union combined operations that added a significant level of uncertainty to Confederate strategy. Moreover, the seizure of coastal positions by amphibious attacks gave added force to the Union blockade, which was one of the major campaigns of the war, cutting off the ability of Confederate blockade-runners to make port, to bring in vital goods, and to get out cash-earning commodities.[14] Given the absence, despite the Mexican War of 1846–1848, of any experience of issues and operations at this scale, and the extent of friction and rivalry between army and navy, the Union proved able to develop a joint military strategy and joint doctrine, but the blockade was more significant as a framer of the context within which the Confederacy had to operate than as a basis for amphibious assaults.

The role of combined operations would probably have been far greater had Britain come into the war against the Union, as seemed possible in 1861 and 1862. The possibilities for action concerned commentators. Henry, Third Viscount Palmerston, then British prime minister, underlined the geopolitical dimension, at once seasonal and international:

> We [Britain] should have less to care about their resentment in the spring when communication with Canada opens, and when our naval force could more easily operate upon the American coast than in winter, when we are cut off from Canada and the American coast is not so safe. But if the acknowledgement [of the South] were made at one and the same time by England, France and some other powers, the Yankee would probably not seek a quarrel with us alone, and would not like one against a European Confederation.[15]

EUROPE

The significance of combined operations for transoceanic Western powers was not generally matched in conflict in Europe during the century, but nevertheless there were important instances. In Spain, during the civil conflicts known as the Carlist Wars (1833–1840 and 1873–1876), there were many combined operations. The Spanish navy relied on the large body of experience accumulated during the war against Napoleon (1808–1814) and in resisting the Latin American Wars of Independence. In 1837, foreign intervention again played a role when, during the First Carlist War, Captain Lord John Hay, commander of the Royal Navy Squadron at nearby Pasajes, landed a Royal Marines battalion at Oriamendi and deployed it along the road to San Sebastián to help halt a rout by Anglo-Cristino forces repulsed from their attack near San Sebastián, only to withdraw because of political demands to observe "non-interference." There had been a furious debate in the House of Commons following Hay's actions.[16] In addition, Admiral Parker's squadron in the Mediterranean effectively operated as a backstop to counterrevolution during the 1836–1837 tumults in Malaga and Barcelona.

In 1849, in a demonstration of the new capability, the French were able to move 7,500 troops and supplies rapidly by steamships across the Mediterranean from Toulon to Civitavecchia, the port for Rome, a deployment that led to the fall of the Roman Republic and the reimposition of papal control over Rome, a major counterrevolutionary success. In addition, Spain sent an expeditionary force of nine thousand troops backed by the navy, which had already sent ships in 1848. Providing transport and logistical support, the Spanish navy also coordinated with the Neapolitan army.

In 1859, France used steamships alongside railways in moving troops to Italy in order to fight Austria. This served to lessen the problems posed by the Alps and in particular the need to move forward in order to prevent

Austrian forces advancing from Milan to overrun France's ally, Piedmont. Rail could serve to transport French troops to the ports of Toulon and Marseilles, from which they could use steamships to Genoa, then under Piedmontese rule, and move on subsequently by train. The French fleet was far greater than that of Austria, and indeed the latter feared the landing of a French expeditionary force on the coast of modern Croatia in order to support an insurrection by southern Slavs and Hungarians. None, however, was attempted, and the French concentrated on dominating the Mediterranean, thus being able to move their troops without hindrance.[17]

The Mediterranean was also a key means for mobility in the case of the ability of Giuseppe Garibaldi and one thousand red-shirted volunteers to sail from Genoa to Marsala in 1860 in order to help a revolt in Sicily against the Neapolitan Bourbons, before pressing on to invade Naples, a key episode in the Risorgimento, the struggle for Italian unification.

Meanwhile, as a protection against combined operations and against the growing strength of warships, with their steel armor and stronger ordnance, there were improvements to shore defenses. These included shore batteries with long-range guns, improved fortifications, and controlled mines that were exploded by electricity from the shore.

These were not the sole factors as constraints on combined operations. In the Crimean War (1854–1856), the Russian fleet chose not to engage in fleet action against the larger British and French fleets. In turn, Britain and France deployed their navies to Russian waters, notably in the Baltic and Black Seas, and used them to bombard coastal positions and dominate the maritime supply situation. The Anglo-French naval bombardments of Odessa and Sevastopol underlined the vulnerability of wooden warships to effective defensive fire. This vulnerability led to the plan for an amphibious attack on Crimea instead of the bombardments. This prefigured the situation in 1915 when the Anglo-French failure to force the Dardanelles by naval means led to the landing at Gallipoli in order to gain control of the Dardanelles.

The British and French were able to land an army in Crimea in 1854 and to support it through an extended campaign. This represented an example of a successful combined operation. However, the campaigning in Crimea demonstrated serious problems in utilizing military capacity and became a slogging match. The Allies surrendered the mobility obtained in launching an amphibious invasion of Crimea by besieging Sevastopol, Russia's Black Sea naval base, a target that indicated the centrality of goals linked to combined capability. The city was well defended, and initial attacks failed. The flexibility offered by combined operations had been lost in the face of fortified positions. The attackers lacked adequate experience in siegecraft and had to face a type of trench warfare that was different to earlier sieges. The Allies also had to confront both particularly bad weather, which hit supply links across the Black Sea, and repeated attempts by the Russian army in Crimea to disrupt the siege. The Turks proposed a landing on the Georgian coast, but Britain and France turned it down.

At the same time, in Crimea, combined operations provided an ability to deploy large forces at a considerable distance. Moreover, Anglo-French naval activity in the region, for example, in the Sea of Azov, made a contribution to eventual successes there. A bland formulation would be to argue that combined operations worked well for limited war. That was the nature of Allied operations in 1854–1856, whereas in contrast Napoleon I, and later Hitler, proposing more major goals, failed to secure the necessary means to achieve their task. More specifically the Allies benefited from steamships in transporting and supporting their forces. In contrast, Russia lacked rail links to Crimea, which made it harder to supply their forces there. In addition, a British Naval Brigade took a role in fighting on land in Crimea, just as it did in the Indian Mutiny.[18]

In the Baltic, the Allies landed on the Åland Islands, capturing the fortress at Bomarsund, which was a threat to Sweden. However, Britain and France were unable to put serious pressure on Russia's Baltic base of Kronstadt: aside from Russia's shore defenses and a network of mines and obstacles, the Russians mobilized a large number of steam-powered gunboats with heavy pivot guns. In 1856, the British deployed ironclad floating batteries, mortar vessels, and light-draft gunboats, but they arrived too late to launch an assault. The British and French naval commanders suffered from inadequate maps. On Kamchatka in the Russian Far East, in 1854, an Anglo-French combined operation experienced the common trajectory of moving from the strength of naval bombardment to the failure of subsequent operations on land.[19] In 1869, British warships off Dover demonstrated how they would provide covering fire for an invasion force, an exercise displayed in the *Illustrated London News* of April 10, but in reality, operations proved more difficult. Nevertheless, the capacity to project power from the sea was a major tool for British foreign policy, ensuring that it rested on an ability to do major damage to the cities of potential enemies.

In the German Wars of Unification (1864–1871), combined operations played only a minor role. The Danes had made a substantial landing in 1848, early in the First Schleswig-Holstein War, which enabled them to flank and defeat the local forces. The Danes would have done better overall, notably in 1864 against the Prussians and Austrians, had they made more use of sea power. Instead, a failure of Danish army-naval cooperation in 1864 enabled the Prussian forces to move from Jutland onto the nearby island of Alsen (Als in Danish). Combined operations were not significant in the Franco-Prussian War of 1870–1871.

MARINES

The century saw the increased differentiation of the military as part of a drive for organization and specialization. In Britain, largely at the instigation of Admiral the Earl St. Vincent, the First Lord of the Admiralty from 1801 to 1804, the Marines were titled the Royal Marines in 1802 by George III and developed as specialized light infantry and artillery. In France, the navy's attempt to arrange for a branch of the army to be for its use failed; instead, a specialized branch of the navy, the Marine Fusiliers, was established in 1856. These troops took part in operations in China, Vietnam, and Mexico. Due primarily to poor leadership, the USMC missed an opportunity to develop its amphibious mission during the Civil War. As a result, it played only a marginal role in the many landings made during the war, being most important at the last major one, at Fort Fisher in 1865.

The development in many countries was somewhat erratic. For example, the origins of the Argentine Marine force go back to the independence years, with soldiers on board the ships, as was usual in the early nineteenth century. The corps was originally created as Coastal Artillery for the Navy in the 1820s and served as shipboard detachments and to protect ordnance warehouses until the beginning of the twentieth century, when battalions were formed. However, the official designation of Infanteria de Marina de la Armada Argentina came only in the 1940s. The Marines participated in the Chaco Campaign of 1884–1885 to suppress Native Americans and played an important role in the defenses of naval establishments, as well as participating in coups, as in 1890 and 1905. In Italy, there was also an erratic process. There was a long-standing Piedmontese Marine force, while Venice, Genoa, and the Papacy used to drill regiments to serve both on ships and land, but the first, the Reggimento Real Navy, was disbanded in 1871 and not really replaced until 1917. Instead, when requiring a landing, every ship had to commit a portion of her crew depending on the size of the ship. A battleship provided a company, a cruiser a platoon, and a smaller ship a team called a *squadra* or squad, but usually small ships were not given this task unless they were alone. In China in 1900, each of the Italian cruisers landed a platoon, and in Tripoli in 1911, when there were plenty of ships, two battalions were landed.

THE LATE NINETEENTH CENTURY

Warships became more sophisticated, more powerful, faster, and more maneuverable in the late nineteenth century, but these capabilities were developed for conflict with other warships rather than for combined operations. The size and complexity of steam engines in the early years of steam technology made their use on ship-to-shore landing boats difficult. Doctrine increasingly looked in the direction of conflict between warships, with the development in the late nineteenth century, in which the American writer Alfred T. Mahan was particularly influential, of an emphasis on the "command of the sea" and an accompanying focus on battleships.

In corresponding terms, the development of general staffs on the German model ensured a focus on large-scale army movements overland, based on the Napoleonic and Prussian examples. From the army point of view, there was no institution or prototype placing a focus on combined operations. Despite British fears, at the time of the Crimean War (1854–1856) and subsequently—fears that led, for example, to defensive fortifications including at Sydney—the Russians did not place any emphasis on a naval or combined attack on the British Empire. Instead, the focus was on the overland threat, both to the British Empire in India and to its Turkish counterpart.

The focus on "command of the sea" contrasted with the continued use of naval strength as an aspect of combined operations, as the basis for power projection from the sea, and for second-rank powers of the time. These were very much seen with the War of the Pacific (1879–1883) and, to a lesser extent, the Spanish-American conflict in 1898. The first was a struggle over the Atacama Desert and its rich nitrate deposits between Bolivia and Peru on one side and Chile on the other, none of which had coastlines that were easy to defend. Chile proved adept in the use of combined operations. It took the initiative and landed an army at the Bolivian port of Antofagasta in February 1879, advancing, after the sinking of the main Peruvian warship, the *Huascar*, that October, to overrun the Bolivian Pacific coastline and then to press on to invade Peru. The capture of the strongly fortified Peruvian port of Arica in 1880 revealed the significance of these operations and threw light on the importance, yet also vulnerability, of fortified positions. Exposed to attack as a result of Chilean naval strength, Arica nevertheless resisted a naval bombardment, but the overrunning of the rest of the province left the garrison exposed. Arica still had to be captured, and after a land bombardment failed to do so, the Chileans had to resort to a nighttime storming. In the autumn of 1880, Chile used its naval strength to ravage the Peruvian coast, and in 1881, forces landed and captured Callao and Lima. Peru thus lost its coastal centers of population, but resistance continued in the interior and was not suppressed until 1883. The peace left Chile with Bolivia's coastline and Peru's southernmost provinces.

In 1898, American combined operations played a major role in the Spanish-American War. However, there was a failure to mesh army and navy operations as effectively as Chile had done. The war was a more obvious triumph for the newly developed and powerful American fleet over the largely obsolete and badly led and manned Spanish fleet than it was for the army. The latter benefited greatly from Spain failing to dispute the American landing in Cuba. In the Philippines, the American force projection was rapidly converted into a counterinsurgency role in which command operations played a major role. These commitments, and even more growing concern about Japan, encouraged the development of ideas about roles for the USMC.[20]

In the case of the Boer War of 1899–1902 between Britain and the Boer republics of Transvaal and the Orange Free State in southern Africa, there were combined operations in the broadest sense, in that naval superiority and maritime strength enabled Britain to support its army in South Africa. However, as the Boer republics did not have a coastline or a navy, this was only true in the broadest sense.

Japan developed a capacity for combined operations as an aspect of its military modernization in the late nineteenth century. The Japanese largely used British experience and expertise as the basis for their own new navy. The expedition sent to Chinese-ruled Taiwan in 1874 was small-scale and involved only 13 ships and 3,600 troops, but from the 1880s, preparations improved, in part to be better able to intervene in Korea. The Grand Manoeuvers held in Nagoya in 1890 included amphibious operations with a high degree of cooperation with the navy. A transport department developed within the army, and in the 1894–1895 Sino-Japanese War, the army planned a major landing in Chihli province in China. However, due to the challenge posed by the Chinese navy, the winter weather, and the wish of the government not to offend the Western powers, the landings were restricted to Korea, the Shantung Peninsula, Manchuria, and Taiwan. Those in practice still represented a major commitment that gave Japan strategic purpose and operational advantages. The seizure of Chinese naval bases provided Japan with great advantages.

The Japanese also participated in the coalition forces that intervened in China during the Boxer Crisis in 1900. The 2,100-strong force of Marines that initially tried to relieve Beijing failed and was replaced by a larger force. In 1904–1905, Japan attacked Russia in the same area, notably the strongly fortified Manchurian naval base of Port Arthur, and the Japanese also invaded the island of Sakhalin in 1905. Port Arthur proved a formidable target due to the strength of the defenses, but the Japanese finally succeeded.[21] The use of the Japanese navy was primarily to convoy troops. This was not a war of opposed landings.

More generally, power projection continued to involve a capability for combined operations, as with the Italian invasion of Libya in 1911, although that became a classic example of an ability to deploy power but not then to determine outcomes.[22] Against a more limited island target, there was a greater opportunity for moving from landing to success. This was seen with Italian and Greek attacks on Turkish-held islands in the Aegean in 1911. The Greek navy cut Turkish communications there and covered amphibious attacks, which resulted in the capture of Chios, Lemnos, Samos, and other islands.[23] At the same time, armies and navies in part fought separate wars, most notably, for both sides, with the Russo-Japanese War of 1904–1905.

Enhanced naval capability expanded the possibilities for planning combined operations, not least with the gaining of naval superiority as a prerequisite for amphibious assaults. By the 1900s, Germany and the United States were planning war with each other, and by 1909, American battleships were being designed with larger coal bunkers, allowing a steaming radius of ten thousand nautical miles.[24] However, preparations and doctrine for combined operations were limited. There was much discussion in the British press and popular fiction, and growing military concern, about the possibility of German invasion in a "bolt-from-the-blue."[25] In practice, there was scant German preparation for such action.

In contrast, British plans for inshore combined operations were developed as part of a range of options against Germany. Coastal assault by warships remained an important goal and means for the Royal Navy, although the change in the strategic outlook from the 1890s, notably Franco-Russian cooperation, affected their viability.[26] The attacks planned on opposing ports did not equate with the plans and attempts seen during the First World War for the large-scale coastal landing of land forces. At the same time, there were differences in approach, both between army and navy and within each. Thus, the idea of an advanced base, an idea developed in the 1890s, was applied against Germany by the Royal Navy, when planning for the seizure of offshore islands in order to support a blockade. In contrast, relying on sea command, the army considered large-scale landings in 1905 and 1908. This was not an idea backed by the navy, but by late 1909, even the feasibility of its ideas had been affected by the increased strength of German coastal defenses and torpedo flotillas. Indeed, to use a later term, access denial was now a major issue affecting even modest plans for combined operations. Despite this, the determination to be seen to attack encouraged the survival of these plans, as well as bolder ones, up to and beyond the outbreak of war in 1914. An army-navy amphibious course at Camberley in 1913 led to the conclusion that troops should not land until the beaches and their approaches had been comprehensively shelled. However, the navy lacked systematic land bombardment training procedures, and its guns were not designed for plunging fire and lacked the right type of ammunition.[27]

In British waters, defenses against amphibious assaults evolved in the context of "flotilla defense." The vexed relationship between army and navy in terms of defending against a German invasion was the victim of much political maneuvering. However, at root, coastal defenses and submarine defenses (mines, torpedoes, and submarines themselves) were putting paid to the prospect of opposed landings.

There was also doctrinal development. In his *Military Operations and Maritime Preponderance; Their Relations and Interdependence* (1905), Charles Callwell, an army colonel, discussed the capture of naval bases by combined operations. A *Manual for Combined Naval and Military Operations* was produced in 1911, with a new edition printed in 1913. Julian Corbett, the lecturer in history at the new Naval War College in Britain, argued in *Some Principles of Maritime Strategy* (1911) that command of the sea permitted an engagement with land warfare as far or as little as desired. He saw this as best expressing the genius of British warfare via combined operations, notably in the eighteenth century, the subject of his *England in the Seven Years' War* (1907). Corbett saw such operations as central to the idea of limited war. Looking back at the Seven Years' War (1756–1763), he wrote approvingly of the idea of Britain fighting a limited war alongside an ally who might be fighting an unlimited war against its neighbors on the Continent. This approach looked toward British ideas in the 1920s and 1930s of being able to wage combined operations when necessary and avoiding war on the Continent whenever possible.

Separately, there was a strand of combined operations focused on river activity. For example, operations on the Paraguay River played a major role in the War of the Triple Alliance of 1864–1870. The ability of the Brazilian fleet to gain control of the river and to arrive off the Paraguay capital, Ascuncion, in 1868 was crucial to the fate of the struggle. The use of the Nile during the British advance from Egypt into Sudan in 1895–1898 proved even more crucial.

Speculation about a very different type of combined operations was encouraged by the development of the use of balloons for war from the 1860s. However, the available technology, not least issues of flight control and vulnerability to weather, limited effectiveness and applicability, even during the static siege operations for which ballooning appeared most useful.[28] Aircraft captured the imagination of many commentators, but the prospect of airborne attacks did not do so. Instead, their amphibious counterparts, past and present, provided attractive visual images. This was seen in a 1905 print by Ohara Koson, "Picture of the Imperial Army Landing from the Rear and Capturing Port Arthur." Alongside the troops, the rising sun was depicted, although not any ships. The focus was on operations on land or at sea.

Chapter Six

The First World War, 1914–1918

Compared to the Second World War, the First was not one that is notable for combined operations. There is one famous one, the Gallipoli offensive of 1915, which was far greater in scale than the combined operations of the Spanish-American War of 1898 and met a resistance greater than that in the Russo-Japanese War of 1904–1905. The Gallipoli offensive, however, failed, and there is nothing comparable, in number or significance, to the sequences of combined operations in the Second World War, those mounted by Germany and Japan and those against Germany, Italy, and Japan. The Gallipoli offensive is highly significant in Australian, New Zealand, and Turkish public history, but not elsewhere.

Winning dominance of the sea had to come before its use for force projection, but this emphasis on dominance had led to a neglect of planning for the latter, a situation that continued during the war. This relative neglect was accentuated by the relative unimportance of combined operations in the 1890s and 1900s, certainly for Britain, Germany, and France, and the greater prominence of commerce raiding and protection during the war that arose from the development of the submarine. Winston Churchill, the First Lord of the Admiralty from 1911 to 1915, and Admiral Sir John Fisher, the First Sea Lord from 1904 to 1915, did not order monitors (shallow-draft armored warships) with anti-torpedo bulges until after the war had begun, and these monitors were too late to help the British Expeditionary Force's race to the sea in 1914 or at the Dardanelles in 1915. Nor had the German navy invested much in coastal assault and defense vessels, like monitors.

The course of the First World War did not really bear out the claim in Charles Callwell's *Military Operations and Maritime Preponderance: Their Relations and Interdependence* (1905) that there was a close connection between command of the sea and control of the shore,[1] a connection he saw as demonstrated by the Japanese army's successful assault on the Russian naval base at Port Arthur. Already, prior to the war, the British had concluded that amphibious operations against Germany were not practical. Plans in 1914–1915 for an attack on Schleswig, the part of Germany south of Denmark and a part exposed to British naval power in the North Sea, were not pursued, although special landing craft were built. However, less significant is not the same as inconsequential. As this chapter will show, combined operations were important in the First World War. Moreover, their strategic advantages and limitations are of more general interest to the study of the subject.

The conventional focus on Gallipoli focuses on a spectacular and serious failure. This failure is then usually supplemented by a discussion of why there were so few combined operations in Europe. Particular attention is devoted to the British decision not to pursue the plans that existed for such operations against German forces, whether on the German coast itself or in the section of Belgium, including most of its North Sea coast, occupied by the Germans from late 1914 until the close of the war. This attention can be supplemented by discussion of the general absence of such operations on the part of the world's second naval power, Germany.

This absence is highlighted by the very use of combined operations by the Germans in 1917 in conquering islands off the western coast of Estonia from Russia. This was the most successful amphibious operation of the war in European waters—and the sole German one. The German success, which matched German successes on land, was helped by the disruptive impact of the February Revolution on Russian forces.[2] In March 1918, the Germans launched a supporting nighttime attack on Allied coastal communications to accompany Operation Michael, the Somme offensive, but this was a matter of destroyers and torpedo boats, not amphibious assaults; it was a peripheral effort, and it failed. As instances of a more general failure to employ such operations, neither Austria nor Italy did so in their conflict despite each launching land attacks on the other and both having vulnerable coastlines on the Adriatic. These points all deserve attention and will be considered in this chapter. At the same time, there will be a discussion of combined operations that require consideration.

THE QUEST FOR EMPIRE

The focus by the combatants on Europe was linked to the war plans they sought to implement in 1914, plans for a quick war. Failures to achieve this outcome meant that the fighting continued and was also largely in Europe. At the same time, Germany had an extensive empire, and this empire provided opportunities as well as issues for its opponents. A similar empire was that of

Turkey, which entered the war on the German side in 1914. Turkish entry opened up an important prospect for Allied combined operations. It also greatly extended the geographical range of the Central Powers, giving them a new front with Russia, in the Caucasus, as well as the possibility of land conflict with the British. The British and Turkish empires had a common border on the Egypt-Palestine frontier, while Turkish rule of Iraq threatened the dominant British position in the Persian Gulf. Thus, the strategic problems facing the Allies increased greatly.

In 1914, Allied sea power was the basis for wide-ranging combined operations against German colonies. These were on a range, simultaneity, and scale not hitherto seen. The Japanese captured undefended German possessions in the Caroline, Mariana, and Marshall Islands in the northwest Pacific, as well as Germany's base of Tsingtao on China's upper east coast: the Germans at Tsingtao were heavily outnumbered and, despite a stubborn resistance, were outfought by a successful British-supported Japanese use of combined operations. The Japanese blockaded and isolated the position, before building up a formidable force and then attacking. The first sea-launched air combat mission took place in September 1914 from the Japanese warship *Wakamiya* against Tsingtao.[3]

The threat posed by the German colonies, both to Allied counterparts and to Allied trade, was demonstrated in September 1914 when the light cruiser *Königsberg* supported the unsuccessful German attack on the British base of Mombasa on the coast of Kenya. In turn, attacks on German colonies did not always achieve success. The costly and unsuccessful British amphibious assault on the port of Tanga (in modern Tanzania), on November 23, 1914, the first major clash in East Africa, exposed the sometimes amateurish nature of British planning and command. There was an absence of adequate coordination between army and navy, one that was serious due to the strength of the opposition as opposed to that encountered in colonial policing. Moreover, the peacetime system of planning and controlling operations appeared unable to cope with the strains of war. A path can then be apparently traced from Tanga to failure at Gallipoli the following year.[4]

It is easy to make such suggestions, but the margin between success and failure is generally close in military history and often so with combined operations. Moreover, another British combined operation, one that displayed the strength of the British Indian army, which deployed a division, captured Basra in southern Iraq from the Turks on November 22, 1914. Furthermore, although failure is usually readily explained, it is necessary to give due weight to the problems facing all operations and to remind ourselves that the far better-prepared Germans did not win in attacking France overland in 1914.

Through combined operations and amphibious assaults, the British and their allies, notably France, were certainly able to destroy the articulation of the German empire. The seizure or destruction of German wireless stations played a major part, with the attack on German East Africa beginning with the shelling of the wireless tower at Dar es Salaam. Other British forces that year destroyed German wireless stations in the Pacific and cut German cable routes. A 1,500-strong New Zealand force supported by Australian and French warships seized western Samoa on August 29–30 without a shot being fired.

These operations continued, with South Africans capturing German Southwest Africa in 1915. Far from being a footnote to the war in Europe, the conquest of the German overseas empire was a difficult struggle. Whereas, prior to 1815, the British essentially had to capture a few bases, principally port cities, in order to secure the conquest of French colonies, many of which were islands, now the German colonies enjoyed control of extensive interiors that posed a more serious military challenge to would-be conquerors. This was one that combined operations were less able to secure. For example, although invaded by British and French forces from August 1914, Cameroon did not finally fall until February 1916, when Mora, the major base in the north, which was far distant from the sea, was captured. The Germans in East Africa (modern Burundi, Rwanda, and Tanzania bar Zanzibar) resisted, in the interior, until the end of the war.[5]

As from the eighteenth century, troops from India were a key resource for the British in the Indian Ocean. They were deployed to East Africa in October 1914, while other units were sent to Egypt and yet others advanced into Mesopotamia (Iraq) in 1915. Indian and other imperial troops also played a prominent role in the Gallipoli campaign of 1915. Sea control was crucial to their use.

THE GALLIPOLI CAMPAIGN, 1915

A campaign that had very different meanings at particular moments, this was an attempt to combine alliance politics with military capability by extending the British bloc and weakening that of Germany. Drawing on the geopolitics of the British Empire and on a series of bases in Gibraltar, Malta, Egypt, and Cyprus, the Mediterranean served as the key fulcrum of British activity and one in which it was possible to employ naval superiority as a force multiplier, both in itself and as a key part of combined operations. These operations offered a chance to attack the center of Turkish power.

For geographical reasons, this was not possible in the cases of Germany, Austria (Austria-Hungary), or Bulgaria. To its supporters, an attack on Turkey appeared to be a viable alternative to the effort required in the damaging confrontation with the Germans on the Western Front. This search for an indirect approach focused on combined operations appeared to conform to

British strategic traditions, notably the strategy of William Pitt the Elder in the Seven Years' War and the emphasis on secondary theaters, especially Portugal and Spain, in the conflict with Napoleon, traditions formulated by Julian Corbett in his *Some Principles of Maritime Strategy* (1911). Such a focus would permit Britain to use its naval power and to achieve success with its relatively modest army without weakening the latter by attacking the main opposing force, in short not matching German war making.[6] As a reminder of the political context of combined operations, this policy would also enable Britain to direct a campaign without relying excessively on France, which was the pattern on the Western Front. The British army's lack of experience with Continental war was also a factor.

Initially, the plan, very much supported by Churchill, was to bring naval pressure to bear on Turkey by destroying its naval forces, cutting communications between its Asian and European territories, and exposing the Turkish capital, Constantinople, to bombardment. This involved first forcing a passage through the Dardanelles, a bold strategic plan but one that was heavily dependent on tactical success. On July 18–19, 1912, an Italian torpedo boat squadron had raided into the Dardanelles, penetrating about twenty kilometers and doing some damage to Turkish shipping before withdrawing without harm. However, the large-scale and far more ambitious Anglo-French naval attempt to force the passage, which began on February 19, 1915, was stopped on March 18 by uncharted mines, shore batteries, and an unwillingness to accept further losses after three battleships (two British and one French) were sunk and two more, as well as a battlecruiser, were badly damaged. The defenses were not suppressed.

This failure was followed by an attempt to gain control of the shores of the Dardanelles by landing troops on April 25: the Gallipoli expedition. This attempt, which had not been part of Churchill's original plan but which he became keen on and which represented an escalation that should have been avoided,[7] represented a continuation of the prewar concept of combined operations as a means to support the bringing to bear of naval power. This concept very much reflected prewar naval thought about amphibious power. Over Gallipoli, however, plans changed from a naval assault (including a few thousand Royal Marines to provide small landing parties) to a combined attack and then into a land campaign sustained from the sea, while the campaign was launched against strongly defended positions and not, as planned prewar, against poorly defended ones.[8]

The Gallipoli expedition was seriously flawed in both conception and execution. A lack of appropriate equipment was a major problem. The British had been building powered landing craft from 1914, but on the general pattern of the period including the USMC, most of the British and French troops that went ashore in amphibious operations were landed from ordinary ships, in other words, steam-driven vessels that could not beach (although SS

River Clyde was run aground at Cape Helles). As a result, troops were landed into ships' boats, a vulnerable situation, or into shallows that in fact were far from shallow. Each method was difficult and left the troops gravely exposed to defensive fire. Casualties were heavy. In addition, the difficulties of navigating accurately at night and of landing at the precisely intended spot were clearly shown.

The Gallipoli landings were further hindered by the extent to which the Turks had strengthened local defenses under German direction and by poor Allied generalship and planning, both of which were affected by poor intelligence. Despite a successful deception that confused the Turks as to the likely landing zones, the Allies, who had no relevant experience, failed to push initial advantages, with the result that their advances were contained. Instead of leading to a rapid advance that outflanked the Turkish anti-ship defenses, the initial assault was not pressed forward hard enough. Instead, troops dug in almost as soon as they were ashore. This failure of initiative left commanding high ground to the Turks, who quickly fortified it building on work that had already been done.

Subsequently, Turkish fighting skills and command capabilities proved important, as was the general strength of defensive firepower especially when unsuppressed by artillery fire. Aside from a failure to anticipate the numbers the Turks could deploy and the strength of the defense, the Allies' seriously flawed assessment of Turkish fighting quality and skill was an issue, not least as it led to an underrating of a resilience and bravery that drew in part on a strong Turkish nationalism. The Turkish element helps explain why arguments that greater Allied efforts would have led to success are highly problematic. British planners and commanders overestimated their own operational and tactical capabilities.[9]

The fighting at Gallipoli rapidly became static, with the tiny, exposed Allied coastal positions made even grimmer by the heat, dysentery, and eventually typhoid. On the night of August 6–7, the British made fresh advances and landings, but a combination of poor command decisions and firm Turkish resistance led again to failure.

Allied failure at Gallipoli was not simply that of combined operations understood simply as landings. The Allies managed to get their forces ashore; they seized a series of beachheads, resisted all attempts by the enemy to drive them back into the sea, and linked their beachheads together. In that respect, the combined part of the operation achieved what it was supposed to, albeit at a heavy cost and without demonstrating any particular skill. The failure was in the follow-up, using the army to achieve broader strategic objects once it was successfully placed ashore. The failure was in part to overestimate what a landing by an Allied force of that size could expect to accomplish once it was ashore.

In part, failure also reflected a lack of experience of modern conflict, notably that the campaign occurred early in the war before the learning curve produced solutions to trench warfare, as was seen with Allied success on the Western Front in 1918. As a result, "tactics ate strategy at Gallipoli."[10] Indeed, Gallipoli was an instance of how, repeatedly during the war, strategic conception was not matched by tactical and operational success. In the case of this conflict, this was partly a matter of the absence of marked capability gaps (comparative advantage) in combat effectiveness between the combatants. This absence should not be seen as the product of military failure, but rather of the fact that there was no failure creating such a gap and that it was difficult to understand the consequences in terms of the constraints of trench warfare, notably providing adequate fire support and ensuring mobility. The contrast between strategic conception and tactical and operational success, of course, is one that is more generally true of military activity but is especially true of combined operations.

Gallipoli has been overrated as an epic failure, but it did demonstrate major issues with amphibious assaults. There were also the specific problems caused by the British failure to develop an amphibious capability and strategy prior to the war. As a result, the Gallipoli campaign rested on a political and strategic drive and suffered from inadequate preparation, specifically the lack of a relevant planning and command structure; although that was a more general problem affecting combined operations and one that became serious largely due to the resolution of the opposition. The Turks were not a peripheral force such as the German units in their colonies. The Allies were also affected by the degree to which the overwhelming concentration of troops and matériel on the Western Front meant that insufficient munitions and high-quality troops were sent to Gallipoli. More specifically, logistics was a major issue in the contexts both of overall resource issues and of the issues involved in moving supplies as far as the Aegean.[11] Major-General Sir Alexander Godley's explanation of failure underlined the need to consider both sides, although, in fact, he also showed questionable leadership:

> The lack of fresh reinforcements, both in April and in August, the strength and superiority of the enemy, in troops, guns and positions, were the true causes of why we did not get across the peninsula and it was not on account of bad plans, or failure of the troops, or bad orders, or want of water, or want of co-operation with the Navy.[12]

Gallipoli captured different aspects of military experience during the war but also the particular problems of a stalled combined operation, or rather a stalled peripheral campaign. John Monash, an Australian brigade commander, commented:

> We have got our battle procedure now thoroughly well organised. To a stranger it would probably look like a disturbed ant-heap with everybody running a different way, but the thing is really a triumph of organisation. There are orderlies carrying messages, staff officers with orders, lines of ammunition carriers, water carriers, bomb carriers, stretcher bearers, burial parties, sandbag parties, periscope hands, pioneers, quartermaster's parties, and reinforcing troops, running about all over the place, apparently in confusion but yet everything works as smoothly as on a peace parade, although the air is thick with clamour and bullets and bursting shells, and bombs and flares. [13]

Aside from putting pressure on the Turks, it was also hoped that the Gallipoli campaign would unlock the Balkans for the Allies, an aspect of a domino theory often advanced by advocates of combined operations (as with Churchill's support for such operations in the Mediterranean in the Second World War) but also in the case of other forms of campaigning. These hopes provided those who were not privy to strategic planning with a sense that the operation had great significance. Indeed, the knowledge of strategic purpose on the part of those engaged in combined operations became a more apparent feature in the twentieth century. For example, Alan Thomson, a British officer, wrote to his wife Edith on September 24, 1915: "Don't worry about me sweetheart. I daresay we shall get Romania and Greece in and if that happens we may be able between us to hold up the Germans in Serbia. . . . If the Germans don't get through to Turkey, I think the latter will give in." He returned to this theme in letters on October 7 and November 20. [14]

The Gallipoli campaign was finally abandoned with the successful withdrawal of the invasion force in nighttime operations on December 18–19, 1915, and January 8–9, 1916, which was the only impressive feature of the operation. These 140,000 troops were to be very useful elsewhere. British hopes from the campaign had been cruelly disabused, and it was not to be repeated.

In Australia, the war remains far more important to national identity than the Second World War, with the Gallipoli campaign, presented as heroic, being the key episode that demonstrated Australian mettle and advanced its nationhood. Peter Weir's iconic film *Gallipoli* (1981) offered a political dimension to disenchantment, one directed against the imperial link with Britain. In this deeply distorted account, one that remains important to the Australian national myth, the British contribution in the campaign was downgraded and seriously misrepresented. The impression offered was of British inefficiency, cowardice, and dilatoriness leading to the sacrifice of Anzac (Australian and New Zealand) troops. [15] This critique is deployed alongside the argument that the British government in the Second World War used Australian forces to pursue its strategy in the Middle East at the expense of Australian requirements against Japan.

AFTER GALLIPOLI

Paradoxically as it might appear, failure at Gallipoli (as later with the Dieppe raid in 1942) led subsequently, in a pronounced learning curve, to greater interest in combined operations, with the development of some of the necessary tools, including, in this case, coastal monitors. However, the core idea—for an amphibious assault on the Belgian coast in 1916–1917 as part of a more general combined operation by land and sea in Flanders—was not brought to fruition. The idea of a landing on the Belgian coast was seen as a way to bring an operational degree of mobility that would have strategic effect. It looked toward successive Allied invasions of North Africa and Europe in 1942–1944 and to the Inchon landing in Korea in 1950. In 1917, the plan was focused on the Third Battle of Ypres, generally called Passchendaele after a ridge that became a key Allied target. The front chosen was that in Flanders, for a number of reasons that reflected the accumulative nature of strategy. Thus, there were combined aspects. The German submarine facilities at Bruges, Ostend, and Zeebrugge provided worthwhile objectives and were given strategic point due to the significance of the damaging German submarine assault on Britain's maritime communications, a significance that helped explain British interest in bombing Belgian harbors. Moreover, Flanders would enable Britain to use its naval dominance, one that had been maintained despite the German attempt to overcome it in 1916, an attempt that had led to the battle of Jutland.

Yet, there were other factors helping explain the selection of Flanders that were not related to combined operations, including the need to lessen the costly vulnerability of the Allied position in the Ypres salient by gaining territory and the German lack of commanding defensive, surveillance, and artillery positions in the low terrain. Landings were not to be launched until the army had achieved gains that it was not in fact to obtain. In practice, there was probably little mileage in the idea that naval power could make a material difference to operations in Flanders, an idea that had been pushed by Churchill as First Lord of the Admiralty in 1914–1915. He claimed:

> If you choose to push your left flank along the sand dunes on the shore to Ostend and Zeebrugge, we could give you 100 or 200 heavy guns in absolutely devastating support. Four or five miles inshore we could make you perfectly safe and superior. Here at last, you have their flank if you care to use it. . . . We could bring men in at Ostend or Zeebrugge to reinforce you in a hard southeasterly push. There is no limit to what could be done by the extreme left-handed push and sea operation along the Dutch frontier.[16]

The strength of the German resistance against the land offensive, however, was the key element in the development of the campaign. There was no landing. Aside from the serious naval problem of operating inshore against a protected coast, there was also the difficulty posed by the strength of German forces, with the added mobility offered them by the railway and quick German reactivity. Once the British heavy monitors appeared off the Belgian coast, they discovered that the Germans had erected ever-heavier shore batteries that could outrange them and had the advantage in terms of ship-versus-shore accuracy.[17]

In addition, earlier pressure on Turkish communications in the Gulf of Alexandretta was not developed. The actions in the gulf and elsewhere on the Turkish coast represented very traditional forms of naval activity. There were numerous minor raids on the coast of Syria designed to harass the Turks, particularly before the 1915 Turkish advance into Sinai. Raiding activity continued later in the war. After the evacuation from Gallipoli in 1916, Vice-Admiral John de Robeck, the British naval commander, suggested using the Royal Naval Division as a dedicated raiding force to harass the coast of Anatolia but was refused permission, and the Royal Naval Division was fed into the mincing machine on the Western Front in France. However, the Royal Navy did undertake some little raids using Greek irregulars, including raids to seize livestock. These were indicative of the desire, seen again with the Second World War, to exploit sea control in order to harass the enemy by any means and also of the failure at this stage to understand what might be achieved by a specialist raiding force: in other words, commandos.[18]

The Allied grand strategy of concerted attacks agreed at Chantilly in late 1915 had very much focused on land operations. The later dispatch of an Anglo-French expeditionary force to Salonica in 1916 neither put much pressure on the Central Powers nor helped Britain's Balkan allies. Instead, the force was hemmed in until just before the close of the war when its eventual success over the Bulgarians was of value largely in helping precipitate the collapse of Germany's alliance system.[19]

The Germans used combined operations successfully in the Baltic in 1917, capturing islands off the coast of modern Estonia from Russia in what was probably the most well-executed amphibious assault of the war.[20] Between the world wars, the USMC studied it along with Gallipoli, although not the successful Spanish landings at Alhucemas in 1925. However, again, this was not a key offensive. The distinction between specific practicality and broader effectiveness was an important one, as it remains.

WIDER CONTEXTS

The First World War therefore did not see the use of combined operations in Europe that might have been anticipated. The size of armies in Europe and the unprecedented mobility brought to the defense by the availability of railways, notably in Western Europe, were such that the prospect of such operations deploying mass and maintaining a dynamic sufficient to overcome resistance was limited. The view of British generals was clearly expressed: "The truth was that this class of operation possibly had some value a century ago, when land communications were indifferent, but now, when they were excellent, they were doomed to failure."[21] The German failure to conquer France (unlike in 1940) meant that there was no need for a decisive large-scale operation to recapture it (as in 1944), and the possibilities for smaller-scale assaults were not pursued.

In terms of opportunity costs, large forces anyway had to be maintained to protect land frontiers; they faced opposing forces, and it was therefore most appropriate to mount offensives overland, not least in order to thwart attacks. In contrast, the burdens and disruption involved in withdrawing forces from the line in order to mount combined offensives, burdens including significant opportunity costs and the frictions that such offensives consistently faced, helped to maintain the emphasis on land offensives.

The situation was very different outside Europe. German imperial possessions were either islands or tended to have a coastal focus, the force ratios were very different to those in Europe, and the impediments against advances overland were far greater, notably those of distance, logistics, and disease. There was also continuity in this sphere with pre-1914 campaigning, for example, the successful intervention of a large Western-Japanese coalition force in China in 1900 during the Boxer Rising. Conversely, there was comparable continuity in the focus on land advances in conflict within Europe.

Allowing for these general points, it may seem still surprising that more use was not made of combined operations during the war. The contrast is certainly apparent. Thus, in 1911, Italy had mounted such operations against the Turkish Empire, which then lacked allies. Not only had a large Italian force been landed in Libya, but there had also been successful operations in the Aegean, notably against Rhodes. In contrast, there was no similar pattern of Italian operations against Turkey (then allied to the Central Powers) after Italy joined the Allies in 1915. Instead, the focus was on attacking Austria overland, and this continued to be the focus despite repeated failures. Italy lacked the capability for a large-scale amphibious assault on the other side of the Adriatic and did not dominate the sea in naval terms, in part because the allied French fleet concentrated on blockading the Strait of Otranto in order to prevent German and Austrian submarines entering the Mediterranean, and did not try to move north into the Adriatic in order to establish control. Such a movement would have exposed it to submarine attack.

In late 1917, Italy organized what became a permanent Marine unit. This reflected the crisis caused by Caporetto, an Austro-German victory over the Italian army that caused heavy losses and created a sense of vulnerability. To defend Venice and the coastline, the navy organized a Brigata Marina or Naval Brigade that comprised an artillery unit and a three-thousand-strong

Reggimento Marina. The regiment performed very well in 1918 in the last campaign of the war and has never disbanded.

In the case of all the powers, preparedness was a factor, as was doctrine in explaining why more use was not made of combined operations, but there were also powerful strategic elements, notably as fed through the politics of command, including differences between politicians and within the military. For France and Russia, the priority was regaining territorial losses to Germany, but for Britain there was a more profound tension between the commitment to the Western Front and an attempt to find alternative areas for attack that were seen as more beneficial and less costly. In January 1915, Arthur Balfour, a member of the Committee for Imperial Defence and a former prime minister, argued:

> The notion of driving the Germans back from the west of Belgium to the Rhine by successfully assaulting one line of trenches after another seems a very hopeless affair, and unless some means can be found for breaking their line at some critical point, and threatening their communications, I am unable to see how the deadlock in the West is to be brought to any rapid or satisfactory conclusion.[22]

Yet to lessen the commitment to the Western Front risked straining Britain's alliance system, as it was unclear if France, under heavy German pressure, would be able to defend its remaining territory unless provided with additional support. Britain itself could not confront Germany by mounting an invasion of the latter, and this led to a variety of "indirect" options, notably mounted at a distance from the principal theater of conflict. The very much more costly commitment on the Western Front was far more direct in that it involved conflict with the main German army.

To a great extent, the inability to mount an invasion of Germany might appear to mean that Britain could not fully use its navy on behalf of the Allies, at least in order to have a direct effect on land. Yet, there were other and far more significant tasks for the navy, notably being able to stop the German High Seas Fleet threatening British dominance of home waters and also protecting oceanic trade routes from German attack, both surface and submarine, all tasks the United States joined in with in 1917. Indeed, two million American troops were convoyed across the Atlantic to Europe in 1917–1918.

Compared to these tasks, mounting combined operations was secondary in strategic terms, while anyway most of the Allied navies were not appropriate for such a task. Indeed, the Gallipoli and colonial operations essentially relied on warships that were not in the line of battle, which greatly lessened the opportunity cost involved, an issue that is always significant for such operations. In addition to the other naval tasks, there was a lack of the necessary preparedness for large-scale amphibious assaults.

At the same time, as with the very different blockade of Germany, the British and Allied navies provided a key element in combined operations by making it very difficult for the Central Powers to block or limit these operations by maritime means. This was seen in (British) Somaliland, where there were not the British troops available to spare for a major offensive against the opposition of the fundamentalist Dervishes. However, the effective naval blockade hit the supply of arms and ammunition to them from Turkey, which had positions in western Arabia, and thus prevented the opening up of a more serious challenge to British power.

There were also combined operations that were not part of the world war, or not directly so, notably the intervention of American Marines in Cuba in 1917, essentially a police action, and of Japanese forces in China. Each corresponded to patterns of activity that preceded the war and that continued after it.

CONCLUSIONS

The likely future pattern of combined operations and amphibious assaults was left unclear by the war, as was their probable impact and possible significance. So much would clearly depend on where conflict focused. This situation was more clearly the case with warfare. The First World War had seen the use of a range of new, or newly improved, weapons and methods, notably airships, aircraft, submarines, tanks, and radio, and the likely consequences of their use attracted planners and commentators. In this situation, combined operations were located as part of a greater flux in conception, doctrine, and speculation, a flux driven on by the intractable costs of the war and the need to avoid as destructive a conflict as the First World War. This need encouraged the search for a magic bullet, as with interest in bombers, but there was little reason to see amphibious assaults in this light. Instead, in the aftermath of Gallipoli, they appeared simply to move the zone of intractable conflict to a new location. Indeed, Gallipoli made any amphibious assault appear foolhardy, if not suicidal.

Combined operations were not at the forefront of attention in 1918. Indeed, in the extensive plans made that year for responding both to developments then and to the prospect of the war continuing into 1919 (as indeed appeared probable until the German military leadership in late October decided to pursue armistice negotiations), the emphasis was very much not on combined operations. The focus instead remained on the Western Front, in response to the threat posed by German forces and not least thanks to the arrival of large numbers of American troops and to the interest aroused by the potential use of tanks to create operational opportunities. Far from focusing on plans for combined operations and amphibious assaults, the Royal

Navy continued to think in terms of victory through blockade and battle against a high-seas fleet.

These were not flawed views or an aspect of a failure to grasp the opportunities. In practice, in terms of the geopolitics of the war in 1918, there was a limit to what could be achieved by combined operations. More particularly, even if successful, they had operational potential rather than likely strategic consequences. Such potential was insufficient due to the state of the war at that stage and the need to deliver rapid strategic results, notably in response to Germany's success in knocking Russia out of the war in 1918, a success achieved as a result of overland attacks. Indeed, the flow of conflict seemed as much set by large-scale advances on land in 1918 as it had done in 1914. Where this left combined operations was unclear but, in practice, required a different type of war to that which was being conducted.

The German overseas empire had largely gone by the start of 1918 (and indeed 1916), but this was not going to determine the course of the war. Indeed, as the Germans attacked on the Western Front with great initial success in the Spring Offensives of 1918, so it appeared that combined operations might be necessary in order to ensure a successful British evacuation from France. This would have been on a far greater scale than Corunna (1809), Gallipoli (1915), or Dunkirk (1940). British plans for a threatening future included the wrecking, without French support, of every French harbor on the Channel as far west as Cherbourg, in order to preempt the risk of a subsequent German invasion of Britain. Both in Operation Michael (March 21 to April 5) and in Operation Georgette, the Lys Offensive (April 9 to 30), the Germans failed to push the British back on the English Channel. The likely outcome had they done so is unclear but would certainly have underlined the varied types of combined operations. That was to be seen even more clearly in the following world war. Might-have-beens are significant today in assessing past potential, not least as they played a major role for contemporaries in considering opportunities, problems, and possibilities. In the latter case, combined operations played a greater role in the First World War than might otherwise appear.

Chapter Seven

The Interwar Period, 1918–1939

1919–1929

Having been of limited significance during the First World War, combined operations were of highly variable importance in the subsequent interwar period. This significance was most pronounced for the United States as it pressed ahead with the use of such operations in order to protect its interests around the Caribbean. There was also the nature of foreign intervention in the Russian Civil War (1918–1921). However, in contrast, many of the conflicts of the period, notably civil wars within China, had only a limited combined dimension. In these cases, such a dimension can be emphasized, but it needs to be set in a broader context of the conduct of wars in which land forces and operations overland played the key role. Indeed, because of the last, moving along and crossing rivers were frequently the most important element of combined operations.

When forces were deployed in combined operations, the dynamic of success or failure was still largely set by campaigning on land. For example, during the Russian Civil War, the Franco-Greek force that had landed at Odessa in December 1918 made scant contribution to the anti-Bolshevik cause in the region and was evacuated the following spring in the face of the Bolshevik advance. The arrival of British and French warships in the Black Sea in 1918 made such intervention far easier. Thus, in late 1918, the British landed troops in the Black Sea port of Batumi, in the modern state of Georgia, in order to establish a strong position in the Caucasus. However, under pressure from too many international commitments, lacking any dynamic of success, and threatened by Bolshevik advances, the British withdrew their forces from there from late 1919, evacuating Batumi in July 1920.

Combined operations proved more significant in the Baltic in 1919 as Bolshevik advances into Estonia and Latvia were stopped by counterrevolutionary forces supported by British naval pressure. The importance of the later was accentuated by the fact that the major cities in Latvia and Estonia—Riga and Tallinn—were ports. This was again significant that October when the attempt by a German unit in the White army to seize Riga, the capital of Latvia, was stopped by Latvian and Estonian forces, helped by the British navy.

Other powers that depended on amphibious power projection into Russia, notably Japan, Canada, and the United States, also ended up having to concede failure. The Americans, Canadians, and Japanese were important to the Allied landings in Archangel, Murmansk, and the Russian Far East. The American Expeditionary Force penetrated 640 kilometers (400 miles) along the Northern Dvina River, starting from the White Sea port of Archangel. Canadian artillery was essential for the Americans. The failure of foreign intervention was not because of an inability to transport, land, and sustain troops, but rather due to the failure to sustain the anti-Bolshevik cause in Russia. Bolshevik forces advanced overland.[1]

In Turkey, in 1919–1922, combined operations enabled the deployment of forces from the victorious wartime Allies. Warships from Britain, France, Greece, Italy, and the United States were deployed to the Bosporus and to Turkish coastal waters. However, the subsequent course of operations and the political context, both in Turkey and in the imperial metropoles, led to failure. In particular, the Greeks, having established themselves on the Aegean coast, were then heavily defeated when they advanced onto the Anatolian plateau in 1921. In turn, British forces backed down when threatened by the Turkish advance in 1922 and agreed to evacuate Constantinople and the Dardanelles.[2] Taking a different political course helped Italy to success. In March 1919, Italian troops from Rhodes landed in Adalya (Antalya) in southern Anatolia and then moved on to Konya, subsequently widening its occupation zone by seizing Makri Budrun, Kuch-Adassi, Alanya Ismidt, and Eskiehir. Italy then aligned with the Turks against France and Greece, which ensured that it was able to sustain its presence until its expeditionary force was withdrawn in April 1922.

Western forces eventually proved successful in Morocco, where France came to Spain's assistance against serious local opposition in the part of Morocco it claimed. The response to the Moors in 1925 escalated, not least when Spain, with French naval support, launched a successful combined operation in the Bay of Alhucemas (al Hoceima). The amphibious assault was supported by naval gunnery and air attack. However, the landing craft carrying the Renault tanks hit a shoal far from the beach, and they could not land on the first day as had been planned. This operation was important but only one among a number of factors that led to the suppression of the Rif rebellion.[3] This operation was very well planned. Francisco Franco, later victor in the Spanish Civil War and dictator of Spain, led the first battalion ashore and wrote a firsthand account of the operation.[4]

The success appears to have created an impression that amphibious attacks were not all that difficult and to have inspired two attempts by the Spanish Republicans during the civil war of 1936–1939. There was an attempted landing on the island of Majorca in 1936. Although largely improvised, the troops from Minorca had command of the seas and gained a beachhead, putting approximately eight thousand troops, mostly militia, ashore. The Nationalists were outnumbered but were able to mobilize reservists on the island. These, together with a couple of aircraft supplied by Italy, gave them the advantage. In 1938, Vicente Rojo, the Republican chief of staff, envisioned a major offensive against the relatively narrow neck of Nationalist territory in Andalusia that separated Republican territory from Portugal. The idea was for an attack westward to sever the corridor, the weakest part of the Nationalist front, combined with an amphibious landing at Motril on the southern coast, unhinging the entire Nationalist front. This plan was rejected partially for political reasons, as many of the Republican troops in Andalusia were Anarchist or Trotskyite, and also for fear that the movement of troops would weaken the defense of the capital, Madrid.

In addition, the Dutch had an amphibious practice to help police their East Indies possessions (modern Indonesia). However, that was not one they translated to Europe, where there was indeed no need.

UNITED STATES

As a parallel with imperial expansion, control, and policing, the Americans dominated the Caribbean militarily. This was not least due to their naval power and to the operational effectiveness of the Marine Corps, a separate service within the Navy Department. The Marines operated in Haiti, the Dominican Republic, and Nicaragua, which, far from receiving short deployments, were occupied in 1915–1934, 1916–1924, and 1926–1933 respectively. However, popular guerrilla movements, notably in Nicaragua, affected their control, and the Americans preferred to rely on local national guard paramilitary forces that they built up and sometimes led. Close air support played a major role. On the pattern of Somalia in the 1990s, the ambush of a small group of Marines in Nicaragua at the end of 1930 helped lead the American government to decide to withdraw the force.[5]

There was a wholesale transformation of purpose and focus between 1933 and 1936, from small wars to amphibious operations. The USMC had made some experiments in "advanced base operations," but the need to deploy most of the Corps abroad had hampered serious progress. By 1927, of the eight USMC regiments, four were in China, one in Haiti, and two in Nicaragua, along with miscellaneous units, including air squadrons. The end of these deployments led to a resumption of landing exercises. The Fleet Marine Force (FMF) was created in 1933 in order to focus on amphibious landings. It was to be organized into two brigades, one based at Quantico, Virginia, for the Atlantic, the other at San Diego for the Pacific. In February 1941, these two brigades were designated the 1st and 2nd Marine Divisions. These became the basis of the First Marine Amphibious Corps, which was landed on Guadalcanal in late 1942.[6] In 1941, the USMC used a battalion in an experimental "special operations" role, which proved the basis for the establishment of Raider Battalions the following year in order to focus on particularly difficult tasks.

Thomas Holcomb (1879–1965) was the key figure in the victory of the amphibious-warfare clique over the small-wars clique. Appointed a second lieutenant in the USMC in 1900, he served in China, in the Philippines, and then on the Western Front in the First World War. Holcomb was commandant of the USMC from 1936 to 1943, overseeing its large-scale expansion from 17,248 to 385,000 men[7] and its reconceptualization from a "small-wars" force to the means for amphibious assault and combined operations. Other prominent figures during the Second World War, including Holcomb's successor, Alexander Vandergrift, and the commander of the Fleet Marine Force, Pacific, Holland "Howlin Mad" Smith, earlier played a significant role in the 1930s in developing techniques and equipment for amphibious operations. The USMC's Schools at Quantico canceled the entire academic year in 1933–1934 to allow faculty and students alike to devote time to analyzing and correcting mistakes at Gallipoli. No other branch of the services did so much with so little to formulate tentative doctrines. The key doctrinal document, the USMC's *Tentative Manual for Landing Operations* (1934), was designed to further War Plan Orange against Japan and its requirement for forcible entry in the shape of the seizure of island bases to support the westward movement of the navy across the Pacific. This was to be influential for the navy's 1938 *Manual for Landing Operations* and the army's 1941 *Landing Operations on Hostile Shores*. The doctrine and planning were to play a major role in American advances in the Pacific in 1943–1945, with particular value attached to practicalities, notably phases, timing, sequencing, and synchronization, although in the 1930s it was not widely perceived that taking islands from the Japanese would be far more difficult than operating in Latin American states against rebels.

In 1946, Admiral Raymond Spruance, then the president of the Naval War College, stated that prior to the Second World War there had been "intensive study" of combined operations by the navy and the USMC, as well as joint army-Marine maneuvers, but no comparable progress with developing a good landing craft capability.[8] In practice, although there were also exercises in which the navy landed army troops to take contested ground, the naval leadership did not focus on combined operations, and the navy's strategic exercises or "fleet problems" did not concern themselves greatly with opposed landings.[9] Separately, coastal defense fortifications were constructed in the Philippines and Hawaii.

SEA-BASED OPERATIONS

More generally, combined operations were not to the fore in interwar naval thinking. In part, this was a consequence of the lack of joint structures and planning, although the absence of a strong drive for such capability was linked to this conservatism. It was particularly apparent with Britain. Looked at differently, there appeared no reason to change the already-established capability and doctrine. Between Britain and the United States, the precise lack of a need for offensive combined operations, rather than for defeating them in the shape of resisting Japanese expansion, was a hindrance in both operational and technological development. An Anglo-American invasion of France in a future war, as was to occur in both northern and southern France in 1944, was not anticipated. Instead, it was assumed that, as in the First World War, France, whatever its territorial losses to German advances, which would be by land, would still hold ports, notably Brest and Cherbourg, where troops could be landed from Britain and the United States. In short, France would have a defensive deep space that would provide safe room for deployment and reinforcement.

That the development of doctrine and capability in the interwar period did not match the subsequent need for sea-based combined operations is not surprising. In part, this can be criticized in terms of sticking to the apparent lesson from the last war, but far more was at stake. It is necessary to look in particular at the focus of naval operations on fleet-to-fleet conflict. This notably was the issue for Japan and the United States as they drew up war plans in the 1920s and 1930s. On the part of the United States, with War Plan Orange, there was an understanding that combined operations would be necessary to seize territory in the western Pacific, but such a seizure was seen as subsequent to victory in naval conflict.[10] That was reasonable and was indeed to be borne out by events, although it was also linked to a general failure, on the part of American naval commanders, to engage with the specifics of combined operations. In the American navy, the internal strategic debate between the "thruster" and "cautionary" admirals was linked to the discussion about the need for combined doctrine and operations, but, in part, the tension between a focus in battleships and one on aircraft carriers left scant role for a wider consideration. Germany held similar discussion about surface warships or submarines. In contrast, in Japan, all naval officers who went through the Etajima Naval Academy in the 1930s were extensively prepared for landing operations.

In the Soviet Union, for which capability in inland seas, the Baltic and Black Seas, and not oceans was then the issue, there was much more interest in cooperation with surface forces. The Young School, who came to the fore in naval planning in 1930, argued that a decisive naval battle was a mistaken goal. Instead, they claimed that the submarines, torpedo boats, and aircraft of the Soviet navy could nullify the impact of the opposing fleet, so as to enable the Soviet navy to assist the army. The annual maneuvers of the Baltic Fleet, which, in the late 1920s, had emphasized a defensive response to an attacking fleet, now focused on amphibious attacks in support of the advancing army. However, those advocating this were swept aside, in the purges that began in 1937, in favor of Stalin's focus on the building and purchase of large surface warships and his determination to be able to oppose those of Britain or Germany. As a result, the effectiveness of the Russian navy in combined operations declined. At the same time, there was a continuing capability for amphibious assaults in support of the army.

Like Germany, the Soviet Union did not develop specialized landing craft. Nevertheless, on the global level, there was more interest in specialized landing craft than there had been prior to and during the First World War. The United States had interest in this capability but, as yet, not the equipment to match their doctrine. Japan made the most progress, both in developing types of landing craft and in building a reasonable number of ships. Their Daihatsu A had an unloading ramp in its bows, and this was to become the key type of landing craft, being copied by the United States and Britain. In 1937, Japan deployed several hundred landing craft, as well as the *Shinshu Maru*, an 8,100-ton landing craft carrier built in 1933. This carrier could hold twenty landing craft inside. There was also the conversion of merchantmen into conventional landing ships.

BRITAIN

Britain had only a weak amphibious warfare capability to match its naval strength as the principal naval power with the United States. The emphasis for Britain continued to be on the display of naval power with troops subsequently landed without resistance and not on mounting opposed landings. There were differences in opinion over how best to organize combined operations in the context of major postwar cuts in resources. These cuts combined with the absence of institutional provision for such operations, and this ensured that they lacked any real constituency, let alone a powerful one. The Royal Navy and the RAF focused on their particular war-fighting requirements, and these emphasized command of the sea and the air as a crucial prelude to anything else. The Royal Navy envisaged a need for combined operations, notably in order to secure or seize naval bases in the Far East in the event of war with Japan, but consideration of these took a secondary role to more pressing requirements. The services did independent war planning, and as the Admiralty's war plans were either purely fleet-based or blockade, it felt no need for combined operations. The army had other things to consider while the Royal Marines had no real ability to press the matter.

At the same time, bolder views were advanced, notably developments of the concept of the Royal Marines. These included independent forces to join the navy on its mobilization in order to seize temporary bases and attack enemy-held coastlines. Even more bold was the idea of a significant permanent landing force, drawn from the Royal Marines and the army.[11] The Royal Marines were under serious threat of abolition, and redefining their role as an amphibious assault force was conditioned as much by this as by an operational imperative.

However, the conflicts of the 1930s in which Britain was involved did not focus on such operations. The most significant were the Arab Rising in Palestine and the Waziristan Campaign on India's northwest frontier in what is now Pakistan. In both, air support was important. War with Italy in the Abyssinian crisis, which appeared a prospect in 1935–1936 and which might have led to such operations (or their prevention) in the Mediterranean, did not come to fruition. The British proposed air attacks on Italy and the protection of Egypt from invasion from the Italian colony of Libya. There was no project for amphibious operations on the pattern of those that were to be mounted in 1943–1944.

As a result, it was scarcely surprising that the British did not mount significant amphibious exercises. This situation only changed in 1938 when, in response to clear signs of Japanese capability, the first was held, only to reveal limited competence and a lack of the necessary equipment.[12] In contrast to the United States, British interwar efforts appear slim, and the Marines did not have an integral role in British naval strategy comparable to that of the USMC in American strategy. Nevertheless, there was some useful progress in terms of doctrine and equipment. The 1938 *Manual of Combined Operations* is, in many respects, a well-founded document, and it established much of the basis for later developments. The manual tended to emphasize the value of surprise, of attacking an undefended beach, and of landing at night, but did not preclude opposed landings in daylight and offered advice on how to conduct these. The manual was possibly as valuable within the context of the European Theater as the nascent American doctrine was to become in the Pacific.

Similarly, the British did not have a dedicated amphibious force to compare to the American Fleet Marine Force, but they did identify ships suitable for conversion to Landing Ship Infantry landing craft, the LCA and LCM, that would later be the mainstay of all major operations. In this respect, the British were in advance of the Americans by the outbreak of the Second World War but did not build many landing craft as there was no obvious immediate need. Subsequently, the British built the first LSTs and LCTs.[13]

CHINA AND JAPAN

Although they took a secondary role, shallow-draft boats played a part in conflict within China in the 1920s, in both coastal waters and on rivers. For example, in December 1920, when Sun Yat-sen, the Guomindang (Nationalist) leader, established his position in Guangzhou (Canton), his arrival was backed by the navy's First Fleet. Five years later, Guomindang gunboats bombarded mercenary positions in fighting outside Guangzhou. In March 1926, three warlord gunboats attacked the Dagu forts, while other warships escorted transports landing five thousand troops nearby. The following spring, the defection to Jiang Jieshi, Sun Yat-sen's successor, of the Fujian Naval Fleet gave him control of the Yangzi River, and he reached Nanjing on one of his new warships.

Meanwhile, foreign pressure on China continued to be possible through combined operations in coastal waters and on rivers, as with the Yangtze Patrol Force organized by the United States in 1921. However, the states in question changed. In 1927, the American, British, French, and Japanese commanders on the China Station considered responding to Guomindang actions against foreign interests by sending warships up the Yangzi, sinking the Guomindang fleet, destroying their arsenals at Hankou and Guangzhou, and possibly preventing Guomindang forces from crossing the Yangzi on their move north.[14] In the event, these steps were not taken, and it was Japan that was to play the key role in applying pressure. Thus, in 1928, Japanese warships were sent up the Yangzi and Special Naval Landing Forces were landed at Wenzhou. In 1931, Japan sought to intimidate China during its occupation of Manchuria by holding naval exercises in the Yangzi and sending ships up the Whangpoo River. In 1932, during the Shanghai Operation, the Japanese navy found it difficult to suppress opposition in Shanghai with its fleet, air power, and Special Naval Landing Forces, until it was reinforced by the landing of an army division behind the Chinese besieging force, which then fell back, giving the Japanese success.

In August 1937, when full-scale war broke out, naval gunfire played a major role in stemming the initial Chinese attack on the positions of the Japanese Special Naval Landing Forces in Shanghai. In response, the Japanese were able to land two divisions to the north, although their rapid success was then lost in a slow progress toward Shanghai in the face of strong resistance, notably at night, in waterlogged terrain. Beyond the range of the navy's guns, and lacking necessary air support, the Japanese lost momentum. As a result, another landing was mounted at Hangchow Bay to the south of the city on November 5, 1937. Successful, the result of this landing threatened to encircle the Chinese and led to their retreat and to the Japanese capture of the city on November 11. In this campaign, the Japanese had benefited greatly from the extent to which rivers and the sea permitted them a mobility and flexibility that they lacked further inland.[15]

The following year, Japanese warships sailed up the Yangzi and directly engaged Chinese positions. The Japanese employed only a portion of their navy in China, and notably few of their aircraft carriers, but had fleets on the Yangzi and off China. In 1938, the ports of Xiamen (Amoy) and Guangzhou (Canton) fell to combined operations, followed, in 1939, by Shantou and the island of Hainan.

The Japanese navy built up its amphibious capability by developing units that specialized as *rikusentai* (landing parties). They were given infantry training, and by the late 1930s, the navy had permanent landing units, Special Naval Landing Forces, that were based ashore and armed with heavy weaponry including artillery. In one respect, this development represented a type of combined operations in that amphibious capability was enhanced. However, these units also reflected the extent to which the Japanese army and navy in part fought separate wars, including with separate air forces. This process was to be greatly accentuated in 1941 when Japan attacked the United States, Britain, and the Dutch.

The Japanese trained several army divisions in landing operations from 1921, and there were joint Japanese army-navy amphibious exercises in the western Pacific in the late 1920s, although the cost restricted such training, as did high-level divisions between army and navy. The tasking of the military helped drive preparedness. While the navy was already focusing on the United States, the army retained its concern with China and Russia. Nevertheless, in response to a rise in enmity toward the United States, the army from the 1920s, and notably 1925, prepared more detailed plans for combined operations against the Americans, especially in the Philippines. Later in the decade, the Japanese army developed Shipping Engineer Regiments that were to be responsible for the operation of landing craft. Moreover, with far more expertise than other powers, the Japanese advanced a combined doctrine and the relevant practice. The Japanese put the emphasis on attacking at night or at dawn and on landing at several points simultaneously and then concentrating on land. Their experience was to stand them in good stead in 1941–1942, notably in their rapid conquests of the British Far East, the Philippines, and the Dutch East Indies (Indonesia).[16]

AIR-LAND

Another reason for a lack of focus by most planners on conventional combined operations was a growing concentration on the capacity for a new form of such operations brought by air power. Part of this involved the development of aircraft carriers. However, although taking part in operations against targets on land, and being deployed to make such action possible, carriers were seen as useful largely in terms of conflict at sea.[17]

A very different account was offered by air-land operations. These appeared likely to help break the impasse of trench warfare and, more particularly, to take advantage of the as-yet-unclear potential of air power. The rapidly enhanced specifications of aircraft, notably their greater size and power, led to interest in the use of airborne troops. A number of states, especially the Soviet Union and Germany, neither of which built aircraft carriers, trained parachute and glider-borne units. The Soviets dropped an entire corps by parachute in 1935 but probably largely to impress foreign observers rather than as a practical military operation. Also in 1935, the Soviets moved a fourteen-thousand-strong rifle division by air from near Moscow to the Soviet Far East. This was a pointed demonstration of an ability to respond to Japan, which had recently seized the neighboring Chinese province of Manchuria. In 1937–1938, the Soviets practiced dropping artillery and tanks by parachute.

Although the army did not show much support, the Germans began training parachutists in 1936. It was the Luftwaffe (air force) that was more enthusiastic. In early 1938, Kurt Student, who had commanded a fighter squadron in the First World War, was appointed to command Fliegerdivision 7, the first German paratroop division. Later that year, Student became inspector of German Airborne Forces and developed DFS230 "attack gliders" to land his forces.[18] Each could lift troops or freight up to 2,500 pounds. Airborne operations were planned when Germany prepared to go to war with Czechoslovakia in 1938, but the crisis did not lead to conflict.

From the late 1920s, Italy made an effort to develop such a capacity, but the first parachute battalion was organized only in 1938, and Italian paratroopers were only dropped on campaign when invading Greece in 1941: they were dropped on Cephalonia in the Ionian Islands. In general, Italian paratroopers were employed as elite infantry in the Second World War. The major use that the Germans were to make of airborne units in 1940 was to surprise many commentators, not least as, prewar, they had focused more attention on tank attacks and on bombing.

CONCLUSIONS

Largely years of peace for the Western powers, the "interwar" period is not associated with combined operations, which indeed proved more important. The legacy of the First World War did not look in that direction, and the largely ad hoc nature of Anglo-American preparations for large-scale combined operations during the Second World War leads to a similar conclusion. In practice, there was more preparation than this might suggest, notably on the part of Japan. The Japanese sought to solve the problems of amphibious assaults under fire by landing uncontested some miles down the shoreline and marching overland and meeting the enemy in inland ground operations. More generally, resource and priority issues played a part in the relative neglect of preparations for combined operations, but so also did the widespread view that power projection would not involve large-scale opposed landings of troops. This indeed appeared vindicated by the early stages of the Second World War, although the situation was subsequently to change.

Chapter Eight

The Second World War, I, 1939–1942

Much of the modern understanding and image of combined operations is based on the Second World War and its presentation. This is true both of amphibious assaults and of the use of airborne troops, each of which were employed to an unprecedented extent in Europe, Asia, and Africa. For both, advantages and limitations clearly emerged. Rather than adopting a chronological approach, this and the next chapter take the following form in order to group together similar episodes for consideration. Sea-based combined operations in the German and Italian war with the Allies up to late 1941 are considered first and then the Japanese advances in the first six months of the war in the Pacific. These are the subject of this chapter. They are followed, in the next chapter, with the American riposte to the Japanese up to the end of the Second World War and then by Allied sea-based combined operations against Germany and Italy in 1942–1945. Lastly, the use of parachutists and glider-borne forces is discussed.

THE GERMAN AND ITALIAN WAR BEGINS, 1939

The use of combined operations at first was very much a matter of initiatives by Germany and Italy. The first in these years was the Italian invasion of Albania on April 7, 1939. Italy had held a combined amphibious training operation on the Tuscan coast in 1929, its first significant such operation. Due to opposition by the army and navy, the air force held a parallel exercise at the same time and over the beach but without coordination with the army and naval commands. The results, which demonstrated that a landing was doomed to failure if made without commanding the air, had not led to any significant planning for such operations, and the results were to be seen in 1939.

The badly managed invasion of Albania, one conducted against a nearby and vulnerable target but planned by a poor High Command, was successful in part because there was little resistance from the outnumbered and divided Albanians. The political decision for the invasion came unexpectedly, largely in response to the German occupation of Bohemia and Moravia and the determination to make a move to bring Italy benefits. The armed forces knew of the assignment only shortly before the invasion: orders were issued from March 31. The suddenness affected the resources available, including merchant shipping, and the planning was inadequate. For example, the depth of the water in the inshore waters was not factored in. Landing areas were Durazzo, where seven thousand troops landed; Valona; San Giovanni di Medua; and Santi Quaranta. The first ship of the convoy entered Durazzo bay by 4:50 a.m., and the garrison there had been swept away by 9 a.m. The Italians lost 12 and had 81 wounded in the entire operation, and the 50,500 men in the Albanian military dispersed, most subsequently joining the Italians. As a result of fog, the ship carrying the army landing parties was late, whereas the army units that were intended as the garrison when Durazzo was seized were landed as the first wave. A lack of wharves made it difficult to unload the ships. The next day, a motorized column advanced on the capital, the inland city of Tirana, although they were delayed because, in the darkness of nighttime preparations, they had been provided with diesel instead of the necessary gasoline.

The column reached the city when the first aircraft of the airlift from Grottaglie airport in Apulia in Italy was landing in Tirana airport. The airlift worked well and carried an entire regiment but could not carry mortars or artillery. A lack of air transports meant that the troops were carried in ninety bombers, with emergency floors of wooden planks added. The flight took only half an hour. The expeditionary force was twenty thousand strong, but only the thirteen-thousand-strong first wave was used, including the two thousand troops who were airlifted. The landing force, which included the Grado Marine battalion, had with it 125 tanks, 860 vehicles, and 1,200 motorbikes. Including the bombers involved in the airlift, air support comprised 384 aircraft. King Zog fled.

In contrast, the major invasion of the year, that of Poland by neighboring Germany in September, was essentially a land-based operation: German warships were deployed but did not play a significant role. The Germans bombarded Westerplatte, a Polish naval depot near Danzig (Gdansk), on September 1, 1939, but a landing there failed. This did not matter as the Germans overwhelmingly won the land campaign.

DENMARK AND NORWAY, 1940

However, combined operations were very important to the German attacks on Denmark and Norway, Operation Weserübung, in 1940. German airborne capability proved tactically and operationally significant, but not strategically so, in what was a surprise assault that the British Chiefs of Staff had wrongly regarded as impractical. Ironically, the British had themselves been considering action in Norwegian coastal waters against German trade, especially the shipping of Swedish iron ore to Germany, although not an invasion. The invasion of Denmark included the first parachute assault. With some German troops already hidden in a German ship in the harbor of the capital, Copenhagen, close to the vulnerable citadel, Denmark rapidly fell to assault from land, sea, and air.

With Norway, separated from Germany by sea, the key element was a series of amphibious operations that captured most of Norway's cities including Kristiansand, Bergen, Trondheim, and Narvik. Mounting simultaneous surprise attacks along a long and winding coastline was an impressive achievement. Oslo, the capital, itself was captured by airborne troops after the loss to the guns and torpedoes of the Oscarsborg fortress of the *Blücher*, a heavy cruiser escorting a landing force that was thereby blocked. Airborne troops also captured the airport at Stavanger. The failure of the British navy to intercept the German troop transports at sea gave the Germans the key strategic advantage, and it was not compensated for by the sinking, then and later, of German warships. Norwegian resistance was badly organized.

Air power gave powerful assistance to the invading Germans. Enjoying the initiative, they proved far more effective than the Allies at coordinating the different arms on both land and sea. This was important to a campaign that revealed the potential of combined operations and thus represented a paradigm shift in war making. German skills and determination interacted with Allied deficiencies in a way that provided opportunities for bold command decisions. The Germans took these and could give successful effect to them.

In response, Allied forces were landed in Norway in an attempt to strengthen the Norwegian resistance and to delay the German advance. It might have been sensible to land all these forces at the same place, but instead three small forces were landed unopposed: near Narvik on April 15, at Namsos on April 16, and at Andalsnes on April 18. The intention was to capture Narvik, the major town in northern Norway and, with the latter two, Trondheim, the major city in central Norway. There was a degree of political commitment to the plan, but German air power discouraged the idea of a direct assault on Trondheim with naval forces. Moreover, the plan for a pincer attack on Trondheim had to be abandoned in the face of heavy German air attacks and a German overland advance from Oslo to the south. In turn, the Allied troops were evacuated from Andalsnes and Namsos.

Subsequently, after Narvik had been eventually captured on May 28, it was evacuated by the Allies on June 8. The German attack on the Netherlands, Belgium, and France made Narvik appear an inconsequential sideshow. Any chance of holding it was also limited by German successes further south in Norway and the probability that the Germans and their air cover would then move north.[1]

For Britain, the Norwegian campaign played an important role in the development of the command ship. It was impossible to run the operation at long range, and the various flagships did not have the necessary communications equipment and personnel, nor any room for all the staffs. This matter was complicated by the fact that, although the overall commitment of force may have been relatively small, there were British, French, Norwegian, and Polish units, as well as land, sea, and air aspects. In addition, using a battleship as flagship proved problematic since, once it was in action, firing the main battery was likely to interrupt communications. The American navy was to learn the same lesson in the Pacific and moved admirals to cruisers, eventually launching command ships as flagships.

BATTLE IN THE WEST, 1940

In the attack on the Netherlands, Belgium, and France, begun on May 10, 1940, the Germans focused on air-land operations. Given British naval strength in the North Sea and the English Channel, there was no potential for amphibious assaults, and the available amphibious German assets had been employed in Denmark and Norway. In contrast, the Germans made effective use of tactical air support. The Germans both gained superiority in the air and took advantage of it, not least by preventing effective Allied attacks on their advancing forces or supply lines. There was also a lack of close air support for the Allied forces.

Belgium and the Netherlands fell rapidly because of the speed of the German advance, especially the use of paratroopers, whose capture of bridges weakened the Dutch reliance on river and canal defenses and hit the morale of the poorly trained and commanded Dutch forces. The Dutch were forced to counterattack and did so without sufficient success. German airborne landings in the Fortress Holland region, where airfields were occupied, denied the Dutch defense in depth, although the key damage was done by the stronger German forces advancing overland. Indeed, the German airborne forces were hemmed in and under some pressure.[2]

In Belgium, the Germans were able to overcome the major obstacle of the Albert Canal. The Eben Emael fortress on the canal north of Liège, a series of emplacements, guarded three important bridges but was attacked by the glider-borne engineers of the Koch Assault Detachment. Other airborne units captured the bridges, although the assault had to be exploited by the advance of ground forces. In response, the Belgium forces pulled back to a new line of defense between Antwerp and Namur, the Dyle Line, although this was outflanked as a result of the German advance through the Ardennes to the south. In strategic terms, the Germans did not need to take the Eben Emael fortress, as the Ardennes advance proved crucial. However, the success contributed to the disorientation of the Allied forces, not least confusion as to the main axis of German attack.[3] This airborne capability was not significant in the German attack on the French, which focused on tank advances.

Combined operations are very much presented in offensive terms as successful assaults and their exploitation. This leaves out the significant role of such operations in retreats and, more particularly, withdrawals in the face of a pursuing enemy. Such withdrawals are more difficult than assaults as there is not the choice of timing and surprise enjoyed by the latter, while there is also the problem of disengagement, as for the British at Corunna in 1809 and at Gallipoli in 1915.

In 1940, one of the most famous withdrawals in history occurred, that of Allied, principally British, troops from northern France, more particularly Dunkirk. Aside from the bravery and fortitude of the many involved, both those who waited exposed to the threat of German air attack before being evacuated to England and those who rescued them, this withdrawal indicated key points, including naval superiority and a nearby base to which to retreat. The British had not been prepared for a fighting retreat in the face of an active and mobile opponent: transport, fuel, and communications all proved insufficient. In the end, simply getting the army out of France became paramount. Having reached the English Channel, the Germans had widened their position to the north, taking the port of Boulogne on May 23 and besieging another, Calais. It held out until May 27, while, defended ably by the First French Army, Lille did not surrender until June 1. Both provided important distractions for the Germans closing in on the encircled Allied forces around Dunkirk.

The British were able to evacuate 338,000 troops, mostly British but also French, but not their equipment from May 26 to June 3. This owed something to skill, luck, and a German halt on May 24, which owed much to Luftwaffe (German air force) pressure to take a leading role, to the need of German tanks for maintenance, to the necessity of allowing the exhausted German tank crews time to recover, and to Hitler's determination to conserve his forces in order to attack the French units near Paris. The Royal Navy evacuated most of the troops, although private boats operated by civilian volunteers also took an important number. The ability of the outnumbered RAF, which lost 177 aircraft, to go on resisting Luftwaffe attacks was important. The weather was also a key element as the Channel was unusually calm.[4] The Allied withdrawal, a combined operation "in reverse," helped distract attention from the striking failure of the land campaign. Other Allied units were evacuated by sea from French ports further west, including St. Valéry-en-Caux, Le Havre, Cherbourg, St. Malo, Brest, and St. Nazaire, although many troops were captured including at Dunkirk.

PLANS TO INVADE BRITAIN, 1940

Once France had surrendered—and with no significant continuing resistance, unlike after Napoleon III's surrender to German invasion in 1870—there was the prospect of a large-scale German combined operation against Britain, one that would bring together land, sea, and air units in an invasion of southern England. Initially, Hitler offered peace, with Britain to retain her empire and navy in return for her acceptance of Germany's dominance of the Continent. The need for Operation Sealion (Seelöwe) depended on the response. Some influential British politicians wanted to pursue negotiations, but Churchill, who had become prime minister on May 10, 1940, was determined not to surrender and not to negotiate with Hitler. Forcing Britain to make peace was the German remedy.

The planned operation, outlined by a directive issued on July 16, was weakened by a lack of the necessary capability, notably of landing craft and warships, but also by a failure of planning and combination, one that resulted in a situation in which none had ownership of the project. The Luftwaffe was instructed to help prepare the way for invasion, especially by driving British warships from the Channel and by covering minesweeping. The Norway campaign, in which a number of German warships had been sunk or damaged, had indicated the serious vulnerability of amphibious assaults to British naval power, and on July 11, the commander of the German navy, Admiral Erich Raeder, expressed his skepticism to Hitler. Although Italy's entry into the war on the side of Germany on June 10, 1940, had greatly increased pressure on the British navy in the Mediterranean, enough warships remained in home waters to challenge any German naval attack.

However, rather than focusing on attacking British warships, Luftwaffe commanders were increasingly concerned to show that they could win by a bombing war on civilian targets, for which the prelude was to be an attack on the RAF and its supporting infrastructure. The lack of clarity in the relationship between air attack and invasion affected German strategy as a whole at this point. Moreover, this factor continued significant, with the Luftwaffe focusing on air attack while the navy's lack of enthusiasm became increasingly apparent.

There were other issues of great significance. The lack of an appropriate force structure was a major problem for the Germans. This included the absence of proper landing craft, an absence for which the proposal to use towed river barges able to travel at only three knots was no substitute. In one respect, this proposal was an instance of the ad hoc planning and make-do expedients that have frequently been so important to combined operations across history. As so often, the nature of the response was crucial: capability does not exist in a vacuum. For example, German Stuka dive-bombers, while a threat to British warships, were highly vulnerable to the modern fighters the British had, the Hurricane and the Spitfire.[5]

There was also the issue of timing, an issue always important for military moves but of particular significance for combined operations due to sea conditions. It was deemed necessary to invade before mid-September, when the weather was likely to become hostile, but this timetable could not be met. Aside from the problems involved in assembling landing vessels, the army needed to be resupplied and moved to the embarkation zones. Victory in the previous campaign in France had involved losses. After delays, the operation was formally postponed on October 17. Irrespective of the serious problems that would have confronted any invasion, notably insufficient naval resources and preparation, it could not be allowed to go ahead without air superiority. Without that, it would be impossible to prevent the still very powerful and determined British navy from challenging any invasion attempt. In addition, air power would have provided the artillery for any invasion.

The British had been greatly weakened by the earlier Battle of France, with much matériel, including large numbers of tanks, left behind in the evacuation from France. Moreover, much of the army was poorly deployed and untrained to resist invasion, while the Home Guard, the "Dad's Army," was a hastily improvised and poorly armed force. Nevertheless, a German invasion of Britain was still a formidable task, not least because of a lack of German experience in large-scale combined operations or in amphibious assaults. Although it had shown that the British navy, however strong, could not be relied upon to block an invasion, the invasion of Norway was no comparison, not least because of the differences in scale, preparedness, and aircraft. In addition, the British army had been considerably strengthened by the arrival of Canadian forces that were successfully convoyed across the Atlantic. The First Canadian Division, which was deployed in Surrey as a mobile reserve, was probably the best-equipped division in Britain, although it lacked effective anti-aircraft guns. It was soon joined by the Second Division.[6]

Had the Germans landed, they would not have faced the prepared defenses that were to be encountered by the Allies in Normandy in 1944. Instead, as far as defenses were concerned, the situation might have been more comparable to the Japanese landing in the Philippines in December 1941, although by July 24, 1940, Admiral Sir Dudley Pound, the First Sea Lord, could write about an invasion that "tremendous strides have been made in the last six weeks in preparing the country for that possibility."[7] Unlike the well-prepared Allies in Normandy, a German invasion would have been improvised and the units employed would have had scant time for resupply after the invasion of France or for preparation, let alone training. The Germans lacked the specialized tanks the British were to use on the invasion beaches in 1944, as well as specialized landing craft. More particularly, the Germans had no relevant training. A surprise invasion of Norway, and occupying the undefended Channel Isles on June 30, islands that were vulnerable to German air attack from nearby France, were no guide to the prospect for a Channel crossing.

The Germans planned to dispatch forces from a number of ports from Rotterdam in the Netherlands south to Le Havre in France (all ports recently conquered), with four corps taking part in the attack. Initially, the invasion force, which was intended to land between Hythe and Rottingdean, with a parachute landing by the Fliegerdivision 7 to cover the right flank, would have been supported by little armor. This would have helped the British contain and counterattack the beachheads. Thus, technology had not altered the fundamental operational constraints that had long affected amphibious assaults. Moreover, continuity in the shape of proximity to France was also reflected in the question of the landing zone chosen in 1940, one envisaged in former German invasion schemes.

However, if the projected beachheads could be resupplied—control of the sea again being the issue—then the situation would have been far more threatening. Furthermore, the successful German attack on Crete in 1941 showed how disruptive a parachute attack could be. Churchill told the House of Commons on June 4, 1940: "We shall fight on the beaches, we shall fight on the landing grounds, we shall fight in the fields and in the streets, we shall fight in the hills; we shall never surrender." Nevertheless, if the first two had failed, it is difficult to see how resistance at his subsequent stages could have succeeded. The Germans aimed to advance first across southeast England, to a line from Gravesend on the Thames estuary to Portsmouth, and then, having captured London, to a line from Maldon on the Essex coast to the Severn estuary.

Yet Churchill's remarks were significant in a general war of morale, one in which the potential of combined operations and of successful opposition both played a major role. In order to keep the psychological pressure on Britain, the Germans ostensibly continued invasion preparations when, in practice, they had scant intention of launching an invasion. This was apparent in late September 1940, as the threat of invasion appeared to give more weight to the German air attack.[8]

Deciding not to mount an invasion led to, and resulted from, a focus on the Soviet Union. Conquering the latter was seen as a way to force Britain to peace by leaving it isolated. This had been outlined as an option by Hitler on July 21, 1940, and was to be pursued from June 1941.

BRITAIN VERSUS ITALY, 1941

The year 1941 saw combined operations on a greater scale although they were still very much subordinated to operations mounted overland. This was very apparent with the war between Britain and Italy. In North Africa, this was a matter of advances across the border between Libya, an Italian colony, and Egypt, a British one, first by Italian forces and then, having defeated the Italian invaders, by those of Britain. In East Africa, where Italy controlled Ethiopia, Eritrea, and most of modern Somalia, the initial moves were mounted by the Italians, notably the conquest of British Somaliland. Again, this conquest was staged overland, and it was not followed by the use of Italian warships in Eritrea or Italian Somaliland to support combined operations against nearby British positions, notably in Aden, Sudan, or Kenya, let alone India.

In turn, it was the British who attacked. There was a combined component. A small force from Aden, supported by warships, crossed the Gulf of Aden and recaptured Berbera, the capital of British Somaliland, on March 16, 1941, against light opposition. Although this recapture of a British colony helped with the logistical situation for forces in East Africa, where supplies were a major problem, the bulk of the British assault on the Italians was mounted overland from Sudan beginning in January 1941 and from Kenya starting in February. At the same time, the conquest of Italian East Africa, a substantial area, was an aspect of the British focus on indirect attacks.[9] The movement of British imperial forces in the wider region was, in a broadest sense, an aspect of combined capability.

Another tradition, that of imperial intervention, was also seen with British combined operations against Iraq and Iran in 1941, in order both to prevent the threat of their nationalist governments turning to Germany and to secure supply routes and strategic depth for a Britain that was under great pressure in the Middle East. Landing in Basra in April 1941, a British division successfully advanced on Baghdad. That August, British troops successfully landed in southern Iran, with warships providing cover at the ports of Abadan, Khorramshahr, and Bandar Shapur, as well as advancing from Iraq. In support, Soviet forces successfully landed on the Caspian coast of northern Iran, at Pahlevi, and, more significantly, advanced overland.

GERMANS CONQUER THE BALKANS, 1941

The German assault in the Balkans in April–May 1941 focused on overland attacks. Yugoslavia and Greece, the targets for Germany and its allies, notably Italy, had long coastlines, and in Italy and its colony Albania, there were ports from which operations could be mounted, particularly Pola and Trieste. However, the attacks came overland, Italian forces converging on Dubrovnik from Istria to the north and Albania to the south, the latter capturing Ragusa. A lack of Italian experience in combined operations, and of the relevant capability, was important, as was the axis of Italian responsibility, namely the Adriatic coast north and south of Albania. The campaign was decided so suddenly by Hitler that the Italians had no time to plan a landing, but already the previous autumn, when attacking Greece, the Italians had rejected the idea of an amphibious assault. Aside from being under pressure in Libya in East Africa, the Italians were also committed against the British in the central Mediterranean, where the British had considered a combined operation against the Italian island of Pantelleria. The British had also considered such action against the Italian islands in the Aegean, the Dodecanese, although again none was mounted.

Attacking on April 6, 1941, the Germans rapidly conquered Yugoslavia and Greece, and British intervention in the latter, intervention that greatly depended on the availability of scarce shipping, made scant difference to the German advance.[10] The German advance was essentially on land, but in the eastern Aegean, the Germans used ships they seized to advance, capturing the islands there, notably Thasos (April 16), Samothrace (April 19), Lemnos (April 25), Lesbos (May 4), and Chios (May 4). Resistance was minimal, especially in the latter stages. To the south were the Italians in the Dodecanese. More generally, the Greek navy had been badly damaged by German air attacks.

The Germans followed on with an attack on Crete, launched on May 20. Parachute and glider troops sent against Canea, Heraklion, Maleme, and Retimo had captured the island by the 31st, although German losses (5,567 dead) were so great that Hitler ordered that no similar operation should be mounted in the future. Despite being warned of German plans by intelligence from Ultra (deciphered German intercepts) material, the British defense was poorly prepared: much of the garrison had hastily retreated from Greece and was short of equipment, especially artillery, and lacking in air support, problems that might have arisen had the Germans invaded Britain in 1940, although not to the same extent. The German success in seizing and holding Maleme airfield provided a beachhead for reinforcements by means of transport aircraft. The airborne aspect of the attack succeeded and led to German victory.

In contrast, British naval superiority, which had already enabled the evacuation of forty-three thousand troops from mainland Greece, led to the failure of the Germans to support their Crete operation by moving troops by sea. Two German convoys doing so were successfully intercepted. Nevertheless, German air attacks hit the British attempt to reinforce, supply, and eventually evacuate Crete by sea. Many warships, including three cruisers and six destroyers, were sunk, and some troops were left behind and captured.[11]

An Italian contribution is a generally overlooked part of the Crete campaign. A force of 2,600 troops from Rhodes was successfully ferried and landed in Sitia bay in nearby eastern Crete on May 28, very early in the morning. It was escorted by one destroyer and ten torpedo boats and was ferried in a convoy of thirteen ships, including almost everything that floated that could be found in Rhodes.

GERMANY ATTACKS THE SOVIET UNION, 1941

Combined operations again played only a limited role when the Germans and their allies attacked the Soviet Union on June 22, 1941. This was very much a campaign waged on land and with air support. The Baltic saw only limited action, which was a continuation of the position during the Finnish-Soviet war of 1939–1940 when the Soviet navy had initially blockaded and bombarded the Finnish coast but then done little, a situation that owed much to a particularly savage winter. In 1941, in contrast, the war began in June, and this allowed for combined operations by the Germans and their allies. For example, the Finns occupied the Åland Islands, without the intervention of the nearby Soviet Baltic fleet. The Germans, who had built up a fleet in Finnish waters as well as deploying warships from German ports, mounted amphibious assaults to capture islands in the Gulfs of Riga and Finland. The Germans also used Finnish ships as well as Soviet ferries that had been seized. However, nothing significant was staged that might have put pressure on the Soviet fallback to defend Leningrad: having annexed Lithuania, Latvia, and Estonia in 1940, the Soviet Union now included a much more extensive Baltic coastline. In part, there was the issue of the strength of the Soviet navy, even if it lacked dynamic leadership and took heavy losses from German mines.

The Soviets, in turn, mounted combined operations to help the movements of their army on land, but again these made no appreciable difference. The Soviets lacked specialized landing craft and the necessary training. Moreover, Soviet landings tended to be poorly planned and implemented. The Soviets could not grasp the practice of maritime warfare. However, Soviet operations included important evacuations of forces from the Baltic islands.

In the Black Sea, the Germans did not have a comparable naval force to that in the Baltic and were in part dependent on the Romanians. Naval operations played a role in 1941 for both sides, but it was a relatively minor one. On September 22, the Soviets landed troops behind Romanian forces besieging Odessa. However, they had scant impact, and the key Soviet amphibious role was a large-scale evacuation of Odessa by sea from October 1 to October 16 in which 86,000 troops and 150,000 civilians were evacuated, an evacuation that reflected the strength of the Black Sea Fleet. These troops were very important to the buildup of Soviet forces in Sevastopol, the major port in Crimea. The latter was attacked on December 17, but this attack was then delayed by the need to respond to Soviet landings in eastern Crimea at the close of the month, landings in which more than 40,000 troops were landed. The Germans succeeded in sealing the Soviet advance, but the diversion delayed the fall of Sevastopol. By the end of 1941, Soviet forces had been pushed back and the Germans were in control of much of Crimea.

MALTA

In the Mediterranean, there was Axis air and submarine pressure on the British base of Malta. Prior to Italy's entry into the war in June 1940, Italo Balbo, an air marshal and the governor-general of Libya, proposed opening hostilities with a surprise assault on Malta. An initial landing by airborne troops and naval infantry was to be followed up by the landing of a division that had been trained for a proposed landing on the Greek island of Corfu. Benito Mussolini, the Italian dictator, decided that the operation was not necessary because, given the imminent fall of France, the war, he felt, was over. The division ended up supporting Italian forces in Albania that were under pressure from an overland Greek advance.

In mid-1942, there was a proposal for an Italian-German assault on the island. By that time, Malta was much better prepared, but the Axis had almost total air supremacy. The attack would have involved more than a division's worth of German and Italian airborne troops, plus a multidivision landing in support. Erwin Rommel, the commander of the Afrika Korps in North Africa, believing that he could reach the Suez Canal quickly by an overland advance in North Africa, helped convince Hitler not to proceed.

BRITISH COMMANDO ATTACKS

The British were developing a capacity for mounting commando raids on the Continent, although this process faced difficulties, not least in the question of organization. The interest in new capacity shown with the opening in May 1938 of the Inter-Services Training and Development Centre (ISTDC), established to assess the problems of landing on a defended beach, had been taken forward after Churchill became prime minister in May 1940 and the British were driven from the Continent. Churchill saw raiding as a vital means to demonstrate that the British were still in the war. On June 4, he sent a memorandum to General Hastings Ismay, his main link with the Chiefs of Staff, arguing that it was important not to concentrate on home defense: "It is of the highest consequence to keep the largest numbers of German forces all along the coasts of the countries they have conquered, and we should immediately set to work to organise raiding forces on these coasts where the populations are friendly." On June 6, Churchill added, "I look to the Chiefs of Staff to propose measures for a vigorous, enterprising and ceaseless offensive against the whole German-occupied coastline." On June 14, the Chiefs of Staff appointed Lieutenant-General Alan Bourne, the adjutant-general of the Royal Marines, as "Commander of Raiding Operations on coasts in enemy occupation, and Adviser to the Chiefs of Staff on Combined Operations." ISTDC and six companies of commandos were put under his command. Churchill, however, felt that Bourne was overly under the influence of the Admiralty. On July 17, Bourne was replaced by Sir Roger Keyes, a friend of Churchill's and the hero of the raid on Zeebrugge in 1918.[12]

Keyes was a keen exponent of the new approach. As "director of combined operations," he very much sought to follow an independent path. An admiral, Keyes nevertheless moved his staff from the Admiralty and established a Combined Operations Headquarters (COHQ) and a Combined Training Centre. Keyes was also committed to scale. He backed the expansion of the commando force and also ensured that the number of landing craft increased. Not short of self-confidence, Keyes, however, clashed with the Chiefs of Staff. He was not ready to focus on the technical and planning side and instead wanted COHQ to be an operational headquarters. His ambitions were in line with a British strategic review of August 1941, which noted the consequences of British forces being unable to compete with the Germans in continental Europe. The response of the weaker power therefore, it argued, was to seek strategic advantage from indirect attack, in the shape of blockade, bombing, and subversion, each being designed to hit the German economy and German morale.[13] Keyes resigned in October 1941 after his title was changed by the Chiefs of Staff from "director" to "adviser."

Keyes was replaced by Lord Louis Mountbatten, another protégé of Churchill and again a naval officer. Mountbatten was a much more astute and far better-connected military politician than Keyes.[14] Appointed chief adviser of combined operations in October 1941, Mountbatten was made chief of combined operations in April 1942 and a de facto member of the Chiefs of Staff Committee. Churchill instructed him to begin raids but also to plan the invasion of France and to develop techniques and equipment accordingly. Thus, as 1941 came toward a close, interest in combined operations rose, being seen as a way to show that Britain was a major player in the war and also as a morale raiser. However, the prospect for such operations on any scale appeared very limited. There were also serious institutional clashes between the commandos and the Special Operations Executive (SOE), which had been established in 1940 to set "Europe ablaze" in Churchill's words. The SOE focused on sabotage and backing for resistance movements.[15]

Commando attacks, notably against the Lofoten Islands in March and December 1941 and the Vaagso Islands in December 1941, helped lead the Germans to station more troops in Norway than was necessary in strategic terms, which was a success for the British. Designed for specific purposes, these attacks also reflected the broader issues posed for British assumptions by the German conquest of Norway, notably concern over German naval access to the Atlantic.[16] Meanwhile, the difficulties the Germans increasingly faced in their operations in the Soviet Union, where their renewed offensive had stalled in late November 1941, suggested that there would be no major German combined operation against Britain. In turn, the British lacked the manpower to mount one of any great scale against German-occupied Europe. Thus, British attacks could only be diversionary at best. This encouraged an emphasis on a bombing offensive against Germany.

JAPAN ATTACKS

The strategic situation was transformed when Japan attacked the Western Powers. The collapse of France and the Netherlands to German attack in May–June 1940, and the weakening position of Britain (already vulnerable in the Far East to Japanese attack) in 1940–1941, created an apparent power vacuum in Southeast Asia. This apparent vacuum encouraged Japanese ambitions southward into the "Southern Resources Area," while leading the Americans to feel that only they were in a position to resist Japan and that they must block Japanese expansion.

On December 7, 1941 (December 8 on the other side of the International Date Line), the Japanese simultaneously launched a series of attacks. The Japanese assault on the American Pacific Fleet at Pearl Harbor was designed to provide security for their conquest of Southeast Asia and the southwest Pacific. As another prelude, the Japanese ability to destroy much of the United States Far East Air Force on the ground in the Philippines on December 8 provided an important advantage and reflected a serious lack of planning and rapid response on the American part.

The most significant Japanese attack in East Asia was on the Philippines, as that was both a forward American position close to the Asian mainland and a threat to any Japanese advance southward to Malaya or the Dutch East Indies. Having gained superiority in the air over the Philippines on December

8, the Japanese used it to attack American installations, seriously hitting morale and removing a threat to Japanese amphibious landings. Understandable fear of Japanese air power, and concern about the relative ratio of naval power after Pearl Harbor and after the sinking of British warships by Japanese aircraft off Malaya on December 8, led the American navy, sensibly mindful of the wider strategic position and in accordance with its prewar planning, to fail to provide the support requested by General Douglas MacArthur, commander of the American forces in the Philippines. This left the defenders in a hopeless position and helped set the wider strategic situation for Japanese success both there and in Southeast Asia.

Hypotheticals can be useful if they can re-create the uncertainties of the period. Had the American navy been able to advance at strength into the western Pacific, then that would have gravely limited Japanese options. That it could not do so in part vindicated the Japanese proponents of the assault on Pearl Harbor, although even had there been no such attack, the prospect of a successful and speedy American deployment would still have been hedged by serious qualifications. The situation prefigures in some respects issues involved in possible Chinese power projection in the future.

Superiority in the air and at sea enabled the Japanese to land where they pleased, and their small forces, certainly far smaller than those deployed in China, initially made rapid gains against poorly prepared and badly led defenders. After preliminary landings, from December 8 when Batan Island to the north of Luzon (not the same as Bataan) was captured, the main invasion of the Philippines was launched on December 22. By then, the Japanese had overrun much of the coast of northern Luzon on which there had been landings from December 10. MacArthur had dispersed his American and Filipino units and supplies to contest Japanese landings on the main island, Luzon. This policy, however, was unsuccessful and also deprived MacArthur of an adequate reserve as well as of necessary supplies once depots had been overrun by the Japanese. The main Japanese force landed in Lingayen Gulf in northwest Luzon (where the Americans themselves were to land in 1944), with supporting units landing in south Luzon at Legaspi (December 12) and Lamon Bay (December 24). The ability to mount combined operations over a broad front both disoriented the defense and ensured that Manila, the capital of the Philippines, was threatened with a pincer attack.

Some of the poorly trained and inadequately equipped Philippine army did not fight well. Moreover, on a long-established pattern, the designation of defense lines to protect Manila proved no substitute for their vigorous defense. MacArthur had made no adequate provision in the event of Japanese success.[17] As a result, he decided to fall back to the Bataan peninsula west of Manila Bay, the initial plan that he had overturned in order to defend all of Luzon. Manila itself fell on January 2, 1942. Eventually, fresh Japanese troops supported by air and artillery attack drove in first the American position at Bataan and then that on Corregidor, an island in the bay, on April 9 and May 6 respectively. Referred to as the Gibraltar of the East, Corregidor was a heavily fortified position designed to control use of the harbor. It was well provisioned, but the fall of Bataan exposed Corregidor to heavy artillery fire, which supplemented frequent damaging air raids. The Japanese attacked as so often at night, on May 5–6, establishing a beachhead through which tanks and artillery were landed. The pummeled garrison surrendered on the 6th, which scarcely reflected the preparations for a long resistance. The fighting determination was not that which was to be shown by many combatants faced with overwhelming odds.

As also elsewhere in response to the unexpected Japanese attack, unprepared Allied forces in the Philippines suffered from poor strategic and operational planning and a lack a synergy of able commanders and troops prepared to take the initiative. MacArthur's incompetence underlined the impact of personality. The Japanese had initially landed only two divisions, whereas there were ten infantry divisions as well as other units among the defenders, although they were dispersed and most had only been under arms about six months and some for only a few weeks before the war began. Part of the Japanese method in the invasion of the Philippines was to keep the Americans guessing where they would land and (as a separate issue) where they would land their main forces.

Outside Luzon, the Japanese attacked across the archipelago, landing at Davao in Mindanao on December 20; on Jolo on December 24, 1941; on Cebu on April 10, 1942; and on Panay on April 16, 1942. The offensive against Mindanao, a large island, reflected the extent to which command of the sea gave the Japanese additional opportunities, for there were significant supporting landings on the west (April 29) and northern (May 3) coasts.

Further east, American islands in the western Pacific also rapidly fell victim to combined operations mounted by the Japanese navy, with Guam falling on December 10, 1941. The first attack on Wake Island was repulsed by the Marine garrison on December 11. This resistance showed that the USMC understood both defense and assault. The Japanese suffered from overconfidence and overextension. Japanese medium bomber crews, which, on December 8, 9, and 10, raided Wake three times preceding the landing attempt, claimed to have completely destroyed the atoll's small air force and its ground defenses. The Japanese High Command accepted these erroneous reports at face value, which accounted for the imprudent tactics adopted by the Wake Invasion Force. Moreover, the ambitious scope of Japan's first Pacific offensive ensured that the Japanese spread themselves thin in places. Wake was a case in point. The Wake Invasion Force consisted of just 3 light cruisers (2 of them obsolescent), 6 destroyers, and 450 landing troops. The operation also proceeded with no air support.

Wake's Marine defenders took able advantage of the enemy's hubris. Because Japanese air raids had knocked out the range equipment of the two Marine five-inch batteries guarding the atoll's south shore, the commander of the Marine ground forces held his fire until the enemy closed to point-blank range for coastal artillery (4,500 yards), which allowed his gun crews to score multiple hits and sink one destroyer. Wake's four remaining 4F4-3 Wildcat fighters completed the Japanese rout, flying repeated sorties to strafe the fleeing ships and drop one-hundred-pound bombs, one of which sank a second destroyer. The Wildcats especially traumatized the Japanese, which was a major reason why the Combined Fleet, which had mounted the Pearl Harbor operation, detached the carriers *Soryu* and *Hiryu* to provide close air support for the second invasion attempt, which was successful. In this, the Japanese landed their first wave in the early morning hours of December 23, letting night neutralize the Marine five-inch guns. Once the sun came up, Japanese carrier aircraft harassed any Marine gun crews who tried to man their ordnance. The inability to relieve the island helped ensure the second attack, although only after heavy Japanese casualties. This brave resistance was important to the rise in the reputation of the USMC. Roosevelt mentioned the resistance in his State of the Union Address.[18]

MALAYA

The British in Malaya considerably outnumbered the Japanese attacking force, but the latter were better prepared, led, and trained; had the operational and tactical initiative; fought well; were more mobile; used light tanks; and enjoyed air superiority and control of the sea. Many of the Japanese units had gained battle experience in China. The British, in contrast, were poorly trained and inadequately led, as indeed were the Australians.

The Japanese landed on December 8 in northern Malaya at Kota Bharu, as well as at Patani and Singora in the south of Japan's ally Thailand. The British had planned to occupy these Thai ports in order to resist such a landing but, lacking ruthless determination, did not do so for political reasons. Moreover, the Japanese were supported by the Malaya Force of the navy and by aircraft that rapidly won air and sea superiority. The Japanese swiftly advanced from their landing sites, translating tactical advantage into operational dynamic. The main axis of Japanese advance was near the west coast of Malaya, and in outmaneuvering successive British defensive positions, the Japanese benefited from both operating through the jungle and from outflanking them by rapidly planned and executed seaborne landings, although the latter were not crucial. The Japanese were able to bundle the defeated British out of Malaya, which they evacuated on January 31, 1942.

In turn, another combined operation, although one mounted across a far shorter distance, as is readily apparent at the site, led to the successful Japanese invasion of the island of Singapore on the night of February 8–9, 1942. A range of factors that were important to the fate of combined operations came into play. The defense was poorly organized, and troop morale among some units was low. The decision to try to defend all of the coastline ensured that there was an inadequate reserve. Moreover, at the point of invasion, there were insufficient defenders. In short, the defense was far worse planned than the attack. As in Malaya, the Japanese ability to concentrate on a limited front and to exploit success on this axis of advance proved crucial. The failure to mount an effective counterattack against the main Japanese landing site was notably a serious error, but one that captured a structural factor in the success or failure of combined operations, namely that those mounting them could not determine the direction, the timings, the size, or even the eventuality of a counterattack.

Once landed on Singapore, the Japanese rapidly exploited their success. As the Japanese fought their way across the island, the defenders were threatened by the loss of water supplies, while morale collapsed. Although ordered to fight on and to engage in street fighting in order to tie down and kill Japanese troops, the British commander, advised by his staff and fellow senior officers, asked for terms on the 15th and surrendered unconditionally with his sixty-two thousand troops that afternoon. The Japanese lost five thousand dead or wounded in the operation. This was a disaster for the prestige, geopolitics, and resources of the British Empire and its military, one that is generally seen as marking a major transition in the fortune of the empire.

The Japanese had also launched a successful combined operation against the far more vulnerable British colony of Hong Kong, which provided military supplies to the Chinese fighting Japan. Hong Kong was attacked by a larger force on December 8, 1941. The fourteen-thousand-strong garrison, recently reinforced by Canadian troops but with inadequate artillery, limited naval support, and only seven outdated aircraft, was too weak for the task, not least because the defensive line in Kowloon on the mainland was too long to hold. The line was breached on the 9th, the defenders retreated to Hong Kong island, and the Japanese were able to make a nighttime amphibious landing on it. Air support enabled them to block interference with their supply routes from British motor torpedo boats. Once on the island, the Japanese wore down their determined but exhausted opponents. The strong Japanese attack was not inexorable, but the repeated pressure put great strain on the defenders. The remaining positions were forced to surrender on December 25. Attacking on December 16, 1941, the Japanese also captured the weakly protected British positions in Sarawak in northern Borneo, notably Kuching airfield.

DUTCH EAST INDIES

On an unprecedented extent for combined operations, the Japanese also attacked the very wide-ranging Dutch East Indies (now Indonesia). This ably planned and finely executed attack began on January 11, 1942, with a landing on Tarakan. That month saw Japanese amphibious forces leapfrog forward through the Straits of Makassar and the Molucca Passage, to the west and east of Sulawesi, capturing ports there and in Borneo: Kendari in east Sulawesi and Balikpapan in east Borneo both fell on January 24, followed by Macassar in south Sulawesi and Benjermasir in south Borneo on February 9 and February 10 respectively. Another force captured Ambon in the Moluccas, and another advanced from Sarawak to leapfrog down the western coast of Borneo, capturing Pamangkat on January 27.

These gains, which outflanked Dutch defenses and were generally achieved in the absence of much resistance, provided bases from which Japanese attacks on the islands of Java, Bali, and Timor further south could be prepared. As already seen with Malaya and Borneo, this was part of a crucial synergy in combined Japanese operations, not least with aircraft moved forward into air bases. The poorly equipped Dutch garrisons were too weak to put up much resistance or to provide mutual support. The lack of adequate air power proved a particular problem for the Dutch.

The Japanese also used paratroopers, as they had not done hitherto. These units, the Yokosuka Special Naval Landing Forces, were developed in 1940–1941 employing German methods, equipment, and instructors. There were 1,688 men in the units but a lack of aircraft. They were directed against operationally significant targets, notably an airfield near Menado in northern Sulawesi on January 11, and against the important oil refinery at Palembang on Sumatra on February 16, a key objective. Japan's need for oil was an important strategic drive. Paratroopers were also used when Dutch Timor was attacked on February 19, hitting the defenders' communications.

In February 1942, a Japanese force that had sailed from Camranh Bay in Vietnam attacked Sumatra. Allied naval forces attempted to protect Java, the major island, unsuccessfully attacking an invasion fleet in the battle of the Java Sea on February 27. Heavy Allied losses, then and subsequently, left the Japanese in a dominant position, and on the night of February 28–March 1, they landed on Java: on a number of sites on the northern coast. With total air superiority, the Japanese rapidly advanced. Batavia (Djakarta), the capital, fell on March 5 and Surabaya, in eastern Java, three days later, the date on which the Dutch East Indies government surrendered, as did its ninety-three-thousand-strong army. In conquering a vast area, Japan's losses had been modest. Its success deserves greater attention in the history of combined operations.[19]

JAPANESE WAR MAKING

The Japanese had benefited from the rapid tempo of their advance, from good operational planning, and from being able to choose their targets. The cumulative nature of Japanese advances was important to this rapid tempo. For example, in the Philippines, the Japanese had initially been stalled by the withdrawal of American forces to the Bataan peninsula. However, having captured Hong Kong and Malaya, the Japanese then moved artillery and aircraft to the Philippines. Operations in the Philippines themselves moved in a sequence. Thus, units sent to Davao in Mindanao in December 1941 moved on to take Jolo, while units from Luzon moved on to attack Cebu and Panay in April 1942 and to land in western and northern Mindanao in May 1942. High morale was also a major advantage for the Japanese.

Japanese success in part reflected the poorly prepared and coordinated nature of the opposition. The American, British, Dutch, and Australian units in the region were insufficient for the vast area they had to cover; they lacked air support; and the ground forces were inadequately trained and equipped and, some of them, low in morale. Infantry units that were essentially colonial gendarmeries and/or all-purpose (rather than specifically tropical warfare) fighting troops were of limited value. Due to a dearth in patrol aircraft and submarines, there was insufficient Allied intelligence. There was no coordinated Allied strategy and no effective central command among the Americans, British, and Dutch.

Combined operations provided a crucial difference in Japanese war making. Whereas the Germans had established their superiority in fast-moving mechanized warfare, the Japanese concentrated on units on foot. In part due to the lightness of their supply "tail," these were fast moving, but the ability to mount effective amphibious assaults provided the vital mobility and speed.[20]

The Japanese, however, found it impossible to sustain their offensive and, as it were, to fix the success of their combined operations as part of a new strategic reality. The Japanese planned to press on to fix and strengthen the defensive shield with which they wished to hold the western Pacific against American attacks. As a reminder of the need to locate combined operations in wider strategic and policy contexts, the extent of this shield was a matter of contention. Although Japan was now overly extended, especially in light of the continuation of the war in China, which was the major commitment for the army, its success led to interest in a more extensive perimeter. The Naval General Staff pressed for an attack on Australia or for operations against India and Sri Lanka. However, the army was unprepared to commit the troops required and instead favored a more modest attempt to isolate Australia.

Having seized Rabaul on the island of New Britain on January 23, 1942, and then the rest of New Britain, as well as the Admiralty Islands, New Ireland, and Bougainville, the Japanese decided to press on to seize Port Moresby, the major town in eastern New Guinea, as well as New Caledonia (where American forces had landed on March 12), Fiji, and Samoa, in order to isolate Australia. By doing so, the prospect for America taking the war to Japan in the western Pacific was to be lessened. On the night of March 7–8, the Japanese landed at Lae and Salamaua in eastern New Guinea without opposition and established bases from which to make further gains on the island. In addition, Tulagi, the capital of the Solomon Islands, fell on May 3.

Moresby Operation, a Japanese combined operation to seize Port Moresby by sea, was designed to protect their positions in New Guinea and New Britain and to increase the threat of an attack on Australia. Having originally thought of the use of self-propelled barges, the Japanese decided on a standard landing and prepared for this by conducting reconnaissance flights. However, they lacked information on opposing strength and were worried about coastal reefs and other navigational obstacles off New Guinea and also about exposure to air attack based in Australia and about the supply of their troops once landed. There was a serious failure to make adequate provision for the American response.

Launched on April 27, 1942, this operation was thwarted as a result of American naval intervention. The first American carrier strike was on May 4, and attacks escalated on May 7 with the major carrier engagement, the Battle of the Coral Sea, on May 8, 1942. The interception of the Japanese invasion fleet led to significant losses for both sides but, more importantly, to the Japanese decision to abandon the operation.[21]

Instead, the Japanese decided to attack Port Moresby overland, launching an offensive in July, only to be affected by disease and supply problems and to be stopped by successful Australian jungle fighting. A supporting amphibious landing in Milne Bay in eastern New Guinea on the night of August 25–26 was defeated by the more numerous Australians. The Japanese did not enjoy the benefit of surprise. Furthermore, the buildup of Allied air strength in the region lessened vulnerability. Indeed, Australian aircraft flying from airstrips helped defeat the Japanese at Milne Bay.

The Japanese amphibious tactics during their sweep through Southeast Asia and the southwest Pacific took advantage of the enormous size of the theater and the relative absence of defenders. They rarely landed against more than token resistance and at times met none at all. At Milne Bay, in contrast, as at Wake, the Japanese landed against a well-organized defense. MacArthur's "leapfrog" operations were, in part, more or less carried out under similar circumstances to those of the bulk of the Japanese advances in 1941–1942, which was why his casualties were relatively lower than those encountered by the navy and USMC across the central Pacific.

More generally, alongside their operational capabilities, the Japanese suffered from systemic problems. In 1941–1942, these included not only a flawed strategy but also a marked difficulty in ensuring cooperation between army and navy.[22] Both these points are significant alongside the impression of success created by the wide-ranging Japanese advance. This contrast invites attention for the consideration of combined operations in the modern world.

Chapter Nine

The Second World War, II, 1942–1945

In the same month as the Germans began Operation Blue, a powerful land offensive against the Soviet Union in the summer of 1942, launched on June 28, that, in the event, was to move to major failure at Stalingrad that winter, the dynamic moved toward the Allies on the oceans, particularly in the Pacific. This situation was much encouraged by the American naval victory over the Japanese fleet at Midway on June 4, 1942. This major victory, in which four Japanese carriers were destroyed, left the Japanese still with a potent navy but also weakened the capacity for any major Japanese advances, not only in the Pacific but also a resumption of that into the Indian Ocean that they had already attempted in early April.

Already in May 1942, contrasting with the abysmally mismanaged attempt to capture Dakar in September 1940, the British had mounted a successful combined operation to capture Diégo Suarez, the main port of Vichy-held Madagascar. This move was intended to preempt its use by Japanese submarines and thus to challenge dominance of the Indian Ocean.

THE PACIFIC, 1942

The fate of Madagascar was significant in terms of strategic hypotheticals, but that of Guadalcanal, an island in the Solomon Islands, was more significant for the strategic actualities of late 1942. The Japanese seized the island on July 7, 1942, only for the Americans to mount an unopposed landing on August 7. The deployment of the 1st Marine Division was in part designed to capture a newly established airfield from which Japan could threaten nearby islands. This was very much a combined operation as a naval conflict offshore was crucial to the ability of the Japanese to support their force on the island. The Americans essentially decided this naval conflict in November, even though some hard mop-up fighting continued on the island itself until February 1943, when the Japanese finally evacuated all remaining troops. The fighting quality of the well-led but often poorly prepared American Marines, in difficult and poorly mapped terrain and against a formidable opponent, was central on the island, ensuring that repeated Japanese attacks on the American beachhead failed. In January 1943, the Americans launched an offensive against the Japanese, and the latter evacuated more than twelve thousand troops from Guadalcanal the following month.

In the campaign, the Americans developed an impressive degree of cooperation between land, sea, and air forces that was to serve them well in subsequent operations, and that, in different circumstances, proved difficult to achieve after 1945. Japanese defeat was also very important to American morale. The role of the USMC was highly important to its rise in reputation. Guadalcanal had strategic importance, but it took on a significance to contemporaries that exceeded both this and the relatively modest size of the Japanese garrison. It was important to demonstrate that the Japanese could be beaten not only in carrier action, as at Midway, but also in the difficult fighting environment of the Pacific islands. For Pacific campaigns to succeed, it was necessary to show that air and sea support could be provided to amphibious forces, both when landing and subsequently. In addition, whereas Coral Sea and Midway had been defensive successes, the latter a triumph and for the navy alone, at Guadalcanal, in contrast, the attack had clearly been taken to the Japanese and, despite much effort, they had been unable to hold the position.[1]

THE PACIFIC, 1943

The time taken to defeat the Japanese on Guadalcanal, the large number of islands they continued to hold, and the casualties that they might cause ensured that it would be necessary to focus American efforts carefully. This policy required the identification of key targets. Thanks to a growingly apparent American superiority in the air and at sea, the Japanese, who failed to mount a submarine campaign against American support units, would be less able to mount ripostes and any bypassed bases would be isolated. Thus the Pacific war was to become one that was far from linear in terms of a clear front line.

In eastern New Guinea, American and Australian forces finally prevailed in particularly arduous fighting conditions: the jungle, the mountainous terrain, the heat, the malaria, and the rain combined to cause heavy Allied casualties. In October 1942, American troops were moved by sea or airlifted to the northern coast of New Guinea. They joined Australian forces advancing overland to capture Gona in November and Buna in December. The poor communications of New Guinea put a premium on sea or airborne moves. Thus, in January 1943, the Australians flew troops into the airstrip at Wau in order to block a Japanese advance. That September, American paratroopers captured the airstrip at Nadzab, after which an Australian division was air-lifted in. It played a key role in the capture of Salamaua and Lae that month. Combined with Guadalcanal, this success ensured that Australia was protected from Japanese advances and prepared the way for further Allied attacks. Allied fighting quality in New Guinea had risen markedly from the situation in 1942.

The Japanese still had substantial forces in New Guinea, and there was fighting there until the end of the war, but successive positions were taken, in part thanks to amphibious attacks, for example, Finschhafen in October 1943, Saidor in January 1944, and Hollandia and Aitape that April. These landings successively outflanked the Japanese. There were further landings at Wakde and Biak islands in May 1944 and Noemfoor and Sansapor that July. Allied landings, however, were often only the beginning of a bitter Japanese resistance, that on the island of Biak from May 27 till mid-August. The landing on Biak indicated many of the factors important to the American advance in the Pacific. Biak was important due to its airfields, and the Americans wanted to seize them in order to assist the advance on the Philippines, which was an aspect of the strategic purpose of combined operations. The Americans faced firm Japanese resistance (as well as many casualties to disease) and needed to mount another landing in order to achieve success there.

The value of supporting American air power was dramatically displayed on March 3–4, 1943, when, in the Battle of the Bismarck Sea, a convoy carrying troops to reinforce New Guinea was attacked by American and Australian aircraft, with the loss of more than 3,600 Japanese troops and 4 destroyers. The defeat of the Japanese Fourth Air Army in American air attacks in August 1943 was a crucial prelude to Allied advances against Lae and Salamanca.

As part of Operation Cartwheel, the attempt to isolate the Japanese base at Rabaul, the Americans began a process of island-hopping in the Solomon Islands in June 1943 with an attack on New Georgia, the main island. As with many of the remarks in this chapter and, indeed, book, this is a bland statement for a very difficult experience of hard fighting that included attritional conflict in difficult jungles and swamps, advancing in the face of determined opponents and their machine guns and snipers, and facing nighttime Japanese infiltration of American positions. The Americans landed Marines and troops, but the strength of the resistance ensured that more units had to be fed in. The Japanese were pushed back onto the nearby islands of Kolombangara and Vella Lavella, from which they successfully withdrew their forces.[2]

Other advances proceeded in similar fashion. Bougainville was invaded on November 1, 1943, and the Americans established a beachhead perimeter from which they beat off a series of Japanese attacks. After a lull in fighting there from April 1944, the Australians took over in December 1944 and cleared much of the island. The American advance culminated with the capture of the Admiralty Islands, which took the 1st Cavalry Division from February 29 to May 18, 1944. The Japanese bases at Rabaul on New Britain and Kavieng on New Ireland were now isolated, while, on Bougainville, Japanese forces that had been beaten away from the defensive perimeter round the Allied beachhead were left stranded.

Island-hopping was crucial to the strategic context of American combined operations. Maps of American advances tend to ignore the Japanese positions that remained, but they lacked strategic relevance and operational point. The notion of a broad-front advance meant less at sea, and notably in the contexts of air and naval superiority, than on land where resistance and vulnerability on the flanks was far more of an issue. Moreover, American strategy depended on an ability to neutralize as well as outfight Japanese units, and in 1943 they were able to demonstrate this ability. It acted as the equivalent to the impressive Soviet development of operational art on the Eastern Front in 1943 and, even more, 1944. As there with German fortress positions, the use of cleaving blows by the attacker left many of the defenders' units isolated and irrelevant.

The consequences of the American approach were also seen at the northern tip of the Japanese advance, in the western Aleutians, off Alaska. After the Americans had gained air and naval dominance and beaten the Japanese on the island of Attu in May 1943—the army division involved trained by USMC instructors—the Japanese garrison on Kiska became of little consequence. The Americans did, however, invade it that August, only to discover that the Japanese had already evacuated the island at the end of July. Kiska, as well as Majuro in the Marshalls in January 1944, were islands invaded by large American forces that the Japanese had already abandoned.

Issues of distance, supply, and international politics (in the shape of Soviet-Japanese neutrality until August 1945) ensured that the North Pacific was not to be the axis of American advance on Japan. An approach route existed, from the Aleutians to Sakhalin, the Kuriles, and Hokkaido, but it was not pursued. Nevertheless, the Japanese had to prepare defenses as if that was an option for the Americans.

In the central Pacific, in contrast, the Americans opened up a new axis of advance in 1943 and with a new structure, the V Amphibious Corps, accordingly established in September. They captured key atolls, especially Makin and Tarawa in the Gilbert Islands, in November. However, these successes were obtained only after difficult assaults on well-prepared and highly motivated defenders. Tarawa, attacked on November 20 in a true amphibious assault, alone cost three thousand American dead and wounded: the preliminary bombardment had failed to destroy the defenses, and a lack of adequate assessment had ensured that the tide was too low for the landing craft, of which there were not enough. The losses, captured with graphic photographs, shocked American public opinion. In comparative terms, losses for Japanese and Soviet units were higher, but the American public did not seek such a comparison.

The Japanese willingness to fight on even in hopeless circumstances, a product of effective indoctrination, including misleading propaganda about horrible penalties the Americans inflicted on prisoners, as well as great bravery, ensured that there were very few prisoners. This willingness to fight on also led the Americans to seek to take few prisoners. This situation has resulted in some discussion of the war as a racist struggle in which there was much hatred and anger.[3] However, although American society was one in which racism played a major role, there are few signs of a policy of indoctrination of troops against the Japanese. Instead, it was the fervent determination of the Japanese to fight on; the difficulty, had they wished to do so, of surrendering given the nature of the battlefield; as well as episodes in which they pretended to surrender and then killed their supposed captors that helped to ensure that the Americans did not anticipate appreciable numbers of prisoners.[4] There have been attempts to incorporate both the ideological and the instrumental perspectives, an approach that is properly grounded in conceptual and methodological complexities.[5]

On the part of the Americans, there was no equivalent to the brutal, murderous treatment of Soviet prisoners by the Germans and of Allied prisoners by the Japanese, and attempts to suggest otherwise reflect a lack of knowledge of the comparative perspective. With the Japanese treatment of Allied prisoners, there was much harshness and gratuitous murder, including the execution of prisoners as well as cases of cannibalism and torture.

THE PACIFIC, 1944

American successes in the Gilberts helped prepare the way, not least in terms of test-running amphibious assaults, for operations against the Marshall Islands in early 1944. This route revived the prewar Plan Orange and represented the shortest route for an advance on the Philippines. The army wanted a southern drive, the navy a central-Pacific drive, but the real story was that the Americans had enough resources to do both and to debate the allocation of units between them at a time when significant Japanese success in China made the prospect of mounting an air war from there against Japan no longer plausible. As a result, the focus would be on gaining Pacific islands from which Japan could be bombed. The choice of strategy was important, alongside the availability of resources, because, however weak the Japanese might be becoming at sea and in the air, there were a large number of Japanese island bases. As a result, combined operations had to be the means while devising an effective strategy that did not involve the loss of too many men or too much time in attacking most of these bases.

The Americans gained cumulative experience in successful amphibious assaults and in their coordination with naval and air support. They developed and used effective techniques, as well as a variety of impressive specialized landing craft, including tracked landing vehicles.[6] However, the difficulties that were to be faced by the Americans on Omaha Beach in the D-Day landings in Normandy in 1944 showed that the lessons learned in the Pacific were not universally applicable. Some that were, however, were not applied in Europe in part because the army commanders in the European theater proved reluctant to learn from the Pacific theater and from USMC experience: D-Day was not a USMC operation. At the same time, there was also the nature of German defensive ideas and constructions to consider, as well as the German ability to move up large tank forces from the hinterland. Moreover, there were other differences, notably the small size of the targets in the Tarawa and Marshall Island assaults, while in Guadalcanal, Bougainville, and New Guinea, it was jungle warfare, not assaults on heavily defended beaches, that was the key element.

The year 1944 saw the collapse of the Japanese empire in the Pacific. Without air superiority, Japanese naval units were highly vulnerable. The Americans could decide where to make attacks and could neutralize bases, such as Rabaul and its one-hundred-thousand-strong garrison and Truk in the Caroline Islands, that they chose to leapfrog. This was part of the more general degradation of Japanese logistics and a key aspect of their lack of strategic capability. Leapfrogging (which was not the same as island-hopping) maintained the pace of the American advance; lessened the extent of hard, slogging conflict; and reflected the degree to which the Americans had and used the initiative. In prewar planning, Truk had been scheduled for capture, the full effectiveness of the combined-arms naval force not yet being understood. In large part, this was because many of the tools were not yet in the inventory, including amphibious doctrine, carrier operations, landing craft, long-range aircraft, mobile airfield construction, and fleet supply trains. In contrast, during the war, the Americans created the tools and developed a dynamic in landings that reflected effective preparations and an appropriate doctrine.

There was, however, a major contrast between the southwest Pacific, where the focus was on surprise landings on relatively lightly defended beaches across a range of possible targets, and the central Pacific, where the Marines faced better-prepared defenses on relatively obvious targets. These required a heavy and sustained preliminary bombardment and thus there was no emphasis on surprise, which was understandable as the targets were small islands, not coastlines backed by large hinterlands where substantial enemy reserves were deployed. In both cases, naval superiority was crucial as the offshore fleet was immobile while protecting the landing parties.

From January 30, 1944, the Americans successfully attacked the Marshall Islands, in part benefiting from the ability to base bombers at Tarawa. By the end of February, the Marshalls had been brought under control, although some isolated positions were still held by the Japanese. The American success reflected the lessons learned at Tarawa, notably the need for closer and sustained inshore bombardment from appropriate ships and the use of underwater demolition teams to clear man-made and natural obstacles, particularly routes through coral reefs.

The Marshalls, in turn, were a valuable asset to American naval and air power and made it easier to strike at the Mariana Islands: Saipan, Tinian, and Guam. Having badly hit Japanese naval power in the Battle of the Philippine Sea on June 19–20, and thus denied Japanese island garrisons the possibility of resupply or reinforcements, the Americans were able to attack the Marianas, which proved a decisive advance into the western Pacific. The determination of the Japanese resistance was shown on Saipan, where nearly the entire garrison—twenty-seven thousand men—died resisting attack and which took three weeks (June 15 to July 9) to capture. The Japanese mounted a strong defense in the jungle-covered mountainous terrain and also launched ferocious frontal counterattacks.[7] Heavy casualties in the latter, however, greatly hit Japanese reserves on Saipan and made the American task less difficult than it would otherwise have been had the Japanese rested on the defensive, as they were to do on Okinawa and Iwo Jima in 1945. Both sides had seen Saipan, the best of the Mariana Islands as a bomber base against Japan, as vital. Its fall led to the resignation of the Japanese cabinet on July 18, 1944. Major defeat therefore had a serious political effect, as might have been the case in the American presidential election later that year.[8]

On Tinian, where the Americans landed on July 24, 1944, the Japanese also fought to the end having made a series of wasteful counteroffensives. The American attack was highly effective, and the island fell in a week. As elsewhere, for example, on Guam, which was conquered on July 21–August 10, those Japanese who were not killed fought on until the end of the war and, in some cases, beyond it. On all these islands, the terrain, especially coastal cliffs, mountains, and dense jungle, made the advance difficult, although on flat Tinian the Americans were able to use tanks with effect. They adapted the force structure they deployed to the particular characteristics of the target. The flat terrain ensured that the island could also be used as a major airbase for B-29 heavy bombers to attack Japan. This was a key instance of strategic-level cooperation in joint operations.[9]

The geographical context was crucial as the Japanese lacked room and capability to maneuver and retreat. On Pacific islands, they could not fall back as they could if obliged in Burma or the Philippines. Moreover, on the islands, the density of troops and defensive fortifications was such as to make the American advance difficult, and the situation provided an opportunity for a glorious "last stand" battle. Farther south, mobility, firepower, and fighting quality brought the Americans further success in New Guinea that year.

The year 1944 saw the activation of a sixth Marine division as the USMC continued to expand under its new Corps commandant, Alexander Vandegrift (1887–1973), a veteran of service in Nicaragua, Haiti, and China and of command at Guadalcanal and Bougainville, and thus of the adaptation of the USMC from a colonial policing force to what presented itself as the amphibious war winner. A force of fewer than twenty thousand men in 1939 was to rise to close to five hundred thousand in 1945.

The Americans used their growing air and naval superiority to mount their largest combined operation in the Pacific during the war: a reconquest of the Philippines. Preliminary moves included attacks on Peleliu and Angaur, two of the Palau Islands that were part of the Caroline Islands group. These attacks are controversial given the argument that the islands could have been bypassed and that their capture was unnecessary. Peleliu, an island with an airstrip, proved a very difficult target. Rather than fighting in an exposed position on the beaches and launching attacks as on Saipan, the 10,600-strong garrison dug their defenses, including tunnels, inland, notably on the Umurbrogol ridge, which had numerous caves. Peleliu was attacked on September 15, 1944, by the 1st Marine Division, whose commander predicted success in four days, but the resistance was not largely subjugated until the end of November and then only after heavy casualties and the replacement of the Marines by an army division. The underground Japanese positions were attacked with flamethrowers, artillery fire, bulldozers, and napalm. Japanese defense techniques, like their American assault counterparts, had evolved over time, with both sides learning lessons.[10]

The invasion of the Philippines began on October 20, 1944, when Leyte was invaded by four divisions. Resistance was initially light with the main threat that of a Japanese naval attack on the landing force, but the Japanese sent fifty thousand reinforcements. The Americans launched a supporting invasion on the west coast of Leyte on December 7 and wiped out the Japanese army units on the island. From December 15, there was a series of invasions of the island of Mindoro, in order to establish air bases to assist in the attack on the main island, Luzon, where the Americans landed in Lingayen Gulf on January 9, 1945, picking the same site chosen by the Japanese in December 1941, 120 miles north of well-defended Manila.

Again, the strategic context requires consideration. In many respects, as in 1941–1942 when the Japanese focus was on China and Southeast Asia, the

Philippines were a cul-de-sac for an American grand strategy focused on Japan. Saipan and Iwo Jima were a more important axis for air attack and advancing on Japan, although control of the central Philippines would increase the number of American bases in the western Pacific. The seizure of Taiwan would have been more important so far as affecting the war in China and, more crucially, helping to keep the pressurized and defeated Kuomintang (Nationalists) in the war against Japan.

However, at the stage when the decision was taken to invade the Philippines, the Americans were still concerned about Japanese-controlled South-east Asia and Indonesia and the Japanese naval forces stationed there. Moreover, as yet there was no proof of B-29 success against Japan. The reasons for recapturing the Philippines were focused and energized by MacArthur's determination to reverse his flight from them in 1942. He insisted that the Americans had obligations to their Filipino supporters. Differences over strategy accentuated divisions between American policymakers, which were also seen in theater in serious rivalry between the army and the USMC, or at least between the commanders and senior officers of both, something that was to be painfully obvious. Major-General William Penney, director of intelligence, HQ supreme Allied commander South-East Asia, who visited Manila in April 1945, reported:

> Feuding between U.S. Army and Navy, including Marines, is openly expressed. In Generals' Mess at Manila I was astounded to listen to the scornful references to operations on Okinawa and other land battles fought under Naval or Marine command.[11]

The acerbic General Holland "Howlin Mad" Smith of the USMC had relieved an army general of active-combat command during the struggle for Saipan, which had increased divisions. As critics of the Philippine campaign had feared, the invasion of the islands indeed led to a delay in the operations planned against Iwo Jima and Okinawa.

The invasion helped ensure a naval battle, that of Leyte Gulf of October 23–26, 1944, that secured American maritime superiority in the western Pacific, as well as checked the Japanese naval threat to the landing force, which had been left poorly protected. Having obtained that superiority, there was no real need to press on with additional landings in the already-isolated Philippines. At the same time, there was a complete breakdown in strategic thought on the part of the Japanese: an inability, in the face of Allied power, to think through any option once the decisive naval battle had been lost. The destruction of naval assets made it difficult to plan for any further large-scale action and reduced the Japanese to a defensive-offensive predicated on a tenacious defense coupled with destructive suicide missions, both designed to sap their opponent's will. The Japanese commanders in the Philippines and elsewhere were simply told to hold on to their positions. They received no logistical support. The weak government that had taken power after the fall of that of General Hideki Tōjō in July 1944 had no plan other than for the military to die heroically.

THE PACIFIC, 1945

The Americans could choose where to land, but the fighting and logistical problems of operations onshore were formidable, and Japanese determination to fight on led to heavy casualties. This was seen both in the Philippines and on the islands of Iwo Jima and Okinawa. The Japanese on the Philippines did not surrender after the Americans landed on Luzon on January 9, 1945. Although the Japanese XIV Area Army, under the newly arrived and highly effective General Tomoyuki Yamashita, the conqueror of Malaya in 1941–1942, had more than 250,000 troops, its condition reflected the degradation of the Japanese war machine. There were only about 150 operational combat aircraft, and most were destroyed by American carrier aircraft before the invasion. Naval support had been destroyed the previous autumn. The troops lacked food and ammunition, and the relatively few vehicles available had insufficient fuel.

Rather than engaging the Americans where they were likely to be strongest—in the invasion zone and the plains between there and Manila—Yamashita deployed his troops to take advantage of areas of difficult terrain. In another instance of army-navy differences, the naval garrison of Manila, however, refused to evacuate the city and vigorously defended it, leading the Americans to turn to an extensive use of artillery. Combined with large-scale Japanese atrocities, this may have led to the death of one hundred thousand Filipino civilians. Manila was not completely regained until March 3, although American troops had entered the city on February 4. MacArthur's decision to engage in the house-to-house battle for Manila remains controversial.

Japanese forces, which held out in mountainous northern Luzon until the end of the war, were able to make little effective contribution to the war effort other than tying down Allied forces and causing heavy casualties: the American army alone suffered 145,000 casualties. This attritional end, however, was an important Japanese goal, not least limiting the numbers available for an invasion of Japan. The Japanese, in turn, suffered heavily from starvation and disease. Such operations raise issues of definition. The presentation of them in the same chapter as, say, the landing on Tarawa certainly involves issues of scale as well as problems of comparison. There are suggestions that campaigning in the Philippines was not a case of combined operations. This was certainly the case if the latter are understood conventionally in terms of hitting the beaches or amphibious assaults. However, if a wider definition of combined operations is allowed, then the Philippines campaign can be included. This was a campaign on islands that was heavily dependent on naval support.

The Luzon operation was accompanied by other combined operations in the extensive Philippine archipelago. With space at a premium and with knowledge of the eventual result of the campaign, it is easy to neglect such attacks in order to focus on the preparations for the assault on Japan, but they are of importance not least for the light they shed on relative capability, on strategic goals, and on the development of impressive American effectiveness and experience in combined operations. The Americans were keen to use the Philippines as a base for the invasion of Japan, which would require a scale of commitment greater than that of earlier Pacific operations, by both them and others. The islands they had already captured were crucial as bases for air attack, but they were not large enough to provide the staging areas required. The Americans gained such positons in central Luzon, especially Clark Field and Manila Bay, where, with the attack aided by a parachute drop, Corregidor fell on February 28.

The Americans also needed to ensure the security of shipping passages. This led to a series of combined operations against the numerous and far-flung islands of the region. Samar was invaded on February 19, Palawan on February 28, and other islands in March and April. American skill in the amphibious assaults, in the coordination of air and sea support, and in the rapid securing and development of beachhead positions was demonstrated and enhanced. Although the scale was very different, this continual process was a useful preparation for planned landings in the Japanese archipelago. Yamashita finally surrendered on September 2.[12]

The islands of Iwo Jima and Okinawa were seized in order to provide airbases for an attack on Japan and to provide rescue bases for damaged B-29s that otherwise would have been ditched at sea. This bland remark gives no guidance to the difficulty of the conquests and the heavy casualties involved in defeating the well-positioned Japanese forces, who fought to the death with fanatical intensity for islands seen as part of Japan, although under heavy pressure from the attacking American Marines with their massive air and sea support. The Japanese were also skillful defenders, well able to exploit the terrain, not least by tunneling into Iwo Jima. This ensured that the bombing and shelling that preceded the landing of the Marines there on February 19 inflicted only minimal damage. As a consequence, the conquest of the island was slow and bloody, and much of the fighting was at close quarters. The Japanese had created a dense network of underground fortifications, and this network not only vitiated the effects of American firepower, both artillery and aircraft, but also made a fighting advance on foot difficult, not least because the network provided the Japanese with a myriad of interconnected firing positions. The Japanese had sufficient artillery, mortars, and machine guns to make their defenses deadly. Their use of reverse-slope positions also lessened the impact of American firepower.

On Okinawa, the major island of the Ryukyu archipelago and sixty miles long, American firepower was too strong for the Japanese to consider defending the beaches. The Americans devoted a formidable effort to the conquest, indeed making it the largest-scale assault prior to what was intended to be the invasion of the main Japanese Home Islands. The Americans deployed 183,000 well-prepared troops, from four army and three Marine divisions, and more than 1,200 warships, while the British Pacific Fleet also provided assistance. The Americans also made highly effective use of tactical ground air support. The Japanese had 77,000 troops as well as 20,000 militia. On March 24, the Americans occupied the Kerama Islands and Keise Island, nearby small islands that both provided an advance base and covered the flank of the main landing by two Marine divisions and two army divisions on April 1. Instead of fighting hard in the landing zone, the Japanese concentrated in part of the interior of the island. This meant that the landings were largely unopposed and the center of the island, including the airfields there, was rapidly seized, ensuring that the island was divided. The Marines were then sent north, where, as it turned out, there were relatively few Japanese troops, and the north was largely conquered by the end of the month.

The army was sent south, where resistance was concentrated near the capital, Naha. The Japanese in the rugged terrain and poor weather created a formidable challenge for the Americans. The coral limestone hills had been fortified with tunnel positions, pillboxes, mortar emplacements, and machine-gun nests. The Japanese made extensive use of caves. American casualties were heavy. The Americans deployed all the facilities of available weaponry to aid their slow progress: they dropped napalm and explosive charges into the entrances of Japanese positions and made extensive use of tank-mounted flamethrowers in order to clear positions. Although the circumstances were very different to operations elsewhere, the successful use of flamethrower and other tanks depended on effective cooperation with infantry, which provided crucial protection for the tanks. Demolition teams of combat engineers also proved an important part of this well-integrated force. Resistance there did not cease until June 22. The Japanese decision to rest on the defensive on land, and not to rely on counterattacks that would cause heavy Japanese casualties, made the American task more difficult. The Japanese, however, used kamikaze attacks against the American warships. The eventual American conquest reflected accumulated experience and saw improvements, notably with cooperation between the army and Marines.[13]

Although much of Iwo Jima had fallen within two weeks, the time anticipated for its capture, it took thirty-six days to conquer the island and more than one-third of the American Marines employed were killed (5,391) and wounded (17,372). Twenty-two thousand Japanese troops were killed. On Okinawa, the American ground losses from all services were about 7,300, and there are about 205 unaccounted for soldiers and Marines.[14] The naval forces lost about 4,300 killed, mostly from kamikaze attacks, while the Japanese lost 110,000 dead and 7,400 prisoners. The heavy American casualty rate inflicted by the defenders of both islands, the vast majority of whom died in the defense, led to fears about the American casualties that an invasion of Japan would probably entail. This was an invasion strongly supported by the army and Marines, whereas the navy and air force backed blockade and air attack respectively.[15]

The heavy American losses on Iwo Jima and Okinawa suggested that the use of atomic bombs was necessary in order both to overcome a Japanese suicidal determination to fight on and to obtain unconditional surrender. MacArthur told Penney that his troops had not yet met the Japanese army properly and that, when they did, they were going to take heavy casualties.[16] Moreover, General George Marshall, the American chief of staff, considered using atom bombs in tactical support of a landing on Kyushu. Planned for November 1945, this was the site for the first projected American landings on the main Japanese Home Islands, and it was there that the Japanese had concentrated most of their forces.

Cumulative experience proved important to American combined operations, which also benefited from their mastery of logistics, not least in ensuring the availability of sufficient oil and ammunition. The transfer of ammunition between ships at sea was tested during the Iwo Jima operation, following success earlier with fuel. The development of Service Squadrons by the navy, and the supporting structure of floating dry docks, was important to American forward movement, not least as existing harbors tended to be distant, exposed to the sea, and limited in their facilities.[17] If American shipping was, in turn, exposed to the risk of Japanese attack, the Americans were well able to protect their shipping. Indeed, the Americans could plan where they wanted to operate and where to mount an invasion. There were also sufficient landing craft and supporting warships.

The Americans were not alone in their use of combined operations against Japan. Although affected by a shortage of landing craft in 1944, which led to the postponement of a plan to recapture the Andaman and Nicobar Islands in the Bay of Bengal, the British launched such attacks in their offensive against the Japanese in Burma in 1945. The focus was inland, on the Irrawaddy valley, but the advance on Rangoon, the main port, was supported by an unopposed amphibious landing, Operation Dracula. Earlier, another force advanced down the Arakan coast, using combined operations to capture the port of Myebon and the offshore islands of Ramree and Cheduba. Throughout, British moves on land were supported by naval action, notably with attacks on Japanese positions.

After the fall of Rangoon on May 3, 1945, it was necessary for the troops to recuperate and resupply. Thereafter, it was unclear whether the British would continue to campaign overland, into southern Burma and/or Thailand, against the Japanese forces in the region or would mount an amphibious advance on the more distant targets of Malaya and Singapore. As an instance of the significance of political factors in the strategic tasking that set the context for combined operations, the recapture of Malaya and Singapore was regarded as very important to British prestige. In September 1944, Admiral Sir Geoffrey Layton, commander in chief of Ceylon, had written of

> the vital importance of our recapturing those parts of the Empire as far as possible ourselves. I would specially mention the recapture of Burma and its culmination in the recovery of Singapore by force of arms and not by waiting for it to be surrendered as part of any peace treaty . . . the immense effect this will have on our prestige in the Far East in post-war years. This and only this in my opinion will restore us to our former level in the eyes of the native population in these parts.

Admiral Louis Mountbatten, the well-connected supreme commander of South-East Asia Command, strongly agreed.[18] Both men were instances of the extent to which command structures involved a combination of men from different services.

In the event, Operation Zipper, an amphibious invasion of western Malaya, was planned for September 9, 1945. It would probably have led to heavy casualties, both British and Japanese, notably as the British did not have enough landing craft and were short of sufficient carrier-based air support. However, the Japanese surrender altered the situation, and the British landed unopposed, although not without serious organizational problems. Planned attacks are repeatedly an important aspect of the history of amphibious operations.

Meanwhile, Australian forces had mounted a series of amphibious attacks on Borneo in May–July, against very varied opposition. Their target was the oilfields near Tarakan and Balikpapan and in Brunei, seized on May 1, June 10, and July 1, respectively. These attacks complemented the British naval air assaults launched against Japanese-held oil installations on Sumatra. As the Japanese were no longer able to transport oil from Borneo to Japan, its value to them was limited. Indeed, there was subsequently to be criticism in Australia of the wastefulness of the attacks. At Tarakan, the outnumbered Japanese fought on for three months against a far larger Australian force landed by an American Amphibious Group. At Balikpapan, the Australians landed in division strength, their largest amphibious assault of the war.

On August 8, 1945, after the surrender of Germany, the Soviet Union declared war on Japan and attacked. The bulk of the attack was overland and focused on the major Japanese forces in Manchuria. However, this offensive included an advance overland, from August 12, into north Korea, as far as the 38th Parallel, that was supported by well-planned and -executed amphibious operations, as well as the conquest of southern Sakhalin and the Kurile Islands, both of which indicated Soviet amphibious capability. The American sinking of the last remaining Japanese warships in late July gave the Soviets freedom to risk their meager naval forces and amphibious capability. Southern Sakhalin was invaded both overland (from northern Sakhalin) and by amphibious forces. Most of the Kuriles were invaded by sea from Kamchatka to the north, but the southernmost ones were occupied by troops that had been involved in the Sakhalin operation. On the island of Shimushu in the Kuriles, the Japanese used the tactics they had displayed in the Pacific against the Americans. The rest of the group fell after the Japanese surrender, although some troops continued to resist.

There were already preparations for what became the Cold War. To match the Soviet invasion of north Korea, the Americans landed troops from Okinawa on September 8 and occupied the south.

COMBINED OPERATIONS AGAINST GERMANY AND ITS ALLIES, 1942

The preparations for the operations against German-occupied Europe were staged against Germany's allies as they occupied peripheral areas that were judged of strategic significance. The initial targets were controlled by Vichy France and were therefore, at once, part of the struggle for control over France's destiny and empire and, at the same time, a stage in the defeat of Germany. These were territories that the Free French had been unable to take from Vichy France in earlier operations in 1940–1941. These operations had been supported by Britain and its allies, as with the takeover of the island of New Caledonia in September 1940, in which an Australian cruiser took a role, and the attack on the port of Libreville in Gabon in November 1940. However, the attack on Dakar, the major French base in West Africa, in September 1940 failed, in large part due to poor planning, including an inadequate understanding of the military and political situation there.

Successfully launched before dawn on May 5, 1942, against the naval base at Diégo Suarez by British troops and commandos backed by carrier aircraft, the Madagascar campaign provided Britain with valuable experience in mounting amphibious assaults. In September 1942, a full-scale attempt, both overland from Diégo Suarez and with fresh landings (at Majunga, Morondava, Tamatave, Tuléar, and Fort Dauphin from September 10 to 29), was launched to seize control of the whole of the island, the largest in the Indian Ocean. These landings were the best way both to seize the entire island and to overcome the logistical problems of operating overland. The isolated

Vichy French put up enough resistance until the surrender on November 5 to justify this major effort. Although this operation was peripheral to the main campaigns, it lessened the danger that the Allied world would be fractured by German and Japanese advances.

Success in Madagascar contrasted markedly with the failure of the amphibious attack on Dakar in September 1940. In large part, the contrast rested on superior situational awareness based on effective intelligence, with this awareness fed through into an effective planning process. Surprise, an important element in combined operations, was also a key contrast, while sea control was firmer in 1942. The actual landing was handled by experienced troops who had been rehearsed, and a tank landing ship was employed. Drawing explicitly on the example of Japanese amphibious assaults in 1941–1942, there was a landing on a broad front.[19]

French North Africa (Morocco, Algeria, and Tunisia) was successfully invaded by Anglo-American amphibious forces, mostly Americans, in Operation Torch on November 8, 1942. The Americans were determined to be seen to act on land in the European theater (however indirectly) as soon as possible.[20] The Allied aim was to squeeze the Axis forces in North Africa from the west and east, the latter the advance from the British in Egypt overland via Libya, as well as to acquire experience in combined operations. The ability to mount the amphibious assaults was a result of the absence of German submarines from near the beachheads. In part, this reflected the limitations of the submarine both as a strategic and as an operational tool. Thanks to successful Allied disinformation, Axis submarines in the Atlantic were positioned farther south to prevent a reported attack on Dakar in Senegal while the Americans were strongly convoyed.

The Americans landing at Casablanca, Port Lyautey, and Safi had sailed directly from Norfolk, Virginia. Given the difficulties experienced in coping with the confusions of a landing and in speedily exploiting the situation, especially in the Casablanca operation, it was just as well that opposition there was relatively light. There was poor planning, a lack of understanding of beach conditions, inadequate training and equipment, and a poor tempo of landing and exploitation. The American landings at Oran and Algiers, which did not face the Atlantic surf seen at Casablanca, were better executed, although the entire operation was affected by the limited time available for preparation, and much of the staff work and logistical support was inadequate, sometimes seriously so. The Americans made use of commandos in the shape of the First Ranger Battalion.[21]

Thanks in large part to a careful cultivation of the French military leaders in North Africa, resistance by far more numerous Vichy forces was rapidly overcome, although some units, especially of the navy, resisted firmly. Negotiations after a general cease-fire ordered on November 10 led the French forces to join the Allies.[22] Despite Allied concerns, Spain, which controlled a portion of northern Morocco, did not intervene against Operation Torch; nor did the Italian surface fleet, which was seriously short of oil.

The wider strategic consequences proved less satisfactory in the mid-term. The Axis were better able to exploit the new situation created by the landings. The refusal of American commanders to include eastern Algeria and Tunisia among the landing zones, in addition to Morocco and western Algeria where the landings occurred, is readily understandable in light of the risk of Axis air attack in the central Mediterranean but had unfortunate consequences. Against no opposition due to the acquiescence of Admiral Jean-Pierre Estéva, the resident-general of Tunisia, German and Italian forces rapidly occupied Vichy-run Tunisia from November 9, moving from Italy by air and sea and denying the Allies their anticipated rapid success in North Africa. Leaving from Livorno, the Italians also landed an army corps in Corsica.

In April and July 1942, General George Marshall, the American chief of staff, had pressed for an invasion of France that year. The success of Operation Torch could not conceal the risks of such an invasion in terms of Atlantic and English Channel weather; lack of Allied shipping, especially landing craft; and German opposition, including U-boats in the Atlantic. Before any invasion of France, there was still a need to win the Battle of the Atlantic against the U-boats and to gain air dominance, as well as to plan operations and train, equip, and move forces.

Allied attacks on Western Europe in 1942 were not encouraging. The British combined-services attack on the French dry dock at St. Nazaire on March 28, an attack launched to limit the possibilities for basing German warships in France, succeeded but was small-scale. Operation Jubilee, the raid on Dieppe, a town on the Channel coast of France, on August 19, 1942, was larger scale (with six thousand troops), but a failure. This poorly planned assault on a well-fortified position led to 60 percent Allied, mainly Canadian, casualties to accurate machine-gun, artillery, and mortar fire. Despite the spin produced to justify the operation, this outcome underlined the problems of amphibious assaults, not least the difficulty of getting adequate information on the defenses. The Dieppe raid also showed that attacking a port destroyed it; hence the need to bring port facilities with the eventual invasion of Normandy in 1944. It was also clear that an invasion would require more intelligence and a greater prior bombardment from air and sea. The Dieppe raid lacked the latter because the RAF, which as yet had not deployed effective tactical support aircraft, was committed to the bombing campaign on Germany. In addition, it hoped to benefit from the element of surprise.[23]

The Germans deployed and used a large amount of resources, troops, aircraft, and matériel preparing to resist attack, which represented a significant case of opportunity costs and a consequence of Germany having lost the initiative and been pushed back onto the defensive. Indeed, there were more

German troops and their allies defending Western Europe in late 1942 than there were British forces in Britain. This was a major Western contribution to the war effort, although far less than that of the Soviet Union. Furthermore, the Germans kept few elite units in Western Europe.

THE MEDITERRANEAN, 1943

The political context for combined operations was again to the fore in 1943. Allied insistence on a German unconditional surrender, a policy announced by Roosevelt at the press conference after the Casablanca Conference of January 14–24, 1943, and the fanatical nature of Hitler's regime combined to ensure that it would be a fight to the finish and thus contributed to the prolongation of the war. Soviet demands for a second front in Western Europe encouraged American pressure for an invasion.

In North Africa, Allied combined operations ensured the surrender of 238,000 German and Italian troops in Tunisia in May 1943. The operations in North Africa demonstrated the importance of logistics. In battle, the Germans were tactically adroit, and in campaign they matched this operationally. However, the fundamentals necessary for their success were lacking. North Africa was peripheral to the main area of German commitment and effectiveness. The Allies not only had superiority in the air and on land but also were able to cut the flow of supplies to Tunisia by sea. Tunisia was in effect an island, and there was to be no equivalent to Dunkirk. The earlier German failure to capture Malta, or to wreck its use as a British base, left the Germans in a weak strategic position in the central Mediterranean, as Malta again proved its value for the interdiction of transport links. The Allied advance on and into Tunisia was greatly assisted by the movement forward of supply points, both ports and airfields, following the advance on land. Allied anti-submarine operations helped secure supply routes.

Victory in Tunisia was followed by an attack on Italy, although in this larger target, one more exposed to German intervention, it proved impossible to repeat the relatively rapid success won in Tunisia. In Operation Husky, Allied forces landed in Sicily on July 10, 1943. Amphibious power and air support allowed the Allies to seize the initiative and helped ensure a wide-ranging attack on Sicily, the largest island in the Mediterranean, one in which 180,000 Allied troops were initially involved alongside 750 warships, 2,500 transport ships, and 400 landing craft. This was to be the second-largest amphibious operation of the war in Europe, D-Day in Normandy in 1944 being the first. The landings were more sophisticated than those mounted in North Africa in 1942. There were appropriate ship-to-shore techniques, notably amphibious pontoon causeways and trained beach parties. The British landed in southeast Sicily and the Americans farther west between Cape Scaramia and Licata.

Once landed, the Allies faced problems from the defenders of the island. The Italian 6th Army, commanded by General Alfredo Guzzoni, defended Sicily. Including navy and air force personnel, Guzzoni had 315,000 men and 40,000 Germans. His troops were primarily composed of Coastal Divisions—five of the nine—and he had only a few obsolete tanks. After considering options, he concentrated his force in the southeastern sector, which was the Allied territorial objective. The SIM—Italian Military Intelligence Service—was sure the Allies were going to land in Sicily, after precise information had been received from its agents in Lisbon, while German intelligence believed the Allies would land in Sardinia or Greece. Kesselring, the German commander, disregarded the Italian intelligence reports and deployed the German tanks of 14th Panzer Corps in central and western Sicily. On July 7, Guzzoni was warned that a landing was expected within two or three days, but despite the information from Lisbon and the Allied seizure of the offshore island of Pantellaria on June 11 after heavy bombing, Kesselring kept his troops in the interior and did not defend the coast. In contrast, the Italian troops were deployed there and on July 10 were able to blow up the ports of Gela and Licata to deny them to the Allies.

The Italian forces resisted but were overwhelmed. For example, when the Eighth Army landed, that part of the coast was defended by the 206th Coastal Division, which was scattered along an eighty-two-mile-long line. The British first wave alone outnumbered the Italian defenders three to one. The Italians, who had no tanks, were annihilated. However, when the British then moved on to attack the Italian-defended city of Catania, it took twenty-three days of hard fighting. The American Seventh Army landed south of Gela. Italian coastal units resisted as best they could but suffered heavy casualties, the 429th Coastal Battalion losing 45 percent of its men. The Livorno Division counterattacked supported by fifty obsolete Italian tanks and by aircraft bombing the beachhead, but the attack failed with the loss of 50 percent of the troops. German tanks were too far away to offer initial support. When they finally arrived, the attack was resumed with initial success, but, supported by naval firepower, American troops fought bravely and enlarged their beachhead. The Allies benefited from support from the local Mafia. Some Italian officers seeking to organize opposition to the Allies were shot, while some American units were guided by Mafiosi.

Subsequently, with British general Sir Bernard Montgomery held before Catania, General George Patton, commanding the Seventh Army, moved north to Palermo, creating and exploiting opportunities for outflanking opposition. The heavily outnumbered Assietta Infantry Division was unable to stop him, and having taken Palermo, Patton moved east on Messina after fighting off counterattacks at Troina.

The Americans proved far more effective than they had done in Tunisia and repeatedly gained and used mobility. However, the Germans fought well, taking advantage of the terrain, which limited the use of armor. The capture of the island was completed on August 16–17, and it provided a valuable base from which mainland Italy could be attacked. Nevertheless, the ability of the Axis to retreat without encirclement and then to evacuate about 102,000 troops—much of their army—seriously compromised the value of the operation. Most of the 132,000 troops captured were Italians. The Americans (repeatedly) and the British launched amphibious landings in advance of their ground forces in an unsuccessful attempt to cut off the retreating forces. The British were less effective but faced more concentrated opposition and called off their critical second-phase landing.[24]

As with Saipan and Japan in 1944, Sicily was a combined operation that had important political consequences. It precipitated a growing crisis of confidence in Mussolini and his overthrow on July 25, 1943. The new Italian government signed an armistice with the Allies on September 3 and announced it five days later. However, a rapid German response left the Germans in control in central and northern Italy and ended a brief opportunity for maneuver by Anglo-American forces. British forces invaded Calabria, the far south of mainland Italy, from Sicily on September 3, meeting no resistance, with fresh landings on September 4 and 8, while, farther north, the major port of Taranto was occupied by a British amphibious force on September 9. From there, the British advanced to capture the ports of Brindisi and Bari, the latter falling on September 14. These operations in Apulia were greatly eased by the Italian armistice as there were no German forces there.

The main invasion force was landed on September 9, 1943, in the Gulf of Salerno, south of Naples, in Operation Avalanche. However, the German response to the overextended Salerno landing proved more rapid and determined than had been anticipated, not least in preventing the Allies from using Montecorvino airfield, which they had captured on landing day. The shallow beachhead was only consolidated and expanded with considerable difficulty, which made it impossible to use the ports of Salerno and Vietri once they had been captured. The Germans proved able to build up their forces faster than the Allies. On September 12, a German counterattack tested the Allies hard, exhausting their reserves and leading to the dropping of American airborne forces into the beachhead. Blocked, the Germans began to withdraw to north of Naples on September 16, while that day there was the first linkup between patrols from Salerno and British troops advancing overland from Calabria. The Allies pressed on to enter Naples on October 1. The Allies were left in control of southern Italy, but the Germans had created a strong line across the peninsula, making plentiful use of the mountainous terrain to create effective defensive positions, from which they were to fight ably and cause heavy casualties for the attacking Allies.

The invasion of Italy also altered the strategic situation in the Mediterranean, creating a new context for combined operations. The Balkans and southern France both now appeared vulnerable to Allied attack, and this situation increased Allied differences over planning. However, because Italy proved a more intractable task than had been anticipated, the resources that might have been freed for such options were not released. That September–October, the Germans were able to withdraw from the islands of Sardinia and Corsica, both of which were occupied by the Allies. The Germans in Sardinia had reached an agreement with the local Italian authorities on September 9 to evacuate the island unopposed. The Allies, in the shape of American parachutists, arrived on Sardinia unopposed on September 14. The Germans withdrew northward to Corsica, but the local Italian garrison there resisted. Germans from Sardinia took the Corsican port of Bastia, but Italian armored units seized it and forced the Germans to leave by sea. Other German units on the island fled when the Allies landed. The Allies made the Italians withdraw to Sardinia, leaving their heavy weapons and vehicles behind.

In contrast, concern about a possible invasion of Greece, deliberately encouraged by Allied deception, led the Germans to reinforce their forces there in June and July 1943. The invasion did not come, but the strength of the German position helped ensure that the British were unsuccessful in the Aegean when they tried to exploit the Italian surrender. This attempt reflected Churchill's long-standing interest in the region, an interest that went back to the First World War, and his hope of bringing Turkey into the war. The Americans sensibly advised against the plan. In the event, a swift German response and the inability of the British to secure air superiority led to a serious failure in the Dodecanese Islands campaign in the Aegean, with the loss of newly inserted British garrisons on Cos (October 3–4) and Leros (November 12–16) as well as of supporting warships. This failure indicated the continued importance of air power and formed a striking contrast with American successes in the Pacific: there, island targets were isolated before attack. In the event, Turkey did not enter the war until March 1, 1945, by when it made scant difference.

The Americans had been reluctant to support an invasion of Sicily and, even more, mainland Italy because they feared that it would detract resources from the invasion of France and the war with Japan and be a strategic irrelevance. American policymakers were opposed to what they correctly saw as the Mediterranean obsession of British policy. The latter commitment indeed reflected British strategic concerns in the region, but these were the product not simply of geopolitical interests but also of the legacy of conflict in the Mediterranean with the Axis since 1940. The British had military resources in the region, as well as commitments, and the former could not be readily reallocated. The British preference for an indirect approach, weakening the

Axis by incremental steps as the preparation for an invasion of France, was also very important.[25] It was an aspect of British strategic culture, greatly strengthened by the experience of the First World War, and also a response to the specific military circumstances of 1942–1943. The British were concerned that a direct attack across the English Channel would expose untested forces to the battle-hardened Germans. Their experience in 1940–1941 had made them wary of such a step until the Germans had been weakened. Fresh defeats at Axis hands in early 1942, in Asia and North Africa, had further hit Britain's military reputation and confidence. The British hoped that a presence in Italy would encourage the already-strong resistance to German occupation in Yugoslavia and, more generally, hold down German forces in the Balkans.

In contrast, the Americans argued that Italy and, in particular, mainland Italy was a strategic irrelevance that would dissipate Allied military strength. Instead, they sought a direct approach, especially an engagement with the major German forces in Western Europe (as in 1918), which meant an invasion of northern France and an advance into Germany itself. German weaknesses in 1943 might suggest that this could have been an option that year. Many key German units were allocated to the unsuccessful Kursk offensive on the Eastern Front, the Germans lacked the buildup in munitions production that 1943 was to bring, and their defensive positions along the French coast were incomplete. There was also a broader strategic context in that the Soviets mentioned their suspicion of their allies' failure to open a Second Front in Western Europe when the Soviets unsuccessfully probed the Germans in 1942–1943 on the possibility of a separate peace. The British were aware of this probing. The link between combined operations and geopolitical alignments was clear and significant.

In turn, Churchill was worried about Soviet expansionist intentions in Eastern Europe and sought to limit these by Anglo-American moves into the Balkans, a policy the United States opposed. Roosevelt indeed informed Churchill in June 1944 that any setback in the invasion of France would be politically disastrous for him if forces had been diverted by being sent to the Balkans. This was a reference to the forthcoming presidential election that November.

At the same time, and not undermining these points, the British were correct to draw attention to deficiencies in Allied preparedness, deficiencies that made any invasion of France in 1943 seriously unwise. As yet, there was only limited experience of (and equipment for) amphibious assaults, while it was unclear at the beginning of 1943 how far it would be possible to vanquish the U-boat threat in the battle of the Atlantic. Aside from the need to build up forces for an invasion, there was also the requirement of assured air and sea superiority. The success of the Torch landings in North Africa in 1942 was only a limited indicator of Allied capability, as opposition to them had been weak. In addition, operations in the Mediterranean in 1943 provided valuable experience in planning and execution, not least in air support, airborne attacks, and the use of landing craft. The landings of 1943, like that of Anzio in Italy in 1944, also provided warnings about the difficulty of invading France, not least in terms of the firm German response and speedy reaction. In 1943, the latter would have been a more serious problem in France than it was to be in 1944, as the Allies did not yet have sufficient air dominance to isolate the area of operations.

Moreover, the fighting in North Africa and Italy had been important in improving Allied military capability on land. The British learned how to respond to German armor and came to place a renewed stress on artillery. The Americans benefited greatly from their first experience in 1942 of fighting the Germans. As it was not feasible to invade France in 1943, the Americans finally agreed to the attack on Sicily. It was the unexpected overthrow of Mussolini on July 25, 1943, that helped lead to the commitment of major forces to invade mainland Italy.

Repeated landings and accumulated planning, preparation, and training gave the Allies experience in a variety of respects, each of which had a cumulative value. For example, the degree to which operations required the collection of data, notably on hydrographic and beach conditions, came to be appreciated and was addressed especially by the work of the British COPPs (Combined Operations Pilotage Parties). These played a major role before D-Day. Comprised of navy and army personnel and helped by infrared equipment and submarines, these parties reconnoitered beaches and were significant both in the landings in Europe and in the 1945 Rhine crossings. For example, Major Logan Scott-Bowden and Sergeant Bruce Ogden-Smith were landed at Ver sur Mer and collected samples from areas of peat marsh on what became the Normandy invasion's Gold Beach, in order to establish whether the peat had a clay base treacherous to heavy vehicles if only lightly covered with sand. Another group were landed on Onival Beach in Picardy (not an invasion beach) in May 1944 in order to report on mines fixed on poles just below high-water mark and on other beach defenses.

THE MEDITERRANEAN, 1944

In 1944, criticism of the Italy campaign increased. The effort employed was criticized. In *Newsweek*, an American journal, on March 13, J. F. C. Fuller, a former British general turned military commentator, argued: "The strategy is execrable. We should never have embarked on this Italian adventure because it was unstrategic from the start." Claiming that the topography helped the defense, which is what the British had mistakenly thought would be the case against the Germans in Greece in 1941, he stated that the forces used in Italy should have been conserved for the Second Front in France. As a result of this topography and its impact, there was interest in amphibious assaults in order to bypass German defense lines.

There was much talk of the use of such assaults in Italy in 1944 but only one major attack. This, launched at Anzio on January 22, bypassed the German defenses near Naples and was designed to open the way to Rome, which was about forty miles away on a flat route and where the Germans were unprepared. Nevertheless, as with Salerno in 1943, the landing was not exploited sufficiently, indeed scarcely exploited at all, which allowed the Germans to gather together a scratch force including air force ground crews, drivers, and soldiers from the telephone centers to resist the Allied advance. Aside from the command flaws to which such a situation gives rise, there was also, as with Gallipoli in 1915, the question of whether the entire operation was misconceived. In particular, limitations in the availability of troops and landing craft and a strategic and political context that was very different to those in which the Sicily and Salerno operations had been launched in 1943 made the situation less propitious. Within forty-eight hours, the Germans were well prepared to resist the Allied forces that had landed. The idea that it would be possible to outflank the Germans on the Gustav Line and cause them readily to abandon their position proved optimistic. Instead, the Anzio beachhead was held, and German counterattacks on February 16 and 29 were beaten off, in part as a result of foreknowledge from signals interception. It proved necessary for the Allies to fight through the Gustav Line, which was done with great difficulty in May as the prelude to a breakout from Anzio. Only then was the way clear to Rome. However, Anzio had led to the commitment of German reserves that might otherwise have been sent elsewhere, notably to France.

This diversion of forces was important to both sides and central to the opportunity-costs element of combined operations. The detachment of six divisions to support landings on the French Riviera in southern France weakened the Allied forces in Italy, as, more generally, did the dispatch of reinforcements to northern France for the D-Day operation rather than to Italy. However, these diversions reflected the sense that Italy had reached an impasse and that it was necessary to open up a new open flank.

The landings on the French Riviera, Operation Dragoon, mounted on August 15 after the D-Day landings in Normandy, were very much an American operation. They were pushed hard by President Franklin Delano Roosevelt, the American Chiefs of Staff, and General Dwight Eisenhower, all of whom were opposed to Britain's Mediterranean strategy, with its commitment to Italy and its interest in an attack from there into Austria. Dragoon was seen as a way to gain the major port of Marseilles, aiding Allied logistics in France, and to cut off German forces in south and southwest France. Although most of the initial landing units were American, much of the follow-up force was French. Due primarily to the weakness of the German defenders who were focused on the struggle in northern France, but also to the strength of Allied naval and air support, the landing did not lead to any major battle comparable to that in Normandy: resistance both on the beaches and inland, where an Anglo-American parachute force landed, was light. Casualties were few. The Allies used 887 warships, 1,370 landing craft, and more than 2,000 aircraft. The heavy naval bombardment, including five battleships and twenty-one cruisers, hit the coastal defenses hard, while overwhelming Allied air superiority prevented German interference.

It was difficult, however, for amphibious forces to transform themselves rapidly for fast-moving advances. In particular, it took time to bring ashore large numbers of vehicles and to prepare for large-scale tank conflict. Advancing rapidly, the Allies took Avignon on August 25, Lyons on September 3, and Dijon eight days later. However, the advance was sufficiently slow for the Germans to be able to withdraw their forces from southern and southwestern France and not to face envelopment.

A smaller-scale landing was launched against the German-held Italian island of Elba, which was invaded on the night of June 16–17, 1944, by a French force sent from Corsica that was covered by British warships. The French took one thousand casualties capturing the island, and two thousand German troops were captured. In strategic terms, the operation accentuated Hitler's fears of Allied landings in Italy and thus encouraged a continuing German commitment to coastal defense that absorbed many troops, for example, near Genoa.

D-DAY

The German withdrawal from southern and southwestern France was already taking place because of the consequences of the Allied landings in northern France on June 6, 1944: D-Day, the launching of the Normandy invasion. American, British, and Canadian forces landed in Normandy, as Operation Neptune (the landings) paved the way for Operation Overlord (the invasion). Under the overall command of General Dwight Eisenhower, the Allies benefited from well-organized and effective naval support for the invasion and from overwhelming air superiority. In addition, a successful deception exercise, Operation Fortitude, ensured that the Normandy landing was a surprise.

The Germans had concentrated more of their coastal defenses and forces, the fixed and mobile aspects of their response to any likely invasion, further east in the Calais region. This appeared an obvious target as it offered a shorter sea crossing from England to France and a shorter route to Germany. Normandy, in contrast, was easier to reach from the invasion ports on the south coast of England, especially Plymouth, Portland, and Portsmouth. The

Germans lacked adequate naval and air forces to contest an invasion, and much of their army in France was of indifferent quality and short of transport and training and, in many cases, equipment. The Eastern Front was a more important call on the army and home defense against Allied bombing on the air force.

There was also a serious issue of operational response. German commanders were divided about where the attack was likely to fall and about how best to respond to it, particularly over whether to move their ten panzer (tank) divisions close to the coast, so that the Allies could be attacked before they could consolidate their position, or to mass them as a strategic reserve. The eventual decision was for the panzer divisions, whose impact greatly worried Allied planners, to remain inland, but their ability to act as a strategic reserve was lessened by the decision not to mass them and by Allied air power that hampered their movements. This decision reflected the tensions and uncertainties of the German command structure, tensions increased by the intervention of Hitler and by disaffection among the Germans about his role and policies.

While the naval side was handled very well, the course of the landings, all mounted in daylight, was very varied. Specialized tanks developed by the British to attack coastal defenses, for example, crab flail tanks for use against minefields, proved effective in the British and Canadian sector: Gold, Juno, and Sword Beaches. Specialized landing craft also performed well, although in the absence of the landing craft gun (medium) (LCG[M]), which were not used until September 1944 in the assault of Walcheren, close-in artillery support was provided by tank landing craft with Royal Marines manning the tanks being carried.[26] The Canadian and British forces that landed on these beaches also benefited from careful planning and preparation, from the seizure of crucial covering positions by airborne troops, and from German hesitation about how best to respond.

The situation was less happy on Omaha Beach. The Americans there were inadequately prepared in the face of a good defense, not least because of poor planning and confusion in the landing, including the launching of assault craft and duplex drive (amphibious) Sherman tanks too far offshore, as well as a refusal to use the specialized tanks and the army's unwillingness to adopt USMC-designed LVTs (landing vehicle, tracked). On land, the topography was a major issue, notably the bluffs behind the beach and the narrow nature of the beach area, both of which would also have affected the use of specialist tanks. The Americans, who had failed to learn sufficient appropriate lessons from American amphibious assaults in the Pacific and Allied ones in the Mediterranean, sustained about three thousand casualties, both in landing and on the beach, from German positions on the cliffs that had not been suppressed by air attack or the overly short naval bombardment, which contrasted with a longer bombardment in the British sector. Air power could not deliver the promised quantities of ordnance on target on time.[27] In contrast, on Utah Beach, the Americans benefited from the disruption to the defense caused by the parachute-landing behind the coastal positions.

Eventually, largely due to the actions of small unit leaders and their subordinates, the Americans on Omaha were able to scale the cliffs, overcome the defenses, and move inland. From Anzio, the Americans had learned the need to advance rapidly from the beach. However, at the end of D-Day, although about 130,000 Allied soldiers had landed, the beachhead was still shallow and the troops in it were fortunate that the Germans had little available armor to mount a response. This owed much to a failure in German command that reflected rigidities stemming from Hitler's interventions. The firepower of Allied aircraft and warships was also a key factor. Nevertheless, had Allied forces at the other landing sites faced German forces of the quality and quantity of those at Omaha, and a similar topography, then the Allies might have suffered heavy casualties and faced the prospect of defeat.

J. C. F. Fuller pointed out that Overlord marked a major advance in amphibious operations as there was no need to capture a port in order to land, reinforce, and support the invasion force. Fuller wrote in the *Sunday Pictorial* of October 1, 1944:

> Had our sea power remained what it had been, solely a weapon to command the sea, the garrison Germany established in France almost certainly would have proved sufficient. It was a change in the conception of naval power which sealed the doom of that great fortress. Hitherto in all overseas invasions the invading forces had been fitted to ships. Now ships were fitted to the invading forces . . . how to land the invading forces in battle order . . . this difficulty has been overcome by building various types of special landing boats and prefabricated landing stages.

To Fuller, this matched the tank in putting the defense at a disadvantage. Fuller's argument was not entirely true, but in the issue of variety and application the point was good. Moreover, the Dieppe operation had shown that attacking a port destroyed it, thus the need to bring two prefabricated harbors, the Mulberry Harbours,[28] composed of floating piers, with the invasion. In 1944, the Germans still mistakenly anticipated that the Allies would focus on seizing ports. The laying of oil pipelines under the Channel was also an impressive engineering achievement that contributed to the infrastructure of the invasion. The experience gained in earlier landings was important, although the scale of the operation, including the naval and air support, and the severity of the resistance on the landing beaches were greater than in North Africa and Italy. At the same time, while thousands of landing craft were deployed and there had been a development of close-support landing craft, there was a lack of sufficient landing ship tanks.[29]

Allied planners focused so much energy on how to secure a beachhead that they failed to think through fully the problem of going inland. It proved difficult for the Allies to break out of Normandy, although with the German armor focusing on the British, the Americans succeeded in breaking out further west in August, outmaneuvering the German forces. The Allies were able then to advance on the German frontier, leaving German coastal positions behind. This was not a process in which amphibious operations played a role until, in the autumn, efforts were made to clear the Scheldt estuary in order to be able to use the port of Antwerp. These operations saw the use by the British of landing craft supplied by the United States, including the DUKW, which had been also used at D-Day, and the LVT, which carried machine guns and, given a level landing area, could climb straight out of the water and move inland before discharging passengers or cargo.[30] By 1944, there were thirteen thousand Marines and forty-eight thousand Royal Navy personnel manning the British amphibious warfare fleet. This was a fleet within a fleet and one that stretched the navy, which was decommissioning battleships in order to release personnel.

In 1945, the emphasis was also on advances overland and, with the exception of the important Rhine crossings in March, not on amphibious attacks, for example, landings in northern Holland or northwestern Germany. The situation therefore was very different to that in the Pacific.

EASTERN FRONT

Combined operations did not play a major role in the Soviet defeat of German forces in Eastern Europe. Nevertheless, the Soviets made many amphibious assaults during the war: in the Baltic and Black Seas and along the Arctic coast. They were largely tactical flanking maneuvers and were not on so lavish a scale as the Anglo-American operations, nor did they have the strategic purpose of the latter. However, Soviet landings were a part of the defeat of the Germans both in the Baltic and in the Black Sea. This was particularly the case with the islands in the Baltic and the near-island of Crimea in the Black Sea. In the former case, the Soviets in September–October 1944 made use of their own, but more particularly Finnish, shipping in order to seize the islands off Estonia and Latvia, while, in the latter case, the Soviets benefited from the vulnerability of eastern Crimea to amphibious attacks. The Germans had tried to seize the Finnish island of Suursaan (Hogland) in the Gulf of Finland on September 15, 1944, but were driven off by Finnish and Russian forces. The Germans also staged major combined operations in the sense of evacuations, in particular from the Baltic islands in 1944 and from coastal enclaves, notably, but not only, in Courland in May 1945.

Attempts to influence campaigning on the mainland were less common than attacks on islands. In January 1944, Soviet ships moved forty-four thousand troops by night to a beachhead around Oranienbaum as part of the operations that led to the end of the siege of Leningrad, but on February 1, 1944, the Soviets were less successful when they launched an amphibious attack on the city of Narva farther west. The entire defense of Leningrad in 1941–1944 was in part a combined operation in that it depended, notably in 1941–1942, on supplies brought across Lake Ladoga—open in the summer and ice-covered in winter.

AIRBORNE OPERATIONS

The Allies employed airborne units in their invasions in the European theater from November 1942. These units were developed as a hasty response to the earlier German use of airborne troops, but there was a lack of relevant experience. The task was primarily to support the intended Second Front in France and thus to assist amphibious assaults. In the meanwhile, airborne troops were used in a range of operations. American and British parachute units were dropped near Bône and Tebessa in eastern Algeria on November 12–16, 1942, although a parachute attack on the airfield at Depienne failed due to the canceling of the supporting ground force. The British first used gliders operationally in an attack in November 1942 on a Norwegian hydroelectric plant at Rjukan that was producing the heavy water available for Germany's atomic bomb program. However, both gliders and one of the towing aircraft crashed.

On July 10, 1943, on a far larger scale, airborne troops were employed in the Anglo-American invasion of Sicily. In what was the first large-scale use of assault gliders, many of them landed in the sea due to strong winds. On land, the gliders were widely dispersed. Many had been released too early. Training was inadequate, often seriously so, but the practical difficulties of the attack at that range, with a long lead-in over water, and in combat conditions had not been understood. As yet, the nature of technology did not permit the greater flexibility that was to be offered from the 1950s by helicopters.

On June 6, 1944, the Allies secured the flanks of their D-Day landing by the use of parachutists and glider-borne troops. Parachutists were particularly important to the American landing on Utah Beach at the eastern end of the Cotentin Peninsula (at the western end of the landings), as the Germans were therefore unable to bring up reserves to support the coastal defenses. The disorganized nature of the airdrop, which matched that of the Sicily operation the previous year, further handicapped the defense as there were no coordinated targets to counterattack. The Americans took very few casualties on Utah, in large part because the crucial fighting had already taken place inland. On the other flank, British airborne forces were dropped to seize the bridges over the Orne River and the Caen Canal in order to prevent the Germans advancing to disrupt the Allied landings to the west. As an instance of cooperation, the airborne troops included forward observers with radio links to British warships.

The British were less successful when they sought to turn the German line on the Rhine by the use of airborne troops in Operation Market Garden, which was launched on September 17, 1944. Tough and skilled German resistance in and near the Dutch city of Arnhem prevented the British from exploiting a skillful parachute and glider assault by the 1st Airborne Division, and the strategic and operational boldness of the offensive was swallowed by tactical failure. The failure resulted from in part a lack of adequate handling of intelligence, in part the consequences of poorly selected drop zones and a lack of a concentrated drop near Arnhem, and in part the problems airborne forces faced when confronted by a mobile opposition. The last drew on a longer-term issue for amphibious attacks. The Arnhem operation lacked adequate preparation and depended on a very difficult linkup with land operations.[31]

However, Anglo-American forces crossed the lower Rhine near Wesel on March 24, 1945, in an operation coordinated with Operation Varsity, an Anglo-American airborne assault by two divisions. In total more than fifteen thousand men were landed, the largest single airborne drop in history. Intended to prevent German counterattacks on the Allied armor as it crossed the Rhine, the operation was successful. Later, there was an airborne crossing of the Elbe River.

That August, in Manchuria, the Soviets used airborne detachments to seize important cities and airfields from the Japanese, notably the cities of Harbin, Port Arthur, Darien, and Fengtien. These landings gave greater depth to the fast-moving Soviet advance and disoriented the Japanese resistance. However, in their earlier war with Germany, the Soviets had not used their airborne forces in large-scale assaults behind German lines, with the exception of the crossing of the Dnieper River near Voronezh in 1943, a crossing supported by troops crossing by ad hoc means, including on oil drums and inner tubes and using short wooden paddles. In general, the Soviets used their airborne units as infantry, which reflected a limited understanding of military opportunity costs.

From 1943, the British deployed ground units, the Chindits, behind the enemy lines in very difficult jungle terrain in Burma. These operations showed that the British could fight the Japanese in the jungle. The Americans subsequently created and deployed the 1st Air Commando Group in the support of the Chindits.

The use of airborne forces did not match that of amphibious assaults, nor was it anywhere near as significant as tactical air power. Nevertheless, as a new aspect of combined operations, such troops provided food for speculation and contributed to the belief that the advantage now increasingly lay with the side able to understand the potential of the offensive. The experience of repeated operations underlined the need to factor in the enemy's response as a key element in planning, while also demonstrating the need to put in relevant expertise at higher command levels.[32] As deployment, airborne forces came into their own for rapidly providing a presence. This was particularly seen at the close of the war when six thousand British troops were flown into southern Norway to disarm and repatriate the Germans there.[33] At the same time, paratroopers in particular generally proved far less valuable as a strategic and even operational tool than they could be on the tactical level.

CONCLUSIONS

Combined operations during the Second World War were very important for subsequent years both because they set the tone for public discussion and as they were the key element in training. The former was particularly significant due to the extent to which war films focused on combined operations, notably for the Americans D-Day and the assaults on Iwo Jima and Okinawa: for example, *The Longest Day* (1962) and *Saving Private Ryan* (1998) for the former and *The Sands of Iwo Jima* (1949). The American television series *The Pacific* (2010) focused on USMC operations. British media displayed a similar focus on Dunkirk and D-Day, as with *Dunkirk* (2017).[34] Indeed, the psychological legacy of the war proved especially significant for American and British audiences.

The legacy was also particularly important for the USMC. The war saw the development of its service culture and an assertion of its significance. These built on prewar trends, but the dynamic and scale were now far greater. High-tempo violent action with conspicuous manliness and heroism was portrayed, a portrayal that drew on undoubted bravery and on a casualty rate that was twice that of the other American services.[35] Marine generals from the war played a major role in the postwar command and ethos of the USMC.[36]

Another, very different, legacy of combined operations was seen in the postwar peace settlement. The acquisition of naval bases was designed to create opportunities or to preempt them. Thus, in ending its war with Finland in 1940, the Soviet Union insisted on the occupation of the port of Hanko in southwest Finland in order to close the entrance to the Gulf of Finland to hostile attack and, in negotiating a new peace in 1944, substituted the port of Porkkala, which was nearer to Helsinki. This presence has ended, but the Americans were to establish bases in Okinawa that have lasted to the present. The American commitment to power projection across the Pacific endures.

Combined operations during the war were particularly important as an aspect of the central role of the world's two leading naval powers on the victorious side. The situation would have been totally different had Japan and the United States not entered the war in 1941 or had France not been knocked out in 1940. Thus, the range of military options was very much set by political contingencies rather than dictating the latter. This was one element of continuity. Another was provided by the similarities between the contested landings in the Pacific and in Normandy in the Second World War and the frontal infantry assaults in the First World War, where unprotected infantry attacked a prepared and dug-in enemy. Both types of attack normally began with a heavy bombardment followed by the human attack. There was a similar iconic character to each type of assault, and, in combination, they helped to shape Western assumptions about the nature of conventional warfare.

Chapter Ten

The Cold War, 1945–1990

In October 1949, Omar Bradley, commander of the American First Army in Normandy in 1944 and the chairman of the Joint Chiefs of Staff in 1949, told the U.S. House of Representatives Committee on the Armed Services, then conducting hearings on "Unification and Strategy" (i.e., the reorganization of the armed forces), that atomic weaponry had made the large-scale amphibious assault anachronistic.[1] This was very much an army and air force view, but one that also appeared to reflect the consequences of rapidly changing technology.

At the same time, the atomic bomb, which the Americans had used in 1945, was not the sole technology at issue. For example, the technological possibilities for combined operations increased greatly in this period as a result of the development of the helicopter, as well as the improved communications technology that increased the range and reliability of radios, although, in turn, such operations were hit by shoulder-fired anti-aircraft rockets.

However, the prime context was set by tasking. There was preparation for combined operations in the case of the confrontation between the major powers in the Cold War, but the large-scale operations that were planned were not executed. The Americans, for example, considered how best to invade Western Europe if it was conquered by a Soviet attack, and the British mapped landing beaches in Pembrokeshire accordingly. In the event, there was no such conquest and thus no invasion. Similarly, Japan in the late 1950s planned to use tank landing ships (LSTs) to contest any Soviet attempt to take over Hokkaido, the most northerly island, which was vulnerable to Soviet combined operations. There was no such attack, although the fear of one continued to affect Japanese military planning, encouraging a focus on the defense of Hokkaido until Chinese expansionism in the East China Sea led to a major reorientation in the early twenty-first century toward that challenge.

The Soviet Union planned amphibious operations as part of any attack on Western Europe in the event of World War III breaking out. This built on Soviet traditions in land-sea operations. During the Cold War, Soviet plans included the use of Soviet, Polish, and East German units in the Baltic and Scandinavia, as well as Soviet amphibious attacks on the Norwegian coast. In the event, there was no Third World War and thus a lack of combined operations in conflict between superpowers.

However, combined operations were seen in more limited conflicts. These were of three principal types: conflicts linked to wars of decolonization, conflicts between newly independent states, and conflicts between major powers and weaker opponents. These will be discussed in order, before looking at common themes and considering the development of technology and doctrine.

WARS OF DECOLONIZATION

Many of the conflicts of the period from 1945 to 1975 were, in part or whole, wars of decolonization. In responding to insurgencies, colonial powers continued to employ the methods that had been adopted prior to the Second World War. In particular, the remedies of naval displays, landing parties, columns of troops, and, more recently, "air policing" all remained significant. At the same time, these methods were in part strengthened by the capabilities, in weaponry and experience, stemming from the recent war. Moreover, the powers involved all still retained conscription for all or much of the period, which provided them with the necessary manpower. At the same time, the context changed, in terms of weaponry and with reference to the political climate: within colonies, in the imperial home countries, and with regard to international power politics.

The discussion of weaponry might well focus on the helicopter and the greatly enhanced mobility it offered, albeit at the cost of severe weight loads that ruled out the movement of armor. It is also necessary to give due place to the "anti-weaponry" deployed by insurgent groups. In large part, this "anti-weaponry" stemmed from arms made available by sponsor powers, notably the Soviet Union and China. Thus, the possibilities for aircraft and helicopters were affected by anti-aircraft guns and then missiles, even if their diffusion would prove slow.

With reference to the politics, colonial powers faced a more pronounced difficulty than prewar in moving from intimidation and coercion as means to dominate colonies to ensuring the control and popular acceptance that were sought. In part, this greater difficulty was due to the organizations and ideologies of opposition, but there was also a sense that colonial control itself was weakening and therefore that resistance had point. Within imperial home countries, support for colonialism became more limited and conditional. And at the international level, the major powers, notably the Soviet Union but also the United States, saw imperial rule (at least by other states) as redundant and indeed as opportunities or problems in global power politics.

This situation was played through a number of counterinsurgency campaigns. In each case, the colonial power was faced not so much by resistance on beaches, as in the D-Day type of operation, but rather by opposition on land within the colony. Partly as a result, airborne operations were used by the colonial powers in order both to overcome the problems with mobility created by ambushes, difficult terrain, and forest cover and an absence of good, or any, roads and also to be able to strike home against opponents.[2] Thus, in the Netherlands East Indies (modern Indonesia), the Dutch in 1946–1949 used shipping to move troops around but also airborne strike forces. They captured Sukarno, the nationalist leader, in a surprise commando-paratrooper assault on Yokjakarta in 1948. The raid was a political failure as it cost much international goodwill, but it showed what could be done.

In Malaya, in the 1950s, air superiority provided the British mobility in anti-guerrilla operations with the deployment of helicopters. In Kenya, against the nationalist Mau Mau movement, British air attack extended the reach of the army and demonstrated the strength of the government. There was also broadcasting from the sky and the dropping of large numbers of pamphlets in order to influence opinion.[3] In 1954, however, at Dien Bien Phu in French Indochina, a forward French base established by a force that had parachuted in was overrun by the Viet Minh in what became a major defeat as it exposed the exhaustion of the French government. In Algeria, later in the decade, the French use of helicopter-borne assault forces successfully took the war to the National Liberation Front (FLN). Local circumstances increased the tactical effectiveness of these attacks. Unlike later insurgent groups, the FLN lacked anti-aircraft missiles, while the upland terrain and limited tree cover were far more exposed to airborne operations than the forested lands of Southeast Asia.

Britain and France launched the Suez operation against Egypt in 1956. This was designed, in cooperation with an Israeli invasion of Sinai, to achieve the overthrow of Colonel Nasser, the nationalist military ruler of Egypt who challenged British and French regional interests. In military terms, this proved slow but highly competent, with the destruction of the Egyptian air force followed by amphibious and airborne landings that led to the conquest of the northern end of the Suez Canal. The operation included the first helicopter-borne assault landing from the sea: 415 Marines and 23 tons of supplies landed by 22 helicopters from the British light carriers *Ocean* and *Theseus*. The after-action reports argued that the use of helicopters had proved effective but that it would be extremely hazardous to enter a hot landing zone, a conclusion that was to be disputed by the Americans.[4] However, it was unclear how the initial success was going to be exploited militarily while politically the governments had failed to win American support. The cease-fire on which the Americans insisted meant that the British forces stopped fairly early on in their advance south from Port Said. Subsequently, the forces that had invaded Egypt had to be withdrawn.

WARS BETWEEN NEWLY INDEPENDENT STATES

Alongside wars of decolonization, there were those between newly independent states. In these cases, the emphasis was on airborne operations, as conflicts were with neighboring states or with insurgencies. Moreover, many African states had no coastlines, but newly independent states that did tended to have only modest navies. The key instances of conflicts with neighboring states were those between Israel and Arab opponents, between India and Pakistan, and between Iran and Iraq. In each case, the emphasis was on land operations. Amphibious capability was limited. Thus, in the 1973 Yom Kippur/Ramadan War, Israeli missile boats successfully engaged Egyptian and Syrian counterparts. There was no capability to mount a landing of anything bar Special Forces. There was the use of airborne troops—for example, by Israel when successfully attacking Egyptian forces in the Sinai Peninsula in 1967 during the Six Days War—but, however tactically significant in weakening Egyptian defenses, this use was generally small-scale. In the Sinai, Israeli tank attacks were far more important.

The 1961 takeover of Portuguese-ruled Goa by India involved a combined assault of air, naval, and ground forces. In the 1971 war with Pakistan, Indian operations in East Pakistan (Bangladesh) involved a major ground assault, air mobile operations (by both paratrooper and heliborne battalions), and an amphibious troop landing operation.[5] The coastal cities in Pakistan and India made both of them vulnerable to coastal attacks, but the armies of both concentrated on landlocked battles.

In 1974, Turkey invaded Cyprus in response to a coup on the island that was followed by the movement in of Greek troops. Cyprus was divided between Greek and Turkish communities. The Turks had long prepared for an intervention, and from 1967, the 39th Marine Infantry Division was ready forty miles to the north at Mersin on the Turkish coast. The coup on July 15, 1974, was followed by a Turkish landing on July 20 west of Kyrenia, although making landfall off target led to delay. As a contrast with World War II landings, the initial Turkish wave was on a very different scale: it consisted of twenty-three landing craft, one of them for tanks; seven warships; and approximately three thousand troops. As so often happens, there was a failure to exploit in order to gain a large enough beachhead. The same day, a Turkish paratroop brigade was dropped into the main enclave of the Turkish Cypriots to the south of the invasion zone. The Turks benefited from air superiority and from nearby bases, and the Greeks, many keener to crush nearby Turkish Cypriot enclaves, failed to focus on the Turkish beachhead, which allowed the Turks to build it up and then advance from it. In the end, the Turks were able to enforce a de facto partition of the island.

CIVIL WARS

More interesting uses of combined operations occurred in the case of civil wars within independent states. China provided a key instance. During the Chinese Civil War (1946–1949), the Nationalists could employ their navy to land troops in Manchuria and to withdraw them from there but not for much more. And landing troops at a port, for example, Qinhuangdao, was of scant value if the troops could not fight their way to Jinzhou where they were needed: the Communists were blocking them at Tashan. American intervention, as was suggested, would not have changed this greatly had it only taken the form of warships and air power. The Communists had strategic depth in the interior.

In turn, the naval limitations of the Communists came into play when they had achieved victory on the mainland in 1949 and had to try to deal with Nationalist forces on offshore islands. The Communists failed badly when they tried to attack the small offshore Jinmen (Quemoy) archipelago in October 1949, which helped lead to the postponement of their planned invasion of Taiwan, a far larger target.[6] When, in contrast, they came to attack the Nationalists on Hainan Island in March 1950, the Communists were better prepared, thanks in part to Soviet advisers. The Fourth Field Army was successful in what was an important amphibious operation, one that deserves to attract more attention, not least as it offered a possible model for an attack on Taiwan.[7]

In turn, the People's Liberation Army's (PLA) first Marine regiment was organized in 1953 in the context of the campaigns to take Nationalist-held islands in the East China Sea, notably the Dachen and Penghu Islands, and to test the American determination to protect Taiwan.[8] However, it was not until 1980, in the context of military modernization, that the PLA established the first Marine brigade, from which the Marine forces grew. Communist China offered no comparable target to Nationalist amphibious attack except for a large-scale invasion, for which the Nationalists lacked the means let alone the backing.

Elsewhere, there was an important use of amphibious operations during the Nigerian Civil War of 1967–1970, a conflict waged against separatism in the southeast of the country, where the state of Biafra was created. The Nigerian navy both imposed a debilitating blockade of the Biafran coast and enabled the army to seize ports and coastal positions, especially the oil-refining center of Port Harcourt. This success increased the number of fronts on which the Biafrans were under attack and contributed to an impression of failure.

Opposition to insurgencies could also involve the deployment of airborne troops by friendly powers, notably the forces of major states. In East Africa, British helicopter-borne Royal Marines, troops flown in by aircraft, and strike aircraft helped against military coup attempts in 1964,[9] while British and Australian naval, air, and land units assisted Malaysia in 1963–1966 against Indonesian pressure on Borneo. In Congo, CIA-provided aircraft and mercenaries, as well as Belgian paratroopers, helped General Mobuto suppress opposition in the east in 1964–1965. Again, in 1978, Belgian and French paratroopers, backed by American and French air transport, helped suppress a Cuban-backed insurgency in the Congolese province of Shaba. In Oman, Britain, Iran, and Jordan supported opposition to a Marxist insurrection, providing a range of support including warships and air assets, such as Iranian helicopter-borne troops. Iran provided backing for a commando attack against rebel bases in South Yemen in 1975.[10]

The use of combined operations against insurgent forces was particularly notable in the case of the Americans in South Vietnam from the early 1960s to 1973 and the Soviet Union in Afghanistan from 1979 to 1988. In each case, the airborne capability was crucial to mobility and also to strike power. Helicopters added much to the possibilities offered by fixed-wing aircraft. For example, in a series of attempts to occupy the Pandsher/Panjshir Valley in Afghanistan, the Soviets concentrated air assets, including using helicopter forces, in order to stop the withdrawal of the mujahideen and to engage them from unexpected directions. However, the deployment from 1985 of American- and British-supplied ground-to-air missiles lessened the effectiveness of Soviet air power: American Stinger missiles had a ceiling of ten thousand feet and a range of five miles. Other powers also used combined operations against insurgents. Indonesia, an archipelago state, employed amphibious assaults against the Gan separatist movement in the Aceh region of Sumatra.

KOREAN WAR

The emphasis in the period could well have been more on combined operations than was in practice the case. This was certainly the case with the United States. During the Korean War (1950–1953), a war essentially waged on land but with most of Korea within one hundred miles of the sea, the

Americans mounted a major amphibious assault at Inchon on September 15, 1950, that helped determine the sway of campaigning for a while and that proved crucial to the developing politics of the war. American naval dominance was a vital prerequisite for such an operation, not least due to proximity to China, which included Soviet naval bases in Manchuria. This daring and unrehearsed landing in particularly difficult tidal conditions applied American force at what proved a decisive point. Carried out far behind the front and with very limited information about the conditions, physical and military, that they would encounter, about eighty-three thousand troops were successfully landed, a situation helped by the North Koreans not deploying the Soviet mines that had been supplied. The benefit of experience gained in the Second World War was apparent as some of the men who took part were veterans of the Pacific war. The USMC called up many reservists. In contrast, the North Koreans and Soviets lacked experience in such an endeavor, either in attacking or in being attacked. This led to a kind of "blind spot" in their strategic, operational, and tactical planning.

The American appreciation of the vulnerability of the North Korean position was also important in 1950. The Americans pressed on to capture nearby Seoul. This threat to communication routes led the North Koreans to pull back their forces that were further south in South Korea, having driven the South Koreans into the Pusan Perimeter. However, with surprise thereby lost, this process could not be repeated. Indeed, an attempt to land on the east coast at Wonsan was delayed due to the extensive mining of the harbor by North Korea's ally the Soviet Union. Moreover, the harbor had very convoluted channels leading into it. As a result, the Americans did not land there until October 26, by which time the North Koreans had already retreated.[11]

Furthermore, the North Koreans were not subsequently in so vulnerable a situation, both because their forces were not so dispersed and because of large-scale Chinese intervention on their behalf from later in the year. At best, another landing might have been the case of Anzio in 1944 after Salerno in 1943 (see chapter 9), but it is more likely that any beachhead would have been driven in by large-scale Chinese frontal attacks. As a result, after it had been successfully used to help American (and other) troops retreat in the face of the Chinese intervention,[12] the amphibious dimension markedly receded during the Korean War and played no significant role in 1951–1953. Indeed, the Inchon Operation, by helping lead to an American advance north of the 38th Parallel and thus to Chinese intervention, ultimately contributed to the stasis that came to characterize the war.

The bravery and endurance of the USMC in Korea, notably in the Chosin Reservoir battle of 1950, contributed strongly to the active molding by the Corps of public and congressional opinion, which helped protect the independence and resources of the Corps.[13] The war was also significant in encouraging the USMC to maintain its engagement with close air support, not least in having a "closer" definition of such support and in training all the pilots as normal Marines.

The North Koreans had undertaken some small amphibious operations in support of their initial offensive in 1950. Most were "end runs" to destabilize the South Korean defenders. The only one of possible strategic consequence took place on the night of June 25, 1950, when they sent about six hundred troops crammed into a small coastal vessel on a very unsophisticated attempt to capture Pusan, well behind the front. The ship was intercepted and sunk by a patrol boat about twenty miles from Pusan.

VIETNAM WAR

The Vietnam War was also instructive. It depended on American naval and air superiority, and there were landings in South Vietnam, as well as an extensive use of American combined operations in the Mekong Delta in the shape of the Mobile Riverine Force (MRF), a "brown-water" navy that combined land and sea capabilities with air support. In part, this force was designed to stop the Viet Cong use of motorized junks. As a result, the MRF included a Coastal Surveillance Force, a River Patrol Force, and a River Assault Force. Its activity involved a blockade used against North Vietnamese coastal supplies, as well as river patrols and gunfire support for South Korean and American operations on land. The flexibility offered by this combined operational capability proved important in the response to the Viet Cong Tet Offensive of 1968.[14] The "brown-water" component was also to be seen in Portuguese counterinsurgency operations in Africa.[15]

However, as one of what became the many counterfactuals of the Vietnam War, the very different possibility of large-scale American landings in North Vietnam, around the port of Vinh and notably of an advance westward in order to cut North Vietnamese supply routes to their forces in South Vietnam, was not followed up. There was to be no second Inchon. The dangers of unlimited consequences from a too-effective "maneuver from the sea," in the shape of a landing in North Vietnam, served in the Cold War as a reason enough not to attempt it. The Americans feared that by threatening the North Vietnamese too directly, they would bring the Chinese in on their side, with possible nuclear escalation as a result. Self-deterrence may thus have nullified the potential effectiveness of amphibious assaults.

Air support for ground operations was important in the Vietnam War, notably with the extensive use of helicopters. The establishment of the separate U.S. Air Force in 1947 had been followed by the development of army aviation focused on the helicopter, with the establishment of the Army Aviation Center in 1955.

The Vietnam War saw the USMC essentially become a helicopter-mobile infantry army, with counterinsurgency becoming more central than the previous focus on amphibious warfare during the Second World War and the opening stages of the Korean War.[16] The operational readiness and combat effectiveness of the Marines, hit in the late 1940s during the postwar force reductions, made this transformation possible and indeed appear desirable, not least due to the global pressures on trained American military manpower. The size of the USMC had fallen from nearly five hundred thousand men in 1945 to approximately two hundred thousand in 1965. Action in Vietnam was necessary to justify these numbers and also made sense of the development of Marine air-ground task forces (MAGTFs). These acted as an anticipation of the 2000s USMC commitment to power projection in inland conflict with irregulars.

AMPHIBIOUS OPERATIONS

And yet, whether alongside airlift or not, amphibious intervention remained important, as when the Americans intervened in Lebanon in 1958 and 1982–1983 and the British in Egypt in 1956, Jordan in 1958, Kuwait in 1961, Tanganyika (modern Tanzania) in 1964, and Lebanon in 1982–1983. Such intervention also continued to be important in the established sphere of American intervention, the Caribbean. This was seen, alongside airlift, in the Dominican Republic in 1965, in Grenada in 1983, and in Panama in 1989.

Earlier, however, American-backed intervention against the Communist regime in Cuba totally failed in the Bay of Pigs episode in 1961. The focus in discussion of the latter has been on decisions on the American side—and notably on President John F. Kennedy's refusal to provide air cover to support the invasion and provide supplies—and on the bureaucratic momentum that left the CIA unwilling to accept that the plan was based on misleading assumptions about the prospects of success, including that a popular uprising might occur. Kennedy certainly allowed political concerns to overwhelm military considerations.[17] This approach, however, with its emphasis on American choices, underestimates the issue of Cuban strength, a matter of resolve and numbers. Castro had successfully infiltrated his opponents, and he commanded his forces well. The Americans underestimated Castro, although as Dean Acheson pointed out, "it doesn't take Price Waterhouse [a major firm of accountants] to figure out that 25,000 Cubans are better than 1,500."[18]

After the Suez Crisis of 1956, the Royal Navy identified amphibious operations as its primary role. Indeed, the 1962 navy estimates justified all other functions with reference to support for amphibious operations in the context of postcolonial world policing. The British exploited new capabilities, especially helicopter-equipped "commando carriers" in order to provide a "joint services seaborne force" designed to promote flexible, limited power projection in a situation where use of land bases was becoming problematic. Many of the arguments deployed then bear a striking similarity to those deployed after the Cold War. This encouraged the development in Britain of a "seaborne-airport concept," designed to integrate amphibious and airborne forces in expeditionary operations, and this eventually evolved into the first *Manual of Joint Warfare*.

The significance of islands, albeit very differently to Cuba, was seen with the reconquest of the Falkland Islands by Britain in 1982 after they had been lost to a surprise Argentinean invasion. The Argentine capture of the Falklands and their subsequent recapture by the British were driven by strong political imperatives. All of the operations achieved strategic surprise largely due to the fact that both sides failed to appreciate the political issues and leadership values of their opponents. The British failed to read the political and financial crisis in Argentina correctly and, by withdrawing the ice patrol ship *Endurance*, appeared to be supporting the Argentine appreciation of the situation. The Argentines did not believe that the British would, or even could, respond and also felt that the weather conditions would preclude a response even if the intention was there.[19]

The Argentine combined operations were planned, led, and executed by the Argentine navy and its Marine Corps. After the successful occupation of the islands, they were declared to be part of the southern province of the country and came within the remit of the Southern Army command. Due to interservice rivalry, the army insisted that it had the responsibility for providing the garrison of the islands. As a result, the well-trained and well-led Marine Corps units were withdrawn (with the exception of one battalion) and were replaced by army units, which consisted mainly of conscripts. The Marine commander of the islands was also replaced by an army brigadier (Mario Menéndez).

Menéndez failed to appreciate his fundamental strategic weakness, especially that he was effectively cut off from support. After the sinking of the Argentine heavy cruiser *Belgrano*, by the British nuclear submarine *Conqueror*, the Argentine navy withdrew its units back to port, notably its aircraft carrier. This meant that not only were the islands effectively cut off from resupply and support, but also that the British naval task force would be free to provide close support for the British landing force, without which it could not have survived. In addition, although Argentine air force squadrons were moved to the south of the country and nearer to the conflict zone, their primary weapon, the "Dagger," was operating at the limit of its range over the Falklands. After its initial efforts to oppose the amphibious landing during the first week of the conflict, which met with some success, the ability to interrupt or interfere with the operations of the task force units, both ashore and afloat, was severely curtailed. Successful attacks on two British landing ships were carried out by Argentine naval aircraft, but again they were operating at extreme range from their mainland bases. Furthermore, they failed to deter the units of the British task force from providing close support to the troops ashore and delivering reinforcements.

For the British, there was a political imperative throughout to demonstrate resolve and a determination to recapture the Falkland Islands. The planning and execution demonstrated just how multidimensional a combined operations approach to the task was. Concurrently with the dispatch of the Carrier Battle Group and the Amphibious Task Group to Ascension Island, a British base in the South Atlantic, Ascension Island itself was being established as a forward operating base and airhead, with long-range bombers sent there. Two nuclear submarines were also dispatched to the South Atlantic, while numerous civilian ships of all categories, from repair vessels to trawlers converted to minesweeping, were requisitioned for service.[20] A major Special Forces operation was initiated to gather intelligence on the ground in the Falklands, an independent landing force of Royal Marines was sent to recapture the island of South Georgia, and a follow-up force began mountain training in Wales.

British success depended in part on the legacy of the expeditionary force built up during the 1960s and somewhat dismantled in the 1970s. Without HMS *Hermes*, the two landing platforms/docks (LPDs), and the landing ship logistics (LSLs), the operation could not have been possible. Had Britain still had the landing platform helicopter (LPH) ships converted in the late 1950s and early 1960s (*Bulwark* and *Ocean*), the operation would have been much easier. Without the LPHs, with their capacity to support "vertical envelopment"–style helicopter operations, the British were forced to adopt an approach to amphibious assaults that would have seemed old-fashioned twenty years earlier.

Despite a major rundown in amphibious capability, as the Royal Navy in the 1970s and early 1980s focused on anti-submarine capability in the northeast Atlantic in the face of the Soviet threat, the British in the Falklands crisis deployed eight thousand miles and then staged a landing not in the face of beach opposition but against Argentinean air attack. This put a premium on the anti-aircraft support that could be offered by the fleet's aircraft and weaponry. By landing on the Falklands, the British had not ensured success, as the Argentinean plan rested on fighting on from fixed positions in order to wear down British numbers and supplies and to take advantage of the onset of the bitter South Atlantic winter.

Nevertheless, British success in the field as they advanced fifty miles across difficult terrain to the capital, Port Stanley, combined with a continued ability to maintain the initiative, destroyed the Argentinean will to fight on, and crucially so as they still had plentiful troops, artillery, and supplies when they surrendered, while the British had nearly run out of artillery shells. The artillery effort was supported by naval gunfire directed by naval gunfire observers attached to ground units. Despite tensions, the British command structure worked to produce cooperation between the services, with a commander task force, Admiral Sir John Fieldhouse, able to provide a cohesion Argentina lacked. At the same time, naval, amphibious, and land commanders all had different priorities. The navy wished to win the air battle but keep the fleet, especially the carriers, safe. The amphibious commander needed to keep his support ships safe, while maintaining the offloading of stores. The land commander wanted to be fully established ashore before continuing the advance inland, which was not included in his original orders.

Once the forces were ashore on the Falklands, neither the headquarters in Britain nor the Carrier Battle Group appreciated the difficulty involved in building up supplies. Conversely, the commanders on the ground failed to appreciate the public relations battle that was being fought in Britain and internationally, and the political imperative of being seen to make progress or "do something." This, in turn, led to the political directive to attack the settlement of Goose Green. The attack was premature as the Parachute Battalion sent to execute the mission did not have adequate artillery support and was not offered the Scorpion light-armored vehicles that would have been of great assistance. The intelligence assessment underestimated the size of the garrison at Goose Green and its support weapons. Moreover, the single gun on the frigate sent to provide direct naval gunfire jammed and it was forced to withdraw, while the effectiveness of the ground-attack Harrier aircraft used as a substitute for artillery was limited by the proximity of civilians, and several were lost. Although the battle was eventually won, it was a costly victory and demonstrated that for modern combined operations, public relations was going to be an additional dimension of crucial importance.

These operations, as well as the presentation of those of the Second World War, strengthened Marine forces in their long-standing attempt to maintain their independence during frequent attempts to restructure the military (for example, as the United States rapidly ran down and sought to reorganize its armed forces in the late 1940s). These attempts involved a determination to define a particular role. In the case of the United States and Britain, this entailed presenting the Marines as the mobile fighting force that both allegedly and in reality contrasted with a slower-moving army, a process aided by the commitment of the latter to tanks, to artillery, and to its share of atomic weaponry. Both lightness and the amphibious dimension looked toward a post–Cold War focus on low-intensity conflict.[21]

AIR POWER

At the same time, there was an increased use in tactical terms by all major powers of helicopters. In Northern Ireland from the 1970s to the 1990s, the British made extensive use of helicopters to supply fortified posts, as roads were vulnerable to ambush by the units of the Provisional IRA, a violent radical Marxist sectarian group based in the Catholic community. In operational terms, the Soviet Union deployed airborne forces in the Cold War, rather than relying on ships that might have been intercepted by the Americans as the 1962 Cuban crisis had demonstrated. Indeed, airlift was a key element, in particular in Angola and Ethiopia. The Cubans supplied the bulk of the troops, but the Soviets provided the aircraft and pilots for the airlift, as well as flying in light tanks, artillery, and helicopters; providing pilots for the helicopters; and using aerial reconnaissance to provide intelligence. The Soviet invasion of Czechoslovakia in 1968, when the reform movement there was forcibly ended, largely depended on troops invading overland, but airborne forces were also significant, notably for seizing control of Prague's airport and radio station. The airlift of troops was also important to the rapid Soviet takeover of major Afghan cities and airbases in late 1979.

The role of airlift was also seen in that by the United States and Britain during the Soviet blockade of Berlin in 1948–1949. Flights numbering 278,228, the majority American, provided 2.3 million tons of supplies, feeding a city of 2.5 million people that was deep in the Soviet zone of occupation despite a shortage of aircraft and landing facilities. Indeed, in this case, air deliveries became greater in scale than pre-airlift rail deliveries. The Soviets harassed the aircraft, for example, firing flak nearby, but did not try to shoot them down and there was no fighting. This was one of the biggest Western wins in the Cold War and one of Stalin's biggest failures.[22]

DOCTRINE

Alongside the specifics of particular moves, there was a more general rise in the significance of combined operations in military doctrine and planning. Moreover, the interoperability of weapons and units for such purposes affected the development and procurement of the former, and the training and deployment of the latter. This was so for a range of taskings, both conventional warfare with other similarly armed powers and for counterinsurgency purposes. The latter, indeed, overlapped with police procurement and training, notably with the use of helicopters.

If combined operations were a key aspect of the jointness that appeared to many to be increasingly relevant, that element was generally countered by the resilience of traditional service distinctions and rationales. These enjoyed a revival in the post-Vietnam world as the Americans reconfigured themselves for conflict with the Soviet Union in Europe, which appeared likely in the early 1980s. The Reagan buildup of the 1980s provided the funds for each service to focus on its own interests and ambitions without being obliged to cooperate.[23] The specific goals and roles of the USMC became part of the debate. At the same time, the possibility of fighting a nonnuclear war encouraged an American and NATO interest in maneuverist techniques, and these techniques enhanced air-land cooperation as a goal and means.

Drawing on the maneuverist ideas of John Boyd, an air force officer,[24] including the OODA loop (observe, orient, decide, act), the USMC pushed "maneuver warfare" to the fore in its doctrine in the 1980s. Officially, *Fleet Marine Force Manual (FMFM) 1, Warfighting,*[25] articulated the new philosophy in 1989. *MCDP (Marine Corps Doctrinal Publication) 1, Warfighting,* was published in 1997, as an update of the same doctrine. *Warfighting* was written by John Schmitt, a young captain, who was influenced by reading Clausewitz and talking with Boyd.

Combined operations in another respect became more significant, with pressure after the Second World War for unified command structures, both to take forward the lessons from the war and in order to address the challenges of postwar restructuring in the context of a still serious international situation. Unified commands were pushed hard, if inconsistently, in the United States, leading to the Goldwater-Nichols Defense Reorganization Act of 1986.[26] In addition, the context of international cooperation, notably NATO, took wartime collaborative military processes forward. Command structures and doctrines coexisted uneasily, both encouraging planning for combined operations and maintaining institutional and cultural resistance.

Serious issues remained, notably the vulnerability of combined operations to counterattack and the extent to which the best place for landing might not be the most appropriate for continued operations.[27] However, the situation had changed greatly with the development of air power. This ensured that combined operations were no longer littoral-based or near littoral-based warfare and, as a result of that factor, different from what can be presented as genuine Continental warfare.

Chapter Eleven

Since 1990

After the end of the Cold War, expeditionary strategies and joint warfare evolved as the dominant form of power projection. As a consequence, rather than a focus on landing and insertion, combined operations were the modus operandi of the entire campaign. Combined capability and operations seemed the crucial means for the military prowess and purposes of America when it appeared the sole superpower in a unipolar world in the 1990s and early 2000s. Their continued role thereafter was perceived as less secure. In both cases, the Americans, as in the "small-wars" days of the USMC in Latin America in the 1920s, sought to deal quickly and selectively from the sea with what were actually intractable problems ashore.

GULF WAR OF 1990–1991

The Gulf War of 1990–1991 proved a dramatic display of combined operations and notably so at the strategic level. What attracted attention was the precision involved in the 1991 air-land battle in which the United States rapidly subjugated the Iraqi forces in Kuwait. There were other elements that were too easy to forget. These included the use of the sea in 1990 to deploy first a rapid-response force to the region in the shape of two Carrier Battle Groups and then to move in a large army. The Maritime Prepositioning Force proved its value. It is part of Military Sealift Command, and the prepositioned equipment is designed to sustain a USMC amphibious brigade for roughly thirty days in action.[1]

Moreover, during the subsequent conflict in 1991, cruise missiles successfully provided a new capability for surface warships, such as the Second World War battleship USS *Wisconsin*. This demonstrated the capacity of these ships for littoral force projection, such that it was no longer necessary to rely solely on aircraft carriers for this capability. However, this deployment was more a justification of the reactivation of battleships in the Reagan naval buildup than for strategic, operation, and tactical reasons. The *Wisconsin*'s unique 405-millimeter guns were of dubious usage as they had no modern rounds available and the ship could deploy only 32 cruise missiles, whereas one Spruance-class destroyer with a vertical launch system could deploy 61 and had a crew of 340 compared to the *Wisconsin*'s 1,921.

SOMALIA

The Americans pressed on to use combined operations in an attempt to stabilize Somalia in 1992–1993, an attempt that reflected the 1992 Navy-Marine Corps White Paper "From the Sea" and the establishment, the same year, of an Expeditionary Warfare Division in the office of the Chief of Naval Operations. Forward deployment appeared to give the navy a relevance in a period of post–Cold War cuts.[2]

In Somalia, in Operation Restore Hope, the Americans initially provided twenty-eight thousand troops of the thirty-seven thousand UN forces. Their advance guard arrived to great publicity, without meeting any opposition, on the Indian Ocean beach of the dusty capital, Mogadishu. The following year, the city, however, proved a difficult environment for the use of Special Operations Forces to capture hostile clan leaders by means of troops inserted by helicopters without the permission to use heavy equipment. As a result, the American forces were vulnerable to small and light arms fire. Political factors, and an overestimate of the capability of the deployed units, led to a serious mistake in this "city battle" in a densely populated area.

The issue also raised the difficulties of determining success and thus capability. Despite heavy odds, the Americans on October 3–4, 1993, were eventually successfully evacuated and several key Somalis were captured. Nevertheless, the operation was perceived as a failure by the relatively risk-averse Bill Clinton administration and by an American population not prepared for losses and unclear about goals in Somalia. There had certainly been overconfidence on the part of the government and commanders alike. The raid was in practice no more than a check, but it led to serious questions being raised in the United States about the purpose of the American commitment and about the long-term prospect. In reaction to their losses, the American government abandoned aggressive operations in Somalia and decided to withdraw its troops from the country. In part, this was very much a response by the Clinton administration to risk. It was not a measured assessment of the consequences of combined operations, and this affected the American response to the very publicly conducted genocide in Rwanda in 1994: there was a global unwillingness to intervene. In February–March

1995, the UN forces in Mogadishu were evacuated after a joint American-Italian combined operation in the face of Somali warlords and guerrillas. The Americans and Italians used helicopters and aircraft in support of Marines that landed near Mogadishu and protected the retreat.

Failure in Somalia serves as a reminder that any counterpointing of the 1990s, when combined operations supposedly "worked," and the 2000s, when they had less strategic effect, is fraught with difficulties. There are also wider implications for the assessment of strategies and methods, not least in terms of the effectiveness of asymmetrical warfare.

Far less attention has been devoted to planning and preparations for combined operations by powers other than the United States in the 1990s. The implosion of the Soviet Union, which lost naval bases in republics that gained independence in the Baltic and Black Seas, and the decline of its naval power ensured that Russia could not play a role. China, however, was seen as a continuing threat to Taiwan, and this led to the blocking forward deployment of the American Seventh Fleet in 1996. Although a deterrent naval action, this could only be seen as part of the equations of combined operations. American reliance on air power alone in the Bosnia and Kosovo crises of 1995 and 1999, and the failure in the latter to move to a NATO invasion, also helped explain the limited use of combined operations in the 1990s. Any such invasion was dependent on the acceptance of casualties by the invaders and on the willingness of neighboring countries to provide access and bases, and the latter was conspicuously lacking in the case of Greece, which denied access and bases in 1999.

THE 2000s

It is too easy to assume that combined operations in the 2000s were ultimately associated with failure, namely that of American-led coalitions to create an acceptable stability in Afghanistan and Iraq, as opposed to overthrowing hostile regimes, tasks successfully and rapidly achieved in 2001 and 2003 respectively. There was also a general strategic misplaying of the process of peace maintenance, notably in Afghanistan.[3] In Libya, in 2011, the failure of interventionism by NATO powers was different, but also a matter of strategy and implementation.

These criteria for success may be overly harsh. If they matched the goals expressed by the United States and its allies, these goals arguably reflected a strategic confusion over the practicality of ends and the viability of means, or rather naïve assumptions concerning both. Interventionism leading to acceptable state transformation proved impossible in these contexts. This was not so much a matter of the advantages or disadvantages of combined operations but rather of broader political and military issues. This point is more generally the case when such operations are considered. At the same time, the military counterpart to these commitments, in the shape of postconquest counterinsurgencies, led to a focus on combined operations as an effective means to conduct irregular warfare by countering that by others. Special Operations Forces, with their focus on process not platform, played a significant role.

At the same time, the doctrinal expansion of goals, notably with the 2006 *American Army and Marine Corps Joint Counterinsurgency Field Manual* (FM 3-24), reflected a degree of hubris.[4] In practice, attempts to change USMC culture by means of a new cultural training center at Quantico, Virginia, and the associated training program had only limited impact. There was also a degree of impracticality in implementation, both by the military and by politicians concerned in particular about election cycles. In the case of the USMC, combat worthiness was not always linked to appropriate interoperability with other services, notably army and air force. The USMC, nevertheless, was a formidable force indeed in May 2010 at 202,000 strong, the largest of its kind and bigger than most armies in the world, including that of Britain. In Iraq and Afghanistan, the USMC was essentially a second army, and one conducting operations far from the sea and effectively so. Afghanistan is landlocked. Multiple tours of duty further ensured this focus, one that underlined a combined dimension further seen with the large number of naval personnel who served in Iraq or Afghanistan.[5]

The Afghanistan operation in 2001–2002 was an extraordinary demonstration of the global range of American power and of naval expeditionary capability. Without sea power, the operation would have been totally impossible. Aside from some B-52/B-1/B-2 missions, almost all air missions were carrier-based. Even that would probably have been impossible were it not for passive support from Iran and, even more, Pakistan, which permitted uncontested overflight and the basing of American tanker aircraft, one of which crashed on January 9, 2002, to support fighter aircraft.[6]

Views of the effectiveness and role of the USMC varied, both within and outside the service. One critique was that the USMC had become excessively like another branch of the army and, in doing so, was overly big and heavy as well as losing sight of its maritime roots, rationale, and therefore effectiveness. In August 2010, in a speech to the Marine Corps Association, Robert Gates, the secretary of defense and a perceptive leader, called for a redefinition of purpose and size while emphasizing the crucial character of a "broad portfolio of capabilities and penchant for adapting" and adding, "Ultimately, the maritime soul of the Marine Corps needs to be preserved." In response, a Force Structure Review Group recommended a cut in the active component to about 186,000 personnel and a combined force operational role as providing formations smaller than traditional army units.[7]

Alongside the impression of failure came amphibious operations that had a degree of success, notably by Russia in Georgia in 2008, by Israel in Gaza in 2014, and by Sri Lanka against Tamil strongholds in the Jaffna Peninsula in 2009. None, however, was a forcible theater-entry campaign of any scale, and in each case, operations on land were far more important. As a different type of operation, river crossings remained significant. Thus, in February 2017, five American-made floating bridges were driven from Baghdad and deployed along the Tigris River in and near Mosul in order to enable Iraqi forces on the east bank to advance to the ISIS-held west: all the city's bridges had been destroyed. At the same time, the key advance on the ISIS-held west that spring came overland.

CAPABILITIES

The significance of combined operations for the United States, and notably so in the Middle East where opportunities for American overland invasions were limited, encouraged a development of weapons platforms designed not so much to assist in such operations as to make them possible. In part, this gave the navy a new role, just as it did for those of America's NATO allies. In the 1980s, these navies had concentrated on preparing for war with the Soviet Union and this had been central to procurement, doctrine, planning, and training. The situation very much changed from the 1990s with a shift of the future "battlefield" to more coastal locations. The stress now was on the development and deployment of "littoral fighting vessels" of various types. These platforms were directly linked to the strategy, tasking, doctrine, and training that characterized NATO forces in particular.[8]

In the 2000s and 2010s, the "anti-access/area denial" (A2/AD) threat forced the American navy and the USMC to come together and jointly rediscover "maritime strategy."[9] The general wisdom in the United States is that the future portends much fighting in crowded, volatile, violent littorals, at least in terms of humanitarian operations, but that the high-end, "near peer" threat will be fought at a long standoff distance. Current thinking stresses the potential for small, distributed units to conduct land-based sea denial or even to further land-based sea control.[10] "Operational maneuver from the sea" (OMFTS) had become the new, "back to our roots" vision of the USMC in the 1990s, but the question arose of how to do it, and especially ship-to-objective maneuver (STOM), if, in the face of A2/AD, it was too dangerous to bring the ships close enough to shore. In the 2010s, discussion focused on this point. Despite the long commitment to Afghanistan and Iraq, the USMC had been honing its amphibious doctrine since Somalia, but the difficulties had become more onerous while it had been landlocked in this commitment.

To get from the ship over the horizon to the shore, vertical insertion is part of the answer, much as when the USMC first developed its doctrine for integrating helicopters in the 1950s and 1960s. Another answer is distributed operations, and for the same reason as in the early Cold War, when it was a matter of not presenting a ready target for tactical nuclear weapons. Today the point, in the face of the threat from hard-to-find but highly precise long-range missile systems, is to complicate targeting and to prevent the loss of any one unit or vessel from compromising the mission. These ends are to be achieved by signal multiplication and by dispersal. Distributed operations were at the heart of "Expeditionary Force 21," the previous USMC doctrine, which was published in March 2014. Published in November 2016, the current MOC (Marine Corps operating concept) does not eliminate it, but aims to develop the expeditionary advance base operations (EABO) operating concept, with the concept placing more emphasis on a larger, more defensible force.

A difficulty with distributed operations, however, is how to reaggregate speedily enough and with sufficient force and firepower to deal with the high-end threat when necessary. This raises questions, seen with the battleship versus battlecruiser debate of the 1900s, as to what vessel will be fast enough and protected enough to be both hard to target and self-defending, and thus what is the proper trade-off between speed and protection. What does the distributed unit deploy with, and where, for day-to-day "engagement" operations if it must also be concerned with potential reaggregation for a high-end fight? In short, what does the twenty-first-century landing unit look like in terms of a world of distributed operations in the face of what the Americans term "the mature precision-strike regime"?

Part of the answer is that "triphibious" warfare—surface, land, and air—must now interact with other domains as well, such as undersea, space, and cyber. Initiatives include, in the United States, unmanned systems and "human-machine teaming," to create "cross-domain synergy," with the unspoken assumption that such synergy would somehow substitute for mass and firepower. This is still unclear and does not affect the point that amphibious assaults, because they are so easily interfered with, involve much luck and demand great courage. Combined operations where the landing is not opposed still face more obstacles than such moves on land.

More conventional capabilities changed in other respects from the 1990s, notably with a greater emphasis on the airlifting of troops. Thus, the NATO military footprint in Europe altered with a major fall in the American presence, from more than four hundred thousand personnel at the height of the Cold War to sixty-four thousand in 2015, including more than twenty-seven thousand soldiers. As a key element, heavy equipment was stockpiled in Western Europe, with the equipment to be used for units airlifted in from the United States in the event of crisis.

The question of a move from a maritime environment to a more land-based one was posed in geopolitical terms in the late 2000s and 2010s as American power appeared to recede, while that of China and Russia increased. Such a conclusion might seem counterintuitive given the major interest of these powers in developing their naval forces and due to the particular significance of disputes over bodies of water, notably the East and South China Seas, or over regions in which seas played a major role, particularly the Baltic and the Black Sea. The deployment of Russia's sole aircraft carrier, as head of a carrier task force, to the Mediterranean in 2016 and its use in the Syrian conflict underlined the issue. As an instance of a major development in the processes and platforms for combined operations, China built up reefs into islands capable of holding military bases. This represented a particular form of combined operations, one that greatly altered the geopolitical and military situation in the South China Sea. The growing Russian threat to the Baltic States in the mid-2010s may lead to a refocus on combined operational capability by NATO powers.

And yet, there was also the issue, as always, of military culture. In both Russia and China, naval power—and everything that came with it—was subordinated to land forces and to a land-based understanding of military power. Indeed, it was the failure of Russia, despite the ambitious claims of President Putin, to sustain Soviet naval strength that was more apparent than its pretensions. The long-range land-attack Kalibr cruise missiles with which Russian surface ships are equipped are a major area-denial threat, but in terms of amphibious assault, Russia is weaker. For example, the Ivan Gren–class landing ship, tanks (LSTs) Russia is currently building are large and impressive, but there are only two of them.

The situation with China is less clear. There is a significant combined capability in China's near waters, but its likely effectiveness is unclear. Sea denial by means of land-based, long-range, precision-strike missile-supported systems is not the same as sea usage.[11] At the same time, while in combined operations the maritime domain remains critical to operational depth on land, archipelagos and individual islands are becoming excellent opportunities for not only sea denial but actual sea control. The United States and its allies and partners have many islands at their disposal, and not merely in the South China Sea, but need to develop the concepts and doctrine for using them in support of expeditionary operations to create and exploit gaps within enemy A2/AD systems. This opportunity has been much discussed in the United States, but it is a challenge to do so without getting attacked by a much larger force operating within easy reach of supplies and support at home. It is not yet clear that the USMC could develop survivability and flexibility at the same time to go in alone and suppress the very systems that would be targeting them, without first some preparatory indirect fire from over the horizon to take out the land-based missile systems threatening approaching vessels and aircraft. So much hinges, in terms of limiting war, on the USMC's ability to get the concepts of distributed operations and expeditionary advanced bases correct. In the United States, it is also assumed that launching an air-sea battle (now termed "joint access and maneuver in the global commons"—JAMGC) would prompt a nuclear retaliation by China.[12]

China has one of the world's largest amphibious assault forces, including, in 2011, twenty-six LSTs of over four thousand tons. The fleet was modernized in the 1990s and 2000s, with the replacement of older ships by more modern types, but overall lift capacity remained about two divisions' worth of troops, which was not sufficient for an attack on Taiwan. A lack of air support was long an issue but was addressed with the launching in 2006 of the Type 071 Kunlun Shan–class LPD (landing platform dock), which is able to employ helicopters in assault roles, and with the development of a carrier capacity, although it was far smaller and less effective than that of the United States. China has also supported development of a helicopter assault ship similar in size to the French Mistral class.

However, the number of troops that could be lifted by this means is limited. Chinese enhanced capability was designed to bolster a presence in the South China Sea, supporting vertical envelopment, as well as to intimidate Taiwan, not least by offering a range able to threaten the vulnerable eastern side of Taiwan. Chinese forces trained in island-seizure exercises in the South China Sea, notably in retaking contested islands. The overall context was the pursuit of an ability to deter American intervention.[13]

Conversely, other states developed or sought to develop capabilities able to oppose China, for example, the naval fast attack craft and coastal-defense anti-ship cruise missiles. China was not alone in building up amphibious capabilities. States that did so included Australia, Brazil, Canada, India, Japan, South Africa, and Singapore.[14] The nature of the preparations varied, not least in accordance with the particular tasking. The latter is a matter of physical as much as political environment. Thus, for Japan, the focus is on China and the East China Sea. To respond to Chinese pressure over the Senkaku Islands, the Japanese built up their amphibious capability, including de facto helicopter carriers (officially called "helicopter destroyers"), landing craft, and amphibious assault vehicles. Joint training with the USMC developed, notably for combined operations.[15]

Australia, from 2012, enhanced its amphibious capability, particularly with its Canberra-class amphibious assault ships, which were designed to offer strength across a broader region. The tasks envisaged were those of presence and deterrence, especially in terms of supporting allies and maintaining stability in the increasingly troubled southwest Pacific. That is a pertinent Australian response to the role of islands in a far-flung region, which is inherently different to the challenge facing Japan. This contrast serves as a reminder of the range of geopolitical and military environments with which the planners of combined operations need to engage. Linked to this comes a requirement for a flexibility in procurement, doctrine, and academic commentary.

There is also the question, for Australia as for other powers, of the likely size of any deployment. The designated size, in terms of ships and troops, has fallen so that the emphasis is on deployment at company level, rather than at battalion, still less brigade. Indeed, the last is understood principally in terms of the USMC, although China and Russia may come to match this potential.

In practical terms, it may be queried whether as much could be achieved with these numbers as doctrine suggested. In 2014, the "Joint Publications 3-02: Amphibious Operations" issued by the American Joint Chiefs of Staff discussed success in terms of the ability to "exploit the element of surprise and capitalize on enemy weakness by projecting combat power precisely at the most advantageous location and time." The Australian Defence Force claimed that amphibious forces "provide government with a cost-effective option for shaping and influencing the geo-political environment,"[16] a doctrine that underplays the risks involved in contested operations.

For Australia, as for other powers, these objectives did not assume a focus on seizing a beach in order to provide a basis for theater entry, for there are not the forces to pursue this outcome. Instead, the focus is on moving from the sea base directly to the target, which tends to mean a political center. Anti-access forces are thus to be bypassed or to be wrong-footed by fast-moving interventions. Moreover, in the case of nonstate actors, there is not the emphasis on a front line, such as a beach. Instead, the stress is on fixing opponents, such as insurgents, in order to defeat them, and this is best secured by mobility. Humanitarian assistance takes a similar form. For both, precision and speed are key elements, with combined operations encompassing air power, special forces, and amphibious capability.

At the same time, precision and speed also offer much to nonstate actors. These tend to be seen as elements that engage on land, with the exception of pirates, but there is also the use of the sea by terrorist and other groups. These can be seen in both the Middle East and South Asia. Terrorists attacking Israel used sea attacks from at least 1975 when eight Fatah men employed a rubber dinghy to reach Tel Aviv, seizing hostages in the Hotel Savoy before being overcome by counterterrorist units. In 1978, there was a similar raid on Israel, which led to the Coastal Road massacre. The Tamil Tigers used the sea to mount raids in Sri Lanka. In 2008, ten Lashkar-e-Taiba Pakistani terrorists, employing a hijacked fishing trawler and an inflatable boat, landed in Mumbai and launched an assault on a number of targets. Such episodes underlined the need for fine-grained surface-control systems designed to prevent such incursions. Stopping, by means of standby naval units (whether ships or helicopters), such incursions before they reach the beach is a necessary goal and means. As another instance of maritime terrorism, in 2000 a boat rammed the side of the USS *Cole* in Aden causing great damage and offering a warning of the threat posed by swarm attacks.

CONCLUSIONS

Moving from specifics, there is also the more profound question of the degree to which combined operations, and the related capability, goals, and strategic consequences, are understood as a package, rather than as a number of independent elements. The likelihood is that military culture as a concept comes into play here but in terms that are not easy to point to precisely. Indeed, "military culture" as a term that in part covers assumptions necessarily points the way to the range of factors significant to, and often instrumental for, strategic, operational, and institutional choices and developments in combined operations. In part, the idea of military culture reflects the extent to which there is learning from experience. This is, to a degree, a significant qualification of the idea of environmentally driven military systems, but also represents the way in which the lessons explicit or implicit to such apparent determinisms are adopted. These issues can be applied to the specifics of airborne as of amphibious warfare, but also relate to more general questions linked to the flexibility necessary to combined operations, however the latter are defined. Ultimately, this flexibility rests on social and cultural assumptions and practices. They may be expressed in institutional forms and be reliant on the availability of resources, but the social and cultural elements are foremost.

Another major element of change is provided by the geopolitical environment. The end of the Cold War was particularly important as it transformed the parameters within which combined operations were generally considered. During the Cold War, especially the post-Vietnam years, the emphasis had been on the use of combined operations as an aspect of any Soviet attack to secure control of the Barents Sea and to deny NATO command of the Norwegian Sea, so that the Soviet submarine force could operate, but, more particularly, as a part of the NATO response. Thus, the British focused their amphibious forces on protecting NATO's northern flank in northern Norway and, like other NATO forces, trained for deployments accordingly. This presence would also limit the chances of the Soviets establishing bases in northern Norway to enhance their challenge to NATO naval forces in the neighboring North Sea and North Atlantic.[17]

From the 1990s, the shift, for Britain, was back toward the out-of-area capability seen in the late 1950s and early 1960s, more especially east of Suez, but also in Africa, as well as making forces capable to prevent further Argentine aggression against the Falkland Islands. The United States very much developed central command and a capability to operate in Southwest

Asia. The possibilities offered by this departure, however, were compromised for the United States and Britain by difficult and lengthy commitments in Afghanistan and Iraq, notably with American and British Marines being used as regular infantry in response to the shortage of the latter. However, the flexibility provided by combined operation capability to forward the pursuit of political objectives was apparent in these commitments, even if these objectives were not shaped accordingly.

Alongside these commitments came an attempt in the late 2000s to reboot an understanding of combined operations and notably to move from a focus on land-based campaigning to one where the naval dimension was to the fore. A doctrine for amphibious operations was issued by the American Department of Defense in August 2009 and identified five categories: assaults, raids, demonstrations, withdrawals, and nonconflict operations such as conflict prevention.[18] Policy, in the shape of a "pivot" toward the Pacific, helped drive this reevaluation. Training and planning followed suit, as with the amphibious training exercise Bold Alligator, conducted by U.S. Fleet Forces Command in 2011.

Yet, as a reminder of the need throughout to adopt a global approach, the United States' approach (and that of Britain) is scarcely typical. It is instructive, for example, to consider in contrast the extent to which historically the South American navies have not invested in amphibious capability. Several inherited war-surplus United States' tank landing ships from the 1960s onward, but at present, only Brazil and Chile have major amphibious ships and then only one apiece. Similarly, Guatemala has a Marine force of about three hundred men. Pakistan has no real capability, as its four small hovercraft can carry only some seventy troops if all are even working at one time. Canada has never had a Marine Corps. Instead, as in 1942 (Dieppe) and 1944 (Normandy), the Canadians trained infantry to assault beaches. Canada will face a major challenge if climate change continues to expose its Arctic islands to foreign intervention.

There are many states in between, but again it is the need not to take the United States as the defining power that stands out. Instead, it is appropriate to consider the extent to which the challenge posed by combined operations, both to those who plan them and to their targets, is a reflection of taskings that arise from very different geopolitical situations and military capabilities and taskings that are understood in that light. For example, Singapore, from the beginning of the twenty-first century, enhanced its force projection (and thus ceased to have primarily a sea-denial navy) by building four Endurance-class landing platform docks, each capable of carrying 350 troops, 4 landing craft, and 2 medium-sized helicopters. At the same time, while valuable, these amphibious assault landing ships[19] can scarcely transform regional geopolitics. They offer presence, rather than the delivery, of a large-scale force.

India has a limited capability with one infantry brigade that practices amphibious landings and a respectable flotilla of landing ships/craft, albeit mostly on the older side. The most potent is the INS *Jalashwa*, the former USS *Trenton*, plus five indigenous Magar-class and four former Soviet Polocny-class ships, as well as about thirty-two landing craft. Strategically, the two cases of potential employment usually cited are the recapture of territory in the Andaman and Nicobar Islands (and a combined arms command, the Andaman and Nicobar Command, has recently been created) and, secondly, threatening the Pakistani coastline. However, it is difficult to see how one brigade could do much, notably in the second case: sustaining it once onshore would represent a major challenge, although India is planning more helicopter carriers.

Interoperability; the diffusion of techniques, weaponry, and doctrine; and the wish to have a cutting-edge effectiveness will all ensure that the approach taken by the leading amphibious power, the United States, is very significant. At the same time, by its very nature, the United States is also atypical, as Britain was before it. This is true not only of resources and tasking, but also of institutional structure and political and public support. For example, the role of the USMC, which in 2015 had 14 percent of the American active-duty armed forces, the highest prestige of the services in public opinion polls, and a minimum size mandated by Congress (three divisions and three wings), is not matched elsewhere. The institutional and political contexts are highly germane to the development of combined operations and to the use of amphibious assaults.

The strength of the USMC suggests that the United States is the power most likely to mount a major combined operation again. However, there are also significant constraints. Aside from the threat of nuclear weapons against a beachhead or air head, many coastal regions and communication nodes have been turned, by population growth, urbanization, and suburbanization, into large-scale potential fortresses. In contrast, smaller undertakings, such as commando raids or the capture of isolated vital installations, will probably remain common. Indeed, the formation and/or expansion of special forces as services of their own is a key element of recent years. They have the idea of combined operations—"delivery by any means"—as their hallmark. In order to achieve that, they have to spend most of their time training, need an enormous logistical apparatus, and can never be very large in terms of manpower. The "War on Terror" could not have been waged without them. Looking ahead, the rise of unmanned air, sea, and, eventually, land vehicles with combat capabilities may well have a major effect on combined operations as well.

Chapter Twelve

Conclusions

"Combined operations" have a number of definitions, as outlined in the preface. This imprecision is an informed response to the protean character of war and to its greatly changing manifestations across space and time and yet also affects the assessment of effectiveness. Separately, there are different, sometimes contrasting strategic, operational, and tactical levels in combined operations. Another important and complicating variety is offered by differences in goals and means. For example, the underlying nature of combined operations can relate in particular to logistics, whether maintaining those of one's own side or harming those of opponents.[1] This may be a matter of army supply, naval supply, or broader societal considerations. Moreover, logistics is an element at the tactical, operational, and strategic levels, and, at each, it is vital and can be a deciding factor.

Organizational factors, notably the idea of network-centric warfare, have attracted much attention.[2] By their very nature, combined operations face major issues in cooperation between institutions, groups, and individuals who have different backgrounds, cultures, training, fighting practices, weaponry, platforms, and often interests, and this is the case even assuming that the enemy does not impose an "information-denial environment." How best to achieve cooperation, and at every level, is a much discussed theme. The need for formal mechanisms for cooperation—for example, between infantry and attack helicopters in the army in the United States—or jointness at operational and strategic levels, is very much the modern approach. This need looks back to earlier periods in which individual commanders cooperated without such a structure, for example, between the German army and air force during the Second World War.[3] Initially, this cooperation was highly effective because of German air superiority and clear lines of advance. However, there was a lack of workable and stable radio communication between the ground and air elements, and after 1942, when Germany faced stronger opposition and lost air control, this was to prove even more problematic.

Such cooperation could be highly successful, as, increasingly although not invariably, with the British in their combined operations and amphibious assaults in their "long eighteenth century" wars with France. But there remained inherent difficulties with some cooperation, not least due to the contrasting requirements and distinctive command cultures of individual services. Cooperation is still extremely difficult even with formal mechanisms and procedures and well-established protocols and routines. The mark of an effective military is one that can work through the friction, both within the system and with the enemy, and still win. Weaknesses in cooperation and issues with friction can also be linked to poor planning, notably based on unrealistic assessments, as with the British attacks on Buenos Aires (1807), New Orleans (1815), Gallipoli (1915), and Dakar (1940), although, in each case, the strength and determination of the opposition were very significant.

The extent to which combined capability is seen in operational terms or as a more strategic expression of political commitment is also significant. The former emphasizes military utility while the latter is more attuned to affecting the geopolitical environment, including influencing allies, neutrals, and domestic opinion. As far as amphibious assaults are concerned, the former is a matter of power projection and the latter a question of to what end. Each approach has very different implications in case of the resources deployed and the time frame allowed. Inserting troops, by means of amphibious assaults or airborne assault and deployment, does not end the questions of effectiveness and purpose, either operationally or strategically. Indeed, that was a major theme in American criticism of British pressure in 1943–1944 to commit forces to Italy and the Balkans.

These and other factors can be related to, but are frequently separate from, the more specific and particular ones of attacks and the overcoming of opposition. In the latter case, effectiveness in combined operations was (and is) in large part in practice a matter of the range of factors, military and crucially political, that led to success for the troops after they arrived. For example, with William III of Orange's successful invasion of England in 1688, success initially rested on the failure of the English fleet to intercept the Dutch, a case of a decisive nonbattle in which luck and political allegiance played a major role, although it is not easy to gauge the latter factor. The subsequent situation on land was also important. James II deployed a larger army to block William's advance on London, but this force rapidly dissolved due to his collapse of will, a collapse that owed much to key betrayals. Finally, William's success rested on political willingness in England, however coerced, to accept the new order. A similar success came with the willingness in Sicily in 1718 to welcome the Spanish invasion force, a willingness that in large part reflected opposition there to the financial demands of the new ruler, Victor Amadeus II of Savoy-Piedmont.

This strategic level is the major concern in this chapter, but at the same time the tactical and operational levels require discussion. Thus, in 1758, discussing British combined operations against Western Europe, Robert, Fourth Earl of Holdernesse, one of the secretaries of state, commented on the need

> to hit upon some place, where, if we have the good fortune to succeed, we may be able to maintain ourselves even against a superior enemy; the very nature of the undertaking proves the difficulty of it, as the same reasons which would enable us to keep our ground, will operate against us in an attempt to seize some post of consequence, unless we have the good fortune to hit upon a spot where the enemy are ill-provided, and may be surprised. . . . As to any attempt upon the coast of Flanders, it would be next to impossible to succeed in it, considering the time that is necessary for disembarking a large body of men and that the enemy would be able to send a superior force to drive us back, before it would be possible to throw up any entrenchment to secure our stores and provisions, not to mention the hazard of reimbarking in the face of a superior enemy.[4]

Holdernesse's comments can be paralleled in terms of the planning during the two world wars. Although technology may be transformed, the operational and, even more, strategic dimensions vary less than might be anticipated. In the eighteenth century, as in other periods, speculation, planning, and operations were also affected by the major difficulties in maintaining an army or smaller units by sea alone.[5] More generally, the evaluation of operations should not be separated from this process of speculation and planning. The politics, both civilian and military, bound up with assumptions of success, moreover, are important to the context of combined operations. Thus, the *Monitor*, an influential London newspaper, in its issue of August 12, 1758, suggested that British forces should have invaded France in order to link up with allied forces in northwest Germany. The paper added, overoptimistically:

> The difficulty of our carrying the war into the heart of France, at the time when their main army was totally routed and dispirited, and their best troops were engaged at the distance of Bohemia [the Czech Republic]; and when the allies, flushed with victory, had nothing to fear, could they have made good their junction with an English army, depended entirely on its landing upon the coast of France; which, experience convinces, is practicable on almost any part, under the cover of our fleets.

Such politics within one country were set within the context of alliance dynamics, as in the Seven Years' War or the two, more famous, world wars of the twentieth century. In April 1758, anticipating Josef Stalin's demands during the Second World War on his American and British allies for a "Second Front," in other words an invasion of Western Europe, Frederick II of Prussia pressed hard for British attacks on the French coast "because he said he was convinced if we made them towards Dunkirk, that it would oblige the Comte de Clermont to detach that way, and that might perhaps give a fair opening to the King's army to pass the Rhine"[6] in order to attack France. Clermont was a French general. In 1760, Frederick II captured the idea of strategically exploiting what he presented as a very divided French ministry when he pressed the British ministry to mount attacks on the French coast, as the reality and fear of such attacks, he argued, "could not fail to raise great murmurings among the people (who were already tired of the war) and might strengthen the hands of those ministers who were disposed to peace."[7] A similar claim about a British attack on the French coast stated: "It cannot do much mischief, though those repeated insults must make France low in the opinion of mankind, as well as in that of Europe."[8]

This issue serves to illustrate the strategic asymmetries generally involved in combined operations, asymmetries that are crucial to questions of impact and effectiveness. For example, during the same war, the use of force to deter or respond to such operations was very different to that involved in mounting them, as was the kind of forces involved. There were also separate army and naval dimensions. For France, the object with the navy during the Seven Years' War was to achieve not so much the sea "control," or at least denial, sufficient to deter invasion, which was not a serious threat for France, but rather mission-focused objectives, as with the force assembled at Louisbourg in 1757 to deter a British attack. Differences in mission, however, made cooperation difficult. Thus, in France there was no doctrine for combined operations. The secretaries of state for war and for the navy were two different administrations without any link and with frequent competition and animosity between them for money, prestige, and reputation. Yet, French invasion plans, as in 1744, 1759, and 1779, involved some kind of combined operations thinking. As with the British, but without the crucial element of frequent experience, the situation improved for France in the second half of the century, which was important to French success during the American War of Independence, notably in the Yorktown campaign.

Aside from the major strategic asymmetries arising from contrasting capabilities (military and diplomatic) and goals, these asymmetries pose difficulties when trying to assess how best to translate the ability to engage in—and win—battles into the outcome of decisive success. This is a long-standing theme in military history and one in which combined operations are not somehow separate. The French success in 1757 in deterring an attack on Louisbourg, which the British expedition commanders themselves thought too hazardous, demonstrated the extent to which strategic implementation was "very uncertain."[9] Strategic and operational choices for all powers in part rested on assumptions about how these choices would affect the policies of opponents, with the arguments often expressed in terms of what was expedient for both sides in political terms, both domestic and international.

There was also a long-standing tendency to exaggerate what could be readily achieved by combined operations, a tendency that of course is shared by other branches of military activity. Thus, in 1788, in response to the Russian capture of the major Turkish fortress of Ochakov on the Black Sea—a fortress the British, seeking to mediate, were insisting should be restored to the Turks as a condition of any peace—Thomas, Seventh Earl of Elgin, the British envoy in Vienna, warned that it might well be followed by that of Constantinople (Istanbul):

> Who could say where the Court of Petersburg would stop if, after forming a solid footing, not only in the Crimea, but in other parts, of the Black Sea, and striking there at the vitals of the Ottoman Porte (and Ochakov alone was perhaps sufficient) she should seize some unlucky moment, when the rest of Europe was unable to assist that country, and erect her standard in Constantinople?[10]

In turn, in 1791, Joseph Ewart, the bellicose British envoy in Berlin and a strong supporter of the dispatch of a British fleet to the Baltic to challenge Catherine II of Russia, wrote:

> The Baltic fleet will consist of 35 sail of the line . . . and the *necessary fireships*, for I have strongly urged the expediency and ease of burning all the B—'s [*sic* for Bitch: Catherine II] ships and docks should she be obstinate. I have likewise represented that the moment our fleet has the command of the Gulf of Finland, it would be very easy to transport ten thousand Prussians across and debark them within a few miles of Petersburg, which could thus be taken at once as the Russians would naturally turn all their efforts towards Livonia.[11]

Counting on Russia thereby deploying to prevent a Prussian attack on the Russian frontier province of Livonia (much of modern Latvia), Ewart therefore projected a knockout military blow at the Russian capital, dealing, as a result of Russia's situation, with a crisis in the Black Sea by sending a fleet to the north. Combined operations thus provided strategic flexibility. There were "pull" factors toward the Baltic including, as in 1855–1856, threatening Russian power at the center of government and securing naval stores. In practice, the viability of Ewart's proposition was unclear given the strength of the Russian galley fleet and the lack of a British counter to it; which was a precursor of the situation with the prospect of British intervention in the face of American monitors during the American Civil War (1861–1865). However, combined operations appeared to offer a chance to strike at the opposing center, a chance that prefigures later ideas of strategic bombing. In the case of 1791, as of 1758, the issue was to the fore in relations with Britain's principal ally, again Prussia.

Overestimating capability remains a common fault of army, navy, air force, and Marine commanders, as well as of politicians. Recent examples include suggestions of what could have been achieved, both militarily and politically, in Syria in 2016 by American and/or British intervention and, arguably, what could have been achieved by earlier such intervention. The need to consider the possible responses of opponents and other powers remains a key element in evaluating capability as a whole as well as practicality in specific terms.

An emphasis today on combined operations, by whatever combination of sea, air, or land, captures a concern with speed and mobility, with, indeed, a "lightness" that still delivers impact. However, the historic advantages of time and space enjoyed by combined operations prior to the twentieth century have been severely reduced in an age of enhanced surveillance: first by air reconnaissance and subsequently by communications monitoring, satellite surveillance, and media coverage. As a result, the prospect of surprise has been lessened, at least for large state-like actors, although smaller actors, such as terror groups in Somalia, could be surprised, not knowing where the troops will land. Ironically, the United States may be endangering its position as the draft budget for fiscal year 2018 proposed a $1.3 billion (11.8 to 14 percent according to estimates) cut to the Coast Guard, including the cut of a ninth national security cutter currently under construction, and the end of the Maritime Safety and Security Teams and the Maritime Security Response Team. The acquisition budget had already been cut between 2010 and 2015 by 40 percent. In comparison, China and Russia have pressed ahead with their ability to meet mission requirements in the Arctic region.[12]

The situation now makes an unopposed coastal landing against a major power less probable, and even with massive support, an opposed landing can be costly. As another instance of change through time, major losses of life may have become politically unacceptable, or more politically unacceptable, in some states, notably in Western Europe, but even for more robust states, such as Israel and possibly the United States. This situation encourages "maneuver warfare" and the idea of not going head-on into obstacles. The earlier embrace of contested landings ("forcible entry") by the USMC brought, in contrast, after the Second World War and especially after Vietnam, the realization that fighting smart trumps brute force. As discussed in chapter 10, the USMC borrowed the ideas of an air force officer, John Boyd, ideas that drew on Liddell Hart. Maneuver warfare, at its core, is not just positional but cognitive. Its explicit objective is to target the enemy's mind and destroy him systematically, with speed and shock as vital. This entails the question of whether speed and shock can be achieved in amphibious warfare or whether they are forfeited in the process of building up the logistical "iron mountain." Indeed, the key to modern distributed operations (as to the very different ones in the Second World War) is logistical speed and flexibility. The Americans are working on it, with the question of how to "generate tempo" throughout the operation. Ship-to-objective maneuver, which relies on "sea basing" rather than on establishing a beachhead, is believed to be part of the answer, although it is unclear how to protect the sea base in the day of long-range precision strike weapons.

In coming in from over the horizon, it is unclear how to sustain or increase operational tempo without sacrificing lethality. It is uncertain which vessels or aircrafts can arrive in sufficient force to create shock and at a sufficient speed to evade A2/AD defenses. Thus, is amphibious warfare going to be anything other than a highly risky mission, as at the time of Gallipoli (1915)? If the USMC cannot crack open the coastal defenses alone, will it be necessary to launch "air-sea battle" from over the horizon, and is this situation limited war? Thus, the question is whether, as the USMC terms it, "amphibiosity" has expanded the state's options or foreclosed them.

Aside from technological change, there are also fundamental difficulties about which consideration of the historical trajectory is instructive, not least in terms of the ability to influence developments in populated areas. There is also the specific issue that littoral regions are becoming less permissive for force projection of any type. In military terms, these regions are becoming cluttered and congested[13] as anti-access policies develop, but there are also the general problems of overawing opposition.

To turn first to Omar Bradley's point, offered in Washington in 1949 and noted at the start of chapter 10, a sense of obsolescence or anachronism may seem apparent when considering the visual images of the Second World War, both captured in photography or imagined in feature films, let alone the presentation of earlier attacks such as Gallipoli in 1915. Moreover, his point about obsolescence in an age of atomic weaponry, while totally disproved by the Inchon landing less than a year later against an opponent (North Korea) that lacked nuclear weapons and had no naval capacity, captured both the vulnerability of mass landings of the 1942–1945 type to technological change and the sense that the latter also opened new possibilities for assault. In practice, landings of the scale of Inchon in 1950 are scarcely credible at present.

Technological change has been, and can be, taken forward across the broad range of anti-access and area-denial weaponry, both present and in potential. How an invasion fleet would be able to respond to anti-ship cruise missiles, drone attacks, smart mines, directed electromagnetic pulses, and other weaponry is unclear; but the very deployment of mass will enhance the target for such weapons and lengthen the time frame for counterattack interception.

From this perspective, large-scale amphibious assaults appear less viable, and the absence of the mass conscript armies of the Second World War, notably in the United States but also across most of the world, is also a factor. That, however, does not rule out smaller, more nimble, readier-to-go forces operating alongside the use of air-mobile units that also offer speed and flexibility. Apart from the United States and, to an extent, China, no other countries, including Russia, have the capability for operations other than small-scale assaults. Indeed, many operations, such as those mounted by Britain against Sierra Leone and Libya, were virtually unopposed. Yet, that point argues for the utility of an amphibious capability for operations short of major conflict.

The key technologies at present are helicopters, vertical- or short-take-off aircraft, precision firepower, and effective command and control. The future here is also unclear. Defending missiles, drones, and other systems, whether protecting against or in support of combined operations, could be electronically suppressed, not least because they are heavily dependent on control systems that can be vulnerable to electronic disruption. At the same time, the willingness of China and Russia to lose platforms and troops may well lessen their concern about losses in mounting amphibious assaults as well as other forms of combined operations, although this situation may change in a state like China or Russia.

These powers still face the major problem of developing relevant expertise. In combined operations, as with much else, such expertise is best obtained through experience. It is the role of the last that helps ensure the emphasis on Britain and then the United States in the history of the subject over the past 325 years. Being the foremost naval power and having interests to pursue by maritime force projection were both key factors, but experience has repeatedly turned out to be a crucial enabler, the product but also cause of the factors just cited.

Alongside narrowly military possibilities for, and constraints on, combined operations, social and cultural assumptions and practices play a key role in defining and discerning capability in combined operations, whether constant or changing capability. This definition of capability indeed is an aspect of the tasking and strategic culture that is specific to individual states and that helps make universal definitions of only limited value. Combined operations need to be understood in this context. They also have to be considered, as suggested in the preface, in terms of the protean nature of definitions. This nature reflects long-standing differences over the meaning of terms, as well as more recent concerns and tasks, and also developing concepts such as hybrid warfare.[14] The discussion of terms is valuable as it encourages us to understand the unfixed nature of conflict and the problems involved in trying to reduce it to a set of rules or maxims. These problems can contribute to failure if they lead to a misunderstanding of the assumptions of opponents.

Notes

PREFACE

1. For an extended and wide-ranging consideration of definitions, see David Trim and Mark Fissel, "Amphibious Warfare 1000–1700: Concepts and Contexts" in *Amphibious Warfare, 1000–1700: Commerce, State Formation, and European Expansion*, ed. David Trim and Mark Fissel (Leiden, Netherlands: Brill, 2006), 1–49.

2. Reviewing the talk, a London newsweekly argued that "tribious—from *tri*, three, and *bios*, life, would be equally correct for denizens of three elements—land, sea and air" but there should not be use of the "meaningless second half of *amphi*. . . . The Greek language and its derivations can't be carved about with a hatchet" (*Spectator*, September 3, 1943, 4).

1. COMBINED OPERATIONS TO 1500

1. Milan Vego, "On Littoral Warfare," *NWCR* 68 (2015): 34–41.

2. George Cawkwell, *The Greek Wars: The Failure of Persia* (New York: Oxford University Press, 2005), but see review by Arthur Eckstein, "Persia and the Greeks: Failure of an Empire," *International History Review* 27 (2005): 807–12.

3. David Lonsdale, "Alexander the Great and the Art of Adaptation," *JMH* 77 (2013): 825–26.

4. Marc C. De Santis, *Rome Seizes the Trident: The Defeat of Carthaginian Sea Power and the Forging of the Roman Empire* (Barnsley, UK: Pen and Sword, 2016).

5. Stephen Dando-Collins, *Legions of Rome: The Definitive History of Every Imperial Roman Legion* (New York: Thomas Dunne Books, 2012), 56–57.

6. Bernard Bachrach's "Some Observations on William the Conqueror's Horse Transports," *Technology and Culture* 25 (1985): 239–55, may be too optimistic on the sailing qualities of the ships. But see also Matthew Bennett, "Amphibious Operations from the Norman Conquest to the Crusades of Saint Louis, c. 1050–c. 1250," in David Trim and Mark Fissel, eds., *Amphibious Warfare, 1000–1700: Commerce, State Formation, and European Expansion* (Leiden, Netherlands: Brill, 2006), 52–53.

7. Charles Stanton, *Norman Naval Operations in the Mediterranean* (Woodbridge, UK: Boydell, 2011) and *Medieval Maritime Warfare* (Barnsley, UK: Pen and Sword, 2015).

8. John Pryor, ed., *Logistics of Warfare in the Age of the Crusades* (Aldershot, UK: Ashgate, 2006).

9. Thomas Madden, "The Venetian Version of the Fourth Crusade: Memory and the Conquest of Constantinople in Medieval Venice," *Speculum* 87 (2012): 311–44.

10. Susan Rose, *Medieval Naval Warfare 1000–1500* (Abingdon, UK: Routledge, 2001).

11. Marios Philippides and Walter Hanak, *The Siege and the Fall of Constantinople in 1453: Historiography, Topography, and Military Studies* (Farnham, UK: Ashgate, 2012).

12. Robert Smith and Kelly DeVries, *Rhodes Besieged: A New History* (Stroud, UK: History Press, 2011).

13. David Trim, "Medieval and Early-Modern Inshore, Estuarine, Riverine and Lacustrine Warfare," in Trim and Fissel, eds., *Amphibious Warfare*, 357–419.

14. John Pryor, *Geography, Technology, and War: Studies in the Maritime History of the Mediterranean 649–1571* (Cambridge: Cambridge University Press, 1988).

15. Benjamin Hazard, "The Formative Years of the Wako, 1223–63," *Monumenta Nipponica* 22 (1967): 260–77.

2. THE EARLY MODERN PERIOD, 1500–1700

1. Jeremy Black, *War in the World: A Comparative History 1450–1600* (Basingstoke, UK: Palgrave, 2011).

2. Malyn Newitt, "Portuguese Amphibious Warfare in the East in the Sixteenth Century, 1500–1520," in David Trim and Mark Fissel, eds., *Amphibious Warfare, 1000–1700: Commerce, State Formation, and European Expansion* (Leiden, Netherlands: Brill, 2006), 103–21; Francisco Bethencourt and Diogo Ramada Cuto, eds., *Portuguese Oceanic Expansion, 1400–1800* (Cambridge: Cambridge University Press, 2007).

3. Giancarlo Casale, *The Ottoman Age of Exploration* (Oxford: Oxford University Press, 2010): 163–78.

4. Arturo Pacini, *"Desde Rosas a Gaeta." La costruzione della rotta spagnola nel Mediterraneo accidentale nel secolo XVI* (Milan: FrancoAngeli, 2013).

5. John Guilmartin, *Gunpowder and Galleys: Changing Technology and Mediterranean Warfare at Sea in the Sixteenth Century*, 2nd ed. (Annapolis, MD: Naval Institute Press, 2013), 42–56.

6. Robert Smith and Kelly DeVries, *Rhodes Besieged: A New History* (Stroud, UK: History Press, 2011).

7. Guilmartin, *Gunpowder and Galleys*, 176–93, and "The Siege of Malta (1565) and the Habsburg-Ottoman Struggle for Domination of the Mediterranean," in Trim and Fissel, eds., *Amphibious Warfare*, 149–80.

8. Elizabeth Bonner, "The Recovery of St Andrews Castle in 1547: French Naval Policy and Diplomacy in the British Isles," *English Historical Review* 111 (1996): 578–98.

9. Trim and Fissel, "Conclusion," in Trim and Fissel, eds., *Amphibious Warfare*, 441–44.

10. Roger Williams, *The Actions of the Low Countries*, ed. John Rigby Hale and David William Davies (Ithaca, NY: Cornell University Press, 1964).

11. Alan James, "A French Armada? The Azores Campaigns, 1580–1583," *Historical Journal* 55 (2012): 1–20.

12. Kenneth Swope, *A Dragon's Head and a Serpent's Tail: Ming China and the First Great East Asian War, 1592–1598* (Norman: University of Oklahoma Press, 2009).

13. Ernst van Veen, "How the Dutch Ran a Seventeenth-Century Colony: The Occupation and Loss of Formosa, 1624–1662," *Itinerario* 20 (1996): 59–77.

14. Armando da Silva Saturnino Monteiro, *Portuguese Sea Battles, I: The First World Sea Power, 1139–1521* (Lisbon: Saturnino Monteiro, 2010).

15. Trim and Fissel, "Conclusion," 445–46.

16. Guy Rowlands, "The King's Two Arms: French Amphibious Warfare in the Mediterranean under Louis XIV, 1664–1697," in Trim and Fissel, eds., *Amphibious Warfare*, 268–69.

17. Victor Ostapchuk, "Five Documents from the Topkapi Palace Archives on the Ottoman Defence of the Black Sea against the Cossacks," *Journal of Turkish Studies* 2 (1987): 49–104, and "The Human Landscape of the Ottoman Black Sea in the Face of Cossack Naval Raids," *Oriente Moderno* 20 (2001): 23–95.

18. Rowlands, "King's Two Arms," 263–314; Émile Laloy, *La Révolte de Messine, l'Expédition de Sicile, et la Politique Française en Italie, 1674–1678* (Paris: Librairie C. Klinckseick, 1929).

19. Jan Glete, "Amphibious Warfare in the Baltic, 1550–1700," in Trim and Fissel, eds., *Amphibious Warfare*, 123–47.

20. Trim, "Medieval and Early-Modern Inshore, Estuarine, Riverine and Lacustrine Warfare," in Trim and Fissel, eds., *Amphibious Warfare*, 388.

21. Fissel, "English Amphibious Warfare, 1587–1656: Galleons, Galleys, Longboats, and Cots," in Trim and Fissel, eds., *Amphibious Warfare*, 244–47.

22. Ibid., 250–54.

23. Philip Aubrey, *The Defeat of James Stuart's Armada 1692* (Leicester: Leicester University Press, 1979).

24. John Stapleton, "The Blue-Water Dimension of King William's War: Amphibious Operations and Allied Strategy during the Nine Years' War, 1688–1697," in Trim and Fissel, eds., *Amphibious Warfare*, 330–34.

25. Hugo O'Donnell and Duque de Estrada, *La Infanteria de Marina Espanola. Historia y Fuentes* (Madrid: Bazán, 1999), 57–130.

26. Tonio Andrade, *Lost Colony: The Untold Story of China's First Great Victory over the West* (Princeton, NJ: Princeton University Press, 2011).

27. Raymond Denis Bathurst, "Maritime Trade and Imamate Government: Two Principal Themes in the History of Oman to 1728," in Derek Hopwood, ed., *The Arabian Peninsula: Society and Politics* (London: Allen & Unwin, 1972), 89–106; Glenn Ames, "The Straits of Hurmuz Fleets: Omani-Portuguese Naval Rivalry and Encounters, c. 1660–1680," *Mariner's Mirror* 83 (1997): 398–409.

28. Atul Chandra Roy, *A History of Naval Warfare under the Mughals* (Calcutta: World Press, 1972).

29. Stapleton, "Blue-Water Dimension," 334.

30. Keith McLay, "Combined Operations and the European Theatre during the Nine Years' War, 1688–97," *Historical Research* 78 (2005): 506–39, "Wellsprings of a 'World War': An Early English Attempt to Conquer Canada during King William's War," *Journal of Imperial and Commonwealth History* 34 (2006): 155–75, "A Mediterranean Amphibian: British Warfare, 1693–1713," *Journal of Mediterranean Studies* 16 (2006): 187–98, and "Sir Francis Wheeler's Caribbean and North American Expedition, 1693: A Case Study in Combined Operational Command during the Reign of William III," *War in History* 14 (2007): 383–407.

31. Andrew Lambert, "The Tory World View: Sea Power, Strategy and Party Politics, 1815–1914," and Brian Holden Reid, "Is There a Tory Strategy?" in Jeremy Black, ed., *The Tory World: Deep History and the Tory Theme in British Foreign Policy, 1679–2014* (Farnham, UK: Ashgate, 2015), 121–48, 265–92.

32. John McNeill, *Atlantic Empires of France and Spain: Louisbourg and Havana, 1700–1763* (Chapel Hill: University of North Carolina Press, 1985).

3. THE EIGHTEENTH CENTURY, 1700–1775

1. Humphrys journal, BL. Add. 45662 fols. 6–7.

2. J. Ellis to Stepney, July 29, 1701, BL. Add. 7074 fol. 45.

3. Methuen to Alexander Stanhope, November 24, 1702, Maidstone, Kent Archive Office, U 1590 029/5.

4. Chetwynd, outletter book, June 25, 1704, Stafford, Staffordshire Record Office, D649/8/2, p. 56.

5. Robert Walpole to Mr. Hopkins, June 22, 1708, BL. Add. 64928 fol. 53.

6. Richard Harding, "The Conduct of Landing Operations," in C. Buchet and G. Le Bouédec, eds., *The Sea in History: The Early Modern World/La Mer dans l'Histoire: La Période Moderne* (Woodbridge, UK: Association Océanides, Boydell Press, 2017), 891–903.

7. Addison to Charles, First Duke of Manchester, July 23, 1708, Beinecke, Manchester papers, vol. 14.

8. Admiral John Norris to Marlborough, July 27, 1710, BL. Add. 61314 fols. 79–80.

9. Admiral Sir Cloudesley Shovell to Charles, Third Earl of Sunderland, Secretary of State for the Southern Department, August 10, 1707, BL. 61311 fol. 50.

10. Blathwayt to Stepney, August 6, 1703, Beinecke, Osborn Shelves, Blathwayt papers, Box 21.

11. James Alsop, "Samuel Vetch's 'Canada Survey'd': The Formation of a Colonial Strategy, 1706–1710," *Acadiensis* 12 (1982): 57.

12. Francis Nicholson, *Journal of an expedition for the reduction of Port Royal* (London, 1711).

13. Gerald Graham, ed., *The Walker Expedition to Quebec, 1711* (London: Navy Records Society, 1953); Richard Harding, "The Expeditions to Quebec, 1690 and 1711: The Evolution of British Trans-Atlantic Amphibious Power," in Peter Le Fevre, ed., *Guerres Maritimes, 1688–1713* (Vincennes, France: Service Historique de la Marine, 1996), 197–212.

14. Lord Gallway to John Hedges, Secretary of State for the Southern Department, September 11, 1705, BL. Add. 61122 fol. 33; Stepney to Harley, December 28, 1706, BL. Add. 7059 fol. 228.

15. Richard Harding, "Anglo-French Attacks on the Coast of Northern Spain, 1719," *Trafalgar Chronicle* 25 (2015): 67–76.

16. Thomas, Duke of Newcastle, Secretary of State for the Southern Department, to Horatio Walpole, envoy in Paris, April 2, 1727, NA. SP. 78/186 fol. 94.

17. Memorandum by Sir George Lowther, RN, "The method for taking St Jago [in Cuba] by sea," c. 1740, BL. Stowe Mss. 256 fols. 319–20.

18. Shinsuke Satsuma, *Britain and Colonial Maritime War in the Early Eighteenth Century: Silver, Seapower and the Atlantic* (Woodbridge, UK: Boydell and Brewer, 2013).

19. Philip Woodfine, "The War of Jenkins' Ear: A New Voice in the Wentworth-Vernon Debate," *Journal of the Society for Army Historical Research* 65 (1987): 67–91; Richard Harding, *Amphibious Warfare in the Eighteenth Century: The British Expedition to the West Indies 1740–1742* (Woodbridge, UK: Boydell and Brewer, 1991), 83–122.

20. William, Duke of Cumberland, to Admiral John Byng, January 11, 1746, Windsor Castle, Royal Archives, Cumberland Papers 9/69.

21. Britt Zerbe, *The Birth of the Royal Marines 1664–1802* (Woodbridge, UK: Boydell and Brewer, 2013).

22. William Pitt to John, Fourth Earl of Loudoun, February 4, 1757, HL. Lo. 2765A.

23. Hugh Boscawen, *The Capture of Louisbourg, 1758* (Norman: University of Oklahoma Press, 2011).

24. Marshall Smelser, *The Campaign in the Sugar Islands, 1759* (Chapel Hill: University of North Carolina Press, 1955).

25. Francis to Jeremy Browne, October 26, 1762, BL. RP. 3284.

26. David Syrett, "The British Landing at Havana: An Example of Eighteenth-Century Combined Operations," *Mariner's Mirror* 55 (1969): 325–31, and *The Siege and Capture of Havana, 1762* (London: Navy Records Society, 1970).

27. Colonel George Monson to Charles Townshend, Secretary at War, October 30, 1762, NA. WO. 1/319, p. 392; Alan Harfield, "The British Expedition to Manila, 1762–1763," *Journal of the Society for Army Historical Research* 66 (1988): 101–11; Nicholas Tracy, *Manila Ransomed: The British Assault on Manila in the Seven Years' War* (Exeter: University of Exeter Press, 1995).

28. Anon., "A Journal of the Occurrences and Military Proceedings at Minorca and particularly at the Castle of St Phillip's commencing the 16th April 1756," Beinecke, Osborn Shelves c 396 fols. 1, 5.

29. Richard Harding, "The Expedition to Lorient, 1746," in Nicholas Tracy, *The Age of Sail*, vol. I (London: Conway Publishing, 2002): 34–54.

30. William Hackman, "English Military Expeditions to the Coast of France 1757–1761" (PhD thesis, University of Michigan, 1968), and "The British Raid on Rochefort, 1757," *Mariner's Mirror* 64 (1978): 263–75.

31. Account of expedition by Lieutenant-Colonel Charles Hotham, Hull, University Library, DDHO/4/172; Alan William Halliday Pearsall, "Naval Aspects of the Landings on the French Coast, 1758," in Nicholas Rodger, ed., *Naval Miscellany*, vol. 5 (London: Navy Records Society, 1984): 207–43.

32. Francis Hebbert, "The Belle Ile Expedition of 1761," *Journal of the Society for Army Historical Research* 64 (1986): 81–93.

33. Bedford to Bute, July 9, 1761, Mount Stuart, Bute, papers of the Third Earl, 1761 correspondence, number 478.

34. David Syrett, "The Methodology of British Amphibious Operations During the Seven Years and American Wars," *Mariner's Mirror* 58 (1972): 269–79.

35. Ira Gruber, *Books and the British Army in the Age of the American Revolution* (Chapel Hill: University of North Carolina Press, 2010), 100–103; Mark Danley, "The British Political Press and Military Thought during the Seven Years' War," in Mark H. Danley and Patrick J. Speelman, eds., *The Seven Years' War: Global Views* (Leiden, Netherlands: Brill, 2012), 359–97, esp. 393–94.

36. Wych to John, Lord Carteret, Secretary of State for the Northern Department, April 10, 1742, NA. SP. 91/31.

37. Brian Davies, *The Russo-Turkish War, 1768–1774* (London: Bloomsbury, 2016), 154–60, 178–80.

38. Christopher Storrs, *The Spanish Resurgence 1713–1748* (New Haven, CT: Yale University Press, 2016).

39. Jean Colin, *Louis XV et les Jacobites. Le projet de debarquement en Angleterre 1743–44* (Paris: R. Chapelot, 1901), 6–24; Eveline Cruickshanks, "The Factions at the Court of Louis XV and the Succession to Cardinal Fleury, 1737–45" (PhD, London, 1956), 262, 382.

40. David McNab, Bruce Hodgins, and Dale Standen, "'Black with Canoes': Aboriginal Resistance and the Canoe: Diplomacy, Trade and Warfare in the Meeting Grounds of Northeastern North America, 1600–1821," in George Raudzens, ed., *Technology, Disease and Colonial Conquests, Sixteenth to Eighteenth Centuries* (Leiden, Netherlands: Brill, 2001), 245.

41. Yingcong Dai, "A Disguised Defeat: The Myanmar Campaign of the Qing Dynasty," *Modern Asian Studies* 38 (2004): 166.

42. Robert Antony, *Like Froth Floating on the Sea: The World of Pirates and Seafarers in Late Imperial South China* (Berkeley: University of California Institute of East Asian Studies, 2003).

43. Lawrence Lockhart, "The Navy of Nadir Shah," *Proceedings of the Iran Society* 1 (1936): 3–18; Willem Floor, "The Iranian Navy in the Gulf during the Eighteenth Century," *Iranian Studies* 20 (1987); Michael Axworthy, "Nader Shah and Persian Naval Expansion in the Persian Gulf, 1700–1747," *Journal of the Royal Asiatic Society* 21 (2011): 31–39.

44. David Syrett, *Shipping and Military Power in the Seven Years' War: The Sails of Victory* (Chicago: University of Chicago Press, 2008).

45. Marlborough to his wife, June 30, 1758, BL. Add. 61667 fol. 22.

46. Hodgson to Lord Barrington, Secretary-at-War, April 29, 1761, NA. WO. 1/165 p. 340.

47. Holdernesse to Andrew Mitchell, envoy in Berlin, June 27, 1758, NA. SP. 90/71.

4. THE AMERICAN REVOLUTION AND THE FRENCH REVOLUTIONARY AND NAPOLEONIC WARS, 1775–1815

1. Roger Smith, "The Failure of Great Britain's 'Southern Expedition' of 1776: Revisiting Southern Campaigns in the Early Years of the American Revolution, 1775–1779," *Florida Historical Quarterly* 93 (2015): 387–414.

2. SRO. GD. 26/9/513/15.

3. Durham, University Library, Grey papers 2239a.

4. I would like to thank James Johnson for letting me have a copy of his MA dissertation "'Making the Best Use of Your Joint Forces': Joint and Combined Operations on the Hudson River, 1777 and 1781" (Naval War College, RI, 1995).

5. NA. WO. 34/112 fols. 164–6.

6. Robert Fallaw and Marion West Stoer, "The Old Dominion under Fire: The Chesapeake Invasions, 1779–1781," in Ernest Eller, ed., *Chesapeake Bay in the American Revolution* (Centerville, MD: Tidewater Publishers, 1981), 443–51.

7. Nottingham University Library, Mellish papers, 172-111/21.

8. George Jones, "The Siege of Charleston as Experienced by a Hessian Officer," *South Carolina Historical Magazine* 88 (1987): 64.

9. Julian Boyd et al., eds., *The Papers of Thomas Jefferson* (Princeton, NJ: Princeton University Press, 1950), 4:312.

10. Charles Smith, *Marines in the Revolution: A History of the Continental Marines in the American Revolution 1775–1783* (Washington, DC: U.S. Government Printing Office, 1975).

11. John Calef, *The Siege of Penobscot by the Rebels . . .* (New York: Arno Press, 1971 [1781]).

12. Alfred Temple Patterson, *The Other Armada: The Franco-Spanish Attempt to Invade Britain in 1779* (Manchester: Manchester University Press 1960).

13. LC, Lincoln's Journal; NA. WO. 34/119 fols. 248–49.

14. Michael Crawford, "The Joint Allied Operation at Rhode Island, 1778," in William Roberts and Jack Sweetman, eds., *New Interpretations in Naval History* (Annapolis, MD: Naval Institute Press, 1991).

15. NA. WO. 34/136 fol. 74; Orwin Rush, *The Battle of Pensacola* (Tallahassee: Florida State University Press, 1966).

16. David Skaggs, "Decision at Cap Français: Franco-Spanish Coalition Planning and the Prelude to Yorktown," in William McBride, ed., *New Interpretations in Naval History* (Annapolis, MD: Naval Institute Press, 1998), 23–46.

17. Piers Mackesy, *Statesmen at War: The Strategy of Overthrow, 1798–1799* (London: Longman, 1974), 184–314.

18. Dundas to Maitland, June 16, 1800, NA. WO. 6/21, p. 21.

19. William to Anne Young, August 30, September 22, 1800, BL. Add. 46712 fols. 8–9, 12.

20. Lowe to father, also Hudson, March 29, 1801, BL. Add. 36297C fols. 12–13. Lowe was later Napoleon's captor on St. Helena.

21. Piers Mackesy, *British Victory in Egypt, 1801: The End of Napoleon's Conquest* (New York: Routledge, 1995).

22. Hill to his mother, December 25, 1801, Hill letters, private hands. I would like to thank Enid Case for granting me access to these letters when in her possession and for permission to quote them at length.

23. Hilary Walton Jackson, *A County Durham Man at Trafalgar: Cumby of the Bellerophon* (Durham: Durham County Local History Society, 1997), 22–23.

24. Rory Muir, *Wellington: The Path to Victory, 1769–1814* (New Haven, CT: Yale University Press, 2013), 185.

25. Ian Fletcher, *The Waters of Oblivion: The British Invasion of the Rio de la Plata, 1806–1807* (Tunbridge Wells, UK: Spellmount, 1991); John Grainger, ed., *The Royal Navy in the River Plate, 1806–1807* (London: Scolar Press, 1996).

26. Popham to Melville, November 23, 1807, BL. Loan 57/108 fols. 18–19.

27. Henry Dundas, Secretary for War, memorandum, Oct. 1796, BL. Add. 59280 fols. 189–90.

28. O'Hara to Sir Evan Nepean, October 1787, Belfast, Public Record Office of Northern Ireland, T. 2812/8/50.

29. Hewes to his father, November 30, 1807, Bristol, Record Office, Mss. 12571(8).

30. Lowe to General Fox, August 12, 1806, BL. Add. 20107 fol. 151.

31. Melville to Popham, August 4, 1812, BL. Loan 57/108 fols. 114–15.

32. Popham to Melville, July 14, 1812, BL. Loan 57/108 fol. 87.

33. Michael Duffy, "Festering the Spanish Ulcer: The Royal Navy and the Peninsular War, 1808–1814," in Bruce Elleman and Sally Paine, eds., *Naval Power and Expeditionary Warfare: Peripheral Campaigns and New Theaters of Naval Warfare* (London: Routledge, 2011), 15–28; Robert Sutcliffe, *British Expeditionary Warfare and the Defeat of Napoleon, 1793–1815* (Woodbridge: Boydell, 2016).

34. Eira Karppinenjed, *The War of King Gustavus III and the Naval Battles of Ruotsinsalmi* (Kotka, Finland: Provincial Museum of Kymenlaakso, 1993); Mikko Huhtamies, "Labyrinth of War: Archipelago Fleets and Society in the Gulf of Finland 1520–1800," *International Journal of Maritime History* 26 (2014): 600–21.

35. David Skaggs and Gerard Altoff, *A Signal Victory: The Lake Erie Campaign, 1812–13* (Annapolis, MD: Navy Institute Press, 1997).

36. Harry Lydenberg, ed., *Archibald Robertson: His Diaries and Sketches in America, 1762–1780* (New York: New York Public Library, 1930), 38.

37. Joseph Whitehorne, *The Battle for Baltimore, 1814* (Baltimore: Nautical and Aviation Publishing Company of America, 1997).

38. NAM. 2002-02-729-1.

39. Ibid.

40. Ibid.

41. NAM. 2001-09-36.

42. Piers Mackesy, "Problems of an Amphibious Power: Britain against France, 1793–1815," *Naval War College Review* 30 (1978): 18–19.

43. NA. WO. 1/141, p. 36.

44. Robert Browning, *Two If by Sea: The Development of American Coastal Defense Policy* (Westport, CT: Greenwood Press, 1983).

5. THE NINETEENTH CENTURY, 1815–1914

1. BL. Add. 40458 fol. 57.

2. BL. Add. 41410 fol. 2.

3. Rebecca Matzke, *Deterrence through Strength: British Naval Power and Foreign Policy under Pax Britannica* (Lincoln: University of Nebraska Press, 2011).

4. Francis Bradlee, *The Suppression of Piracy in the West Indies, 1820–1832* (New York: Library Editions, 1970).

5. Michael Birkner, "The 'Foxardo Affair' Revisited: Porter, Pirates and the Problem of Civilian Authority in the Early Republic," *American Neptune* 43, no. 3 (1982): 165–78.

6. Donald Cannery, *Africa Squadron: The U.S. Navy and the Slave Trade, 1842–1861* (Washington, DC: Potomac Books, 2006).

7. Sir Robert Peel to Edward, Earl of Ellenborough, First Lord of the Admiralty, March 17, 1846, BL. Add. 43198 fol. 122; Karl Jack Bauer, *The Mexican War 1846–1848*, 2nd ed. (Lincoln: University of Nebraska Press, 1992), 166.

8. Karl Jack Bauer, *Surfboats and Horse Marines: U.S. Naval Operations in the Mexican War 1846–48* (Annapolis, MD: U.S. Naval Institute, 1969).

9. George Buker, *Swamp Sailors in the Second Seminole War* (Gainesville: University of Florida Press, 1996).

10. Gordon Chang, "Whose 'Barbarians'? Whose 'Treachery'? Race and Civilization in the Unknown United States–Korea War of 1871," *Journal of American History* 89 (2003): 1331–65.

11. Earl Hess, *Civil War in the West: Victory and Defeat from the Appalachians to the Mississippi* (Chapel Hill: University of North Carolina Press, 2012).

12. Graham to Raglan, January 10, 1854, BL. Add. 29696 fol. 87.

13. Daniel Canfield, "Opportunity Lost: Combined Operations and the Development of Union Military Strategy, April 1861–April 1862," *JMH* 79 (2015): 687–89. For the argument that Union generals were slow and that victory was possible much earlier, Donald Stoker, *The Grand Design: Strategy and the U.S. Civil War* (New York: Oxford University Press, 2010).

14. Craig Symonds, *The Civil War at Sea* (Oxford: Oxford University Press, 2012); Gary Ohls, "Fort Fisher: Amphibious Victory in the American Civil War," *NWCR* 59, no. 4 (Autumn 2006): 81–99.

15. Palmerston to John, Earl Russell, October 2, 1862, G. P. Gooch, ed., *The Later Correspondence of Lord John Russell, 1840–1878* (London: Longmans, 1925), II:326–27.

16. Mark Lawrence, *Spain's First Carlist War* (Basingstoke, UK: Palgrave, 2014), 163–64.

17. Frederick Schneid, "A Well-Coordinated Affair: Franco-Piedmontese War Planning in 1859," *JMH* 76 (2012): 412–14, 421–25, and *The French-Piedmontese Campaign of 1859* (Rome: Uffico Storico, 2014).

18. Richard Brooks, *The Long Arm of Empire: Naval Brigades from the Crimea to the Boxer Rebellion* (London: Constable, 1999).

19. Andrew Rath, *The Crimean War in Imperial Context, 1854–1856* (Basingstoke, UK: Macmillan, 2015).

20. Jack Shulminson, *The Marine Corps' Search for a Mission, 1880–1898* (Lawrence: University Press of Kansas, 1993), and "The Influence of the Spanish-American War on the U.S. Marine Corps," in Edward Marolda, ed., *Theodore Roosevelt, the U.S. Navy, and the Spanish-American War* (New York: Palgrave, 2001), 81–94.

21. Mark Grove, "The Development of Japanese Amphibious Warfare, 1874 to 1942," in Geoffrey Till, Theo Farrell, and Mark Grove, eds., *Amphibious Operations* (Camberley, UK: Strategic and Combat Studies Institute, 1997), 26–29.

22. Bruce Vandervort, *To the Fourth Shore: Italy's War for Libya, 1911–1912* (Rome: Stato Maggiore dell' Esercito Ufficio Storico, 2012).

23. Zisis Fotakis, *Greek Naval Strategy and Policy, 1910–1919* (London: Routledge, 2005).

24. William McBride, "Strategic Determinism in Technology Selection: The Electric Battleship and US Naval-Industrial Relations," *Technology and Culture* 33 (1992): 249.

25. David Morgan-Owen, *The Fear of Invasion: Strategy, Politics, and British War Planning, 1880–1914* (Oxford: Oxford University Press, 2017).

26. Richard Dunley, "Technology and Tradition: Mine Warfare and the Royal Navy's Strategy of Coastal Assault, 1870–1890," *JMH* 80 (2016): 389–409.

27. Shawn Grimes, "Combined Operations and British Strategy, 1900–9," *Historical Research* 89 (2016): 866–84.

28. Jeffrey Stamp, "Aero-Static Warfare: A Brief Survey of Ballooning in Mid-Nineteenth-Century Siege Warfare," *JMH* 79 (2015): 767–82.

6. THE FIRST WORLD WAR, 1914–1918

1. Charles Callwell, *Military Operations and Maritime Preponderance: Their Relations and Interdependence* (Annapolis, MD: U.S. Naval Institute Press, 1996), 163.

2. Michael B. Barrett, *Operation Albion: The German Conquest of the Baltic Islands* (Bloomington: Indiana University Press, 2008).

3. Charles Burdick, *The Japanese Siege of Tsingtao: World War I in Asia* (Hamden, CT: Archon Books, 1976).

4. Ross Anderson, *The Battle of Tanga 1914* (Stroud, UK: Tempus, 2002).

5. Phillip Pattee, *At War in Distant Waters: British Colonial Defense in the Great War* (Annapolis, MD: Naval Institute Press, 2013).

6. Geoffrey Till, "Richmond and the Faith Reaffirmed: British Naval Thinking between the Wars," in Geoffrey Till, ed., *The Development of British Naval Thinking* (Abingdon, UK: Routledge, 2006), 110.

7. Christopher Bell, *Churchill and the Dardanelles* (Oxford: Oxford University Press, 2017).

8. Richard Harding, "Command, Control, Communication and Intelligence: The Case of the Gallipoli Campaign, 1915," First Sea Lord's Lecture on Naval History and Strategy, July 8, 2015.

9. Edward Erickson, *Ordered to Die: A History of the Ottoman Army in the First World War* (Westport, CT: Praeger, 2001), *Ottoman Army Effectiveness in World War I: A Comparative Study* (London: Routledge, 2007), *Gallipoli: The Ottoman Campaign* (Barnsley, UK: Pen and Sword, 2010), and *Gallipoli: Command under Fire* (Oxford: Osprey, 2015).

10. Tim Travers, *Gallipoli* (Stroud, UK: Alan Sutton, 2001), 310. See also Robin Prior, *Gallipoli: The End of the Myth* (New Haven, CT: Yale University Press, 2009); and Peter Hart, *Gallipoli* (New York: Oxford University Press, 2011).

11. Rhys Crawley, *Climax at Gallipoli: The Failure of the August Offensive* (Norman: University of Oklahoma Press, 2014).

12. Godley to Lieutenant-General Sir William Birdwood, February 27, 1915, AWM, 3 DRL/3376, 11/4.

13. Monash to wife, May 30, 1915, AWM, 3 DRL/2316, 1/1, p. 72.

14. Alan to Edith Thomson, September 24, October 7, November 20, 1915, Thomson papers.

15. Mark Connelly, "*Gallipoli* (1981): A Poignant Search for National Identity," in James Chapman, Mark Glancy, and Sue Harper, eds., *The New Film History: Sources, Methods, Approaches* (Basingstoke, UK: Palgrave, 2007), 41–53.

16. Andrew Wiest, *Passchendaele and the Royal Navy* (London: Greenwood Press, 1995), 8.

17. David Massam, "British Maritime Strategy and Amphibious Capability, 1900–40," (PhD, Oxford University, 1995).

18. Paul Halpern, *The Naval War in the Mediterranean, 1914–1918* (Crows Nest, NSW: Allen & Unwin, 1987).

19. Richard Hall, *Balkan Breakthrough: The Battle of Dobro Pole 1918* (Bloomington: Indiana University Press, 2010).

20. Barrett, *Operation Albion*; Richard DiNardo, "Huns with Web Feet: Operation Albion, 1917," *War in History* 12, no. 4 (November 2005): 396–417.

21. Arthur Marder, *From the Dreadnought to Scapa Flow* (London: Oxford University Press, 1966), I:391.

22. BL. Add. 49703 fols. 137–38.

7. THE INTERWAR PERIOD, 1918–1939

1. Carl Richard, *When the United States Invaded Russia: Woodrow Wilson's Siberian Disaster* (Lanham, MD: Rowman & Littlefield, 2013).

2. Paul Halpern, ed., *The Mediterranean Fleet 1919–1929* (Farnham, UK: Ashgate, 2011).

3. José Alvarez, "Between Gallipoli and D-Day: Alhucemas, 1925," *JMH* 63, no. 1 (January 1999): 75–78; José Pérez, "The Spanish Military and the Tank, 1909–1939," *JMH* 80 (2016): 762; Shannon Fleming, "Primo de Rivera and Abdel Krim: The Struggle in Spanish Morocco, 1923–1927" (unpublished PhD dissertation, Wisconsin, 1974), 247–361.

4. Francisco Franco, "Diario de Alhucemas," *Revista de tropas colonials* 2, nos. 9–12 (September–December 1925). For the plans, "El Proyecto de desembarco en Alhucemas del General Martinez Anido," *Revista de historia military* 49 (1980): 139–69.

5. Hans Schmidt, *The United States Occupation of Haiti, 1915–1934* (New Brunswick, NJ: Rutgers University Press, 1995); Lester Langley, *The Banana Wars: United States Intervention in the Caribbean* (Wilmington, DE: Scholarly Resources, 2002); Bruce Calder, *The Impact of Intervention: The Dominican Republic during the US Occupation of 1916–1924* (Austin: University of Texas Press, 1984).

6. David Ulbrich, "The U.S. Marine Corps, Amphibious Capabilities, and Preparations for War with Japan," *Marine Corps University Journal* 6, no. 1 (Spring 2015): 71–105.

7. David Ulbrich, *Preparing for Victory: Thomas Holcomb and the Making of the Modern Marine Corps, 1936–1943* (Annapolis, MD: Naval Institute Press, 2011).

8. Hal Friedman, "The Quiet Warrior Back in Newport: Admiral Spruance, the Return to the Naval War College and the Lessons of the Pacific War, 1946–1947," *NWCR* 64, no. 2 (2011): 120.

9. Craig Felker, *Testing American Sea Power: U.S. Navy Strategic Exercises, 1923–1940* (College Station: Texas A&M University Press, 2007); Albert Nofi, *To Train the Fleet for War: The U.S. Navy Fleet Problems, 1923–1940* (Newport, RI: Naval War College Press, 2010).

10. Edward Miller, *War Plan Orange: The U.S. Strategy to Defeat Japan, 1897–1945* (Annapolis, MD: Naval Institute Press, 1991).

11. Geoffrey Till, "Amphibious Operations and the British," in Geoffrey Till, Theo Farrell, and Mark Grove, eds., *Amphibious Operations* (Camberley, UK: Strategic and Combat Studies Institute, 1997), 18–19.

12. Nigel Hamilton, *Monty: The Making of a General, 1887–1942* (New York: McGraw-Hill, 1981), 286; Richard Harding, "Amphibious Warfare, 1930–1939," in Richard Harding, ed., *The Royal Navy 1930–2000: Innovation and Defence* (London: Frank Cass, 2005), 42–68.

13. David Massam, *British Maritime Strategy and Amphibious Capability, 1900–40* (PhD dissertation, Oxford University, 1995).

14. Report by the Chiefs of Staff Sub-Committee, April 4, 1927, NA. CAB. 24/186 fols. 108–9.

15. Peter Harmsen, *Shanghai 1937: Stalingrad on the Yangtze* (Havertown, PA: Casemate, 2013).

16. Edward Drea, *In the Service of the Emperor: Essays on the Imperial Japanese Army* (Lincoln: University of Nebraska Press, 1998), 14–25; Allan Millett, "Assault from the Sea: The Development of Amphibious Warfare between the Wars—The American, British, and Japanese Experiences," in Allan Millett and Williamson Murray, eds., *Military Innovation in the Interwar Period* (Cambridge: Cambridge University Press, 1996), 50–95.

17. For a discussion, see Jeremy Black, *Naval Warfare since 1860* (Lanham, MD: Rowman & Littlefield, 2017), 102–5.

18. Anthony Farrar-Hockley, *Student* (New York: Ballantine, 1973).

8. THE SECOND WORLD WAR, I, 1939–1942

1. Graham Rhys-Jones, *Churchill and the Norway Campaign* (Barnsley, UK: Pen and Sword, 2008); Geirr Haarr, *The German Invasion of Norway, April 1940* (Annapolis, MD: Naval Institute Press, 2009).

2. Jeffery Gunsburg, "*La Grande Illusion*: Belgian and Dutch Strategy Facing Germany, 1919–May 1940 (Part II)," *JMH* 78 (2014): 652–53.

3. Gilberto Villahermosa, "Rudolf Witzig, The Eagle of Eben Emael," *Strategy and Tactics* 291 (March–April 2015): 22–29.

4. Harold Winters, *Battling the Elements: Weather and Terrain in the Conduct of War* (Baltimore: Johns Hopkins University Press, 1998), 23.

5. Anthony Cumming, *The Royal Navy and the Battle of Britain* (Annapolis, MD: Naval Institute Press, 2010).

6. Jack Lawrence Granatstein, *Canada's Army: Waging War and Keeping the Peace* (Toronto: University of Toronto Press, 2002), 186.

7. Pound to Admiral Andrew Cunningham, Commander in Chief of the British Mediterranean Fleet, July 24, 1940, BL. Add. 52560 fol. 152.

8. Theodore Gatchel, *Defense at the Water's Edge* (Annapolis, MD: Naval Institute Press, 1996), puts Sealion into the perspective of defensive operations from Gallipoli on.

9. Andrew Stewart, *A Very British Experience: Coalition, Defence and Strategy in the Second World War* (Brighton, UK: Sussex Academic Press, 2012).

10. Craig Stockings and Eleanor Hancock, *Swastika over the Acropolis: Re-interpreting the Nazi Invasion of Greece in World War II* (Leiden, Netherlands: Brill, 2013).

11. Callum MacDonald, *The Lost Battle: Crete 1941* (New York: Free Press, 1993).

12. Christopher Bell, *Churchill and Sea Power* (Oxford: Oxford University Press, 2013), 206–14.

13. Strategic Review for Regional Commanders, August 16, 1941, AWM. 3 DRL/6643, 1/27.

14. Adrian Smith, *Mountbatten: Apprentice War Lord* (London: I.B. Tauris, 2010).

15. Tom Keene, *Cloak of Enemies: Churchill's SOE, Enemies at Home and the "Cockleshell Heroes"* (Stroud, UK: Spellmount, 2012).

16. Christopher Mann, *British Policy and Strategy towards Norway, 1941–45* (Basingstoke, UK: Palgrave Macmillan, 2012).

17. Richard Meixel, "Major-General George Grunert, WPO-3, and the Philippine Army 1940–1941," *JMH* 59, no. 2 (April 1995): 324.

18. Gregory Unwin, *Facing Fearful Odds: The Siege of Wake Island* (Lincoln: University of Nebraska Press, 1997).

19. Peter Boer, *The Loss of Java: The Final Battles for the Possession of Java Fought by Allied Air, Naval and Land Forces in the Period of 18 February–7 March 1942* (Singapore: NUS Press, 2010); War History Office of the National Defense College of Japan, *The Invasion of the Dutch East Indies* (Leiden, Netherlands: Leiden University Press, 2015).

20. Mark Grove, "The Development of Japanese Amphibious Warfare, 1874 to 1942," in Geoffrey Till, Theo Farrell and Mark Grove, eds., *Amphibious Operations* (Camberley, UK: Strategic and Combat Studies Institute, 1997), 23.

21. Milan Vego, "The Port Moresby–Solomons Operation and the Allied Reaction, 27 April–11 May 1942," *NWCR* 65, no. 1 (2012): 93–151.

22. Chi Kwong, "The Failure of Japanese Land-Sea Cooperation during the Second World War: Hong Kong and the South China Coast as an Example, 1942–1945," *JMH* 79 (2015): 69–91.

9. THE SECOND WORLD WAR, II, 1942–1945

1. William Bartsch, *Victory Fever on Guadalcanal: Japan's First Land Defeat of WWII* (College Station: Texas A&M University Press, 2014); Richard Frank, *Guadalcanal* (New York: Random House, 1990).

2. Hale Bradt, *Wilber's War: An American Family's Journey through World War II.* Vol. 2, *Combat and New Life* (Salem, MA: Van Dorn Press, 2016).

3. John Dower, *War without Mercy: Race and Power in the Pacific War* (New York: Pantheon, 1986); Craig Cameron, *American Samurai: Myth, Imagination, and the Conduct of Battle in the First Marine Division, 1941–1951* (Cambridge: Cambridge University Press, 1994); Peter Schrijvers, *Bloody Pacific: American Soldiers at War with Japan* (Basingstoke, UK: Palgrave, 2010).

4. Eric Bergerud, "No Quarter: The Pacific Battlefield," *Historically Speaking* 3, no. 5 (June 2002): 8–10.

5. Matthew Hughes, "War Without Mercy? American Allied Forces and the Deaths of Civilians during the Battle for Saipan, 1944," *JMH* 75 (2011): 93–125, esp. 122–23.

6. Jerry Strahan, *Andrew Jackson Higgins and the Boats That Won World War II* (Baton Rouge: Louisiana State University Press, 1994).

7. Kathleen Williams, *The Measure of a Man: My Father, the Marine Corps, and Saipan* (Annapolis, MD: Naval Institute Press, 2013).

8. Sharon Lacey, *Pacific Blitzkrieg: World War II in the Central Pacific* (Denton: University of North Texas Press, 2013).

9. Nathan Prefer, *The Battle for Tinian: Vital Stepping Stone in America's War against Japan* (Havertown, PA: Casemate, 2012).

10. Bobby Blair and John DeCioccio, *Victory at Peleliu: The 81st Infantry Division's Pacific Campaign* (Norman: University of Oklahoma Press, 2011).

11. Penney to Major-General John Sinclair, Director of Military Intelligence, War Office, May 2, 1945, LH. Penney 5/1.

12. William Breuer, *Retaking the Philippines: America's Return to Corregidor and Bataan, October 1944–March 1945* (New York: St. Martin's Press, 1986).
13. Roy Appleman et al., *Okinawa: The Last Battle* (Washington, DC: US Army Center of Military History, 2005), 4–7.
14. Ian Spurgeon, "The Fallen of Operation Iceberg: U.S. Graves Registration Efforts and the Battle of Okinawa," *Army History* 102 (Winter 2017): 19.
15. Charles Brower, *Defeating Japan: The Joint Chiefs of Staff and Strategy in the Pacific War, 1943–1945* (New York: Palgrave Macmillan, 2012).
16. Penney to Sinclair, May 2, 1945, LH. Penney 5/1.
17. Peter Nash, *The Development of Mobile Logistic Support in Anglo-American Naval Policy, 1900–1953* (Gainesville: University Press of Florida, 2009).
18. Layton to First Sea Lord, September 13, Mountbatten to Layton, September 15, 1944, BL. Add. 74796.
19. Tim Benbow, "'Menace' to 'Ironclad': The British Operations against Dakar (1940) and Madagascar (1942)," *JMH* 75 (2011): 769–809, esp. 805, 809.
20. Keith Sainsbury, *The North African Landings 1942: A Strategic Decision* (London: Davis-Poynter, 1976).
21. George Howe, *Northwest Africa: Seizing the Initiative in the West* (Washington, DC: Office of the Chief of Military History, Department of the Army, 1957).
22. Arthur Funk, *The Politics of Torch: The Allied Landings and the Algiers Putsch, 1942* (Lawrence: University Press of Kansas, 1974).
23. Denis Whitaker, *Dieppe: Tragedy to Triumph* (Toronto: McGraw-Hill Ryerson, 1992).
24. Richard Harding, "The End of the Amphibious Option? The Cancellation of Operation Chopper, Sicily, July 1943," *Northern Mariner* 15 (2005): 1–14.
25. Douglas Delaney, "Churchill and the Mediterranean Strategy: December 1941 to January 1943," *Defense Studies* 2, no. 3 (Autumn 2002): 17–18.
26. R. Gwilliam, *L.C.G. (M)s* (Privately printed, 1989), 6.
27. Adrian Lewis, *Omaha Beach: A Flawed Victory* (Chapel Hill: University of North Carolina Press, 2001).
28. Colin Flint, *Geopolitical Constructs: The Mulberry Harbours, World War Two, and the Making of a Militarized Transatlantic* (Lanham, MD: Rowman & Littlefield, 2016).
29. Craig Symonds, *Neptune: The Allied Invasion of Europe and the D-Day Landings* (Oxford: Oxford University Press, 2014).
30. Stephen Bull, *Churchill's Army 1939–1945: The Men, Machines and Organisation* (London: Bloomsbury, 2016), 287.
31. Sebastian Ritchie, *Arnhem Myth and Reality: Airborne Warfare, Air Power and the Failure of Operation Market Garden* (London: Robert Hale, 2011).
32. Sebastian Ritchie, "Learning the Hard Way: A Comparative Perspective on Airborne Operations in the Second World War," *Air Power Review* 14, no. 3 (Autumn/Winter 2011): 13–16.
33. John Greenacre, "Shadows of Arnhem: British Airborne Forces and the Aftermath of Operation Market Garden," in John Buckley and Peter Preston-Hough, eds., *Operation Market Garden: The Campaign for the Low Countries, Autumn 1944: Seventy Years On* (Solihull, UK: Helion, 2016), 276.
34. Joshua Levine, *Dunkirk: The History Behind the Major Motion Picture* (London: William Collins, 2017), 10, 15.
35. Aaron O'Connell, "A Harsh and Spiritual Unity: A New Look at Culture and Battle in the Marine Corps' Pacific War," *International Journal of Naval History* 7, no. 3 (December 2008), and *Underdogs: The Making of the Modern Marine Corps* (Cambridge, MA: Harvard University Press, 2012).
36. George Clark, *United States Marine Corps Generals of World War II: A Biographical Dictionary* (Jefferson, NC: McFarland, 2008).

10. THE COLD WAR, 1945–1990

1. *The National Defense Program: Unification and Strategy: Hearings before the U.S. House of Representatives Committee on the Armed Services*, 81st Cong., 1st sess., October 1949 (Washington, DC: U.S. Government Printing Office, 1949), 521.

2. John Cann, *Flight Plan Africa: Portuguese Airpower in Counterinsurgency, 1961–1974* (Solihull, UK: Helion, 2015).

3. Stephen Chappell, "Air Power in the Mau Mau Conflict," *RUSI* 156, no. 1 (February/March 2011): 64–70.

4. Employment of Joint Helicopter Unit on Operation Musketeer, January 14, 1957, NA, WO 288/76/JEHU/S. 816/G; Helicopters at Port Said, Air Ministry Secret Intelligence Summaries, 1957, NA, AIR 40/2771, vol. 12, no. 5:12.

5. Gulab Hiranandani, *Transition to Triumph: History of the Indian Navy, 1965–1975* (New Delhi: Lancer, 2000).

6. Maochun Yu, "The Battle of Quemoy: The Amphibious Assault That Held the Postwar Military Balance in the Taiwan Strait," *NWCR* 69 (2016): 91–107.

7. Odd Westad, *Decisive Encounters: The Chinese Civil War, 1946–1950* (Stanford, CA: Stanford University Press, 2003), 303–4; Li Xiaobing, *A History of the Modern Chinese Army* (Lexington: University Press of Kentucky, 2007), 129–35; He Di, "The Last Campaign to Unify China: The CCP's Unrealised Plan to Liberate Taiwan, 1949–1950," in Mark Ryan, Michael Finkelstein, and Michael McDevitt, eds., *Chinese Warfighting: The PLA Experience since 1949* (Armonk, NY: East Gate Books, 2003).

8. Bruce Elleman, *Taiwan Straits: Crisis in Asia and the Role of the U.S. Navy* (Lanham, MD: Rowman & Littlefield, 2015).

9. Tim Benbow, *British Uses of Aircraft Carrier and Amphibious Ships: 1945–2010* (London: Corbett Centre for Maritime Policy Studies, 2012).

10. Geraint Hughes, "Demythologising Dhofar: British Policy, Military Strategy, and Counter-Insurgency in Oman, 1963–1976," *JMH* 79 (2015): 423–56, esp. 440–50.

11. Donald Boose, *Over the Beach: U.S. Army Amphibious Operations in the Korean War* (Fort Leavenworth, KS: CSI Press, 2008).

12. Donald Chisholm, "A Remarkable Military Feat. The Hungnam Redeployment, December 1950," *NWCR* 65, no. 2 (2012): 105–44. This article has wide-ranging value.

13. Aaron O'Connell, *Underdogs: The Making of the Modern Marine Corps* (Cambridge, MA: Harvard University Press, 2012); Thomas Hammes, *Forgotten Warriors: The 1st Provisional Marine Brigade, the Corps Ethos, and the Korean War* (Lawrence: University Press of Kansas, 2010).

14. John Sherwood, *War in the Shallows: U.S. Navy Coastal and Riverine Warfare in Vietnam, 1965–1968* (Washington, DC: Naval History and Heritage Command, 2015).

15. John Cann, *Brown Waters of Africa: Portuguese Riverine Warfare, 1961–1974* (Petersburg, FL: Hailer Publishing, 2007).

16. Robert Coram, *Brute: The Life of Victor Krulak, U.S. Marine* (New York: Little, Brown, 2010).

17. Trumbull Higgins, *The Perfect Failure: Kennedy, Eisenhower, and the CIA at the Bay of Pigs* (New York: Norton, 1987).

18. Juan Rodriguez, *The Inevitable Battle: From the Bay of Pigs to Playa Girón*, trans. Rose Ana Berbeo (Havana: Editorial Capitán San Luis, 2009).

19. Lawrence Freedman, ed., *The Official History of the Falklands Campaign* (London: Routledge, 2005).

20. Kenneth Privratsky, *Logistics in the Falklands War* (Barnsley, UK: Pen and Sword, 2015).

21. O'Connell, *Underdogs*.

22. Robert Slayton, *Master of the Air: William Tunner and the Success of Military Airlift* (Tuscaloosa: University of Alabama Press, 2010); Robert Owen, *Air Mobility: A Brief History of the American Experience* (Washington, DC: Potomac Books, 2013).

23. Frederick Hartmann, *Naval Renaissance: The U.S. Navy in the 1980s* (Annapolis, MD: Naval Institute Press, 1990); John Hattendorf and Peter Swatz, eds., *US Maritime Strategy in the 1980s: Selected Documents* (Newport, RI: U.S. Naval War College, 2008).

24. John Olsen, ed., *Airpower Reborn: The Strategic Concepts of John Warden and John Boyd* (Annapolis, MD: Naval Institute Press, 2015); Boyd's slide presentation, "Patterns of Conflict," http://dnipogo.org. Accessed March 10, 2017.

25. http://www.marines.mil/Portals/59/Publications/MCDP%201%20Warfighting.pdf. Accessed March 10, 2017.

26. Steven Willis, "The Effect of the Goldwater-Nichols Act of 1986 on Naval Strategy, 1987–1994," *NWCR* 69 (2016): 21–40. For a more positive account of the value of such command, David Jablonsky, *War by Land, Sea, and Air: Dwight Eisenhower and the Concept of Unified Command* (New Haven, CT: Yale University Press, 2011).

27. Martin Van Creveld, *More on War* (New York: Oxford University Press, 2017), 121.

11. SINCE 1990

1. Paul Westermeyer, *Liberating Kuwait: U.S. Marines in the Gulf War, 1990–1991* (Quantico, VA: Marine Corps Division, 2014).

2. Theo Farrell, "United States Marine Corps Operations in Somalia: A Model for the Future," in Geoffrey Till, Theo Farrell, and Mark Grove, eds., *Amphibious Operations* (Camberley, UK: Strategic and Combat Studies Institute, 1997): 49; Peter Haynes, *Toward a New Maritime Strategy: American Naval Thinking in the Post–Cold War Era* (Annapolis, MD: Naval Institute Press, 2015).

3. Jack Fairweather, *The Good War: Why We Couldn't Win the War or the Peace in Afghanistan* (New York: Basic Books, 2014).

4. Caroline Holmqvist, *Policing Wars: On Military Intervention in the Twenty-First Century* (Basingstoke, UK: Palgrave, 2014).

5. Robert Gates, "Remarks of Secretary of Defense Robert M. Gates," May 3, 2010, *NWCR* 63, no. 4 (2010): 9–10.

6. http://www.arlingtoncemetery.net/010902-crash.htm. Accessed March 10, 2017.

7. Robert Kozloski, "Marching toward the Sweet Spot: Options for the U.S. Marine Corps in a Time of Austerity," *NWCR* 66, no. 3 (2013): 11–36.

8. Wayne Hughes, *Fleet Tactics and Coastal Combat*, 2nd ed. (Annapolis, MD: Naval Institute Press, 2000); Colin Gray, *The Navy in the Post–Cold War World: The Uses and Value of Strategic Sea Power* (Philadelphia: Pennsylvania State University Press, 2004).

9. Sam Tangredi, *Anti-Access Warfare: Countering A2/AD Strategies* (Annapolis, MD: Naval Institute Press, 2013).

10. Andrew Erickson, *Chinese Anti-Ship Ballistic Missile (ASBM) Development: Drivers, Trajectories and Strategic Implications* (Washington, DC: Jamestown Foundation, 2013).

11. Toshi Yoshihara and James Holmes, *Red Star over the Pacific: China's Rise and the Challenge to US Maritime Strategy* (Annapolis, MD: Naval Institute Press, 2010).

12. Aaron Friedberg, *Beyond Air-Sea Battle: The Debate over US Military Strategy in Asia* (Abingdon, UK: Routledge, 2014).

13. Daniel Kostecka, "From the Sea: PLA Doctrine and the Employment of Sea-Based Airpower," *NWCR* 64, no. 3 (2011): 11–30.

14. Calvin Manganyi, "Resurrection of the Marine Capability in the South African Navy: The Maritime Reaction Squadron," *Scientia Militaria* 40 (2012): 429–71.

15. Justin Goldman, "An Amphibious Capability in Japan's Self-Defense Force: Operationalising Dynamic Defense," *NWCR* 66, no. 4 (2013): 117–34.

16. Peter Roberts, "The Future of Amphibious Forces," *RUSI* 160, no. 2 (April/May 2015): 43.

17. Jacob Børresen, "Alliance Naval Strategies and Norway in the Final Years of the Cold War," *NWCR* 62, no. 2 (2011): 97–115.

18. U.S. Defense Department, *Joint Doctrine for Amphibious Operations* (Washington, DC: Joint Staff, 2009).

19. Laura Chua, "Singapore's *Endurance* Class LST," *Naval Forces* 20, no. 2 (1999): 26–29.

12. CONCLUSIONS

1. For example, Elaine Murphy, *Ireland and the War at Sea 1641–1653* (Woodbridge, UK: Boydell and Brewer, 2012).

2. Norman Friedman, *Network-Centric Warfare: How Navies Learned to Fight Smarter through Three World Wars* (Annapolis, MD: Naval Institute Press, 2009).

3. Joel Hayward, "A Case Study in Early Joint Warfare: An Analysis of the *Wehrmacht*'s Crimean Campaign of 1942," *Journal of Strategic Studies* 22 (1999): 103–30.

4. Holdernesse to Joseph Yorke, envoy in Berlin, May 3, 1758, NA. SP. 90/71.

5. Count Maffei, Sardinian envoy in Paris, to Victor Amadeus II, January 23, 1730, AST. LM. Francia 165.

6. Yorke to Holdernesse, April 13, 1758, NA. SP. 90/71. For the need for a diversion, Newcastle to Field Marshal John Ligonier, the Commander in Chief, June 17, 1758, BL. Add. 35417 fol. 236. The "King's army" was that of German forces subsidized by George II.

7. Mitchell to Holdernesse, April 20, 1760, NA. SP. 90/75.

8. Ross to Forbes, September 15, 1758, Edinburgh, Scottish Record Office, GD 45/2/20/13.

9. Reporting views of Newcastle, Hugh Valence Jones, MP and Solicitor to the Treasury, to Hardwicke, August 30, 1757, BL. Add. 35417 fol. 38.

10. Elgin to William Pitt the Younger, First Lord of the Treasury, December 20, 1790, NA. PRO. 30/8/132 fol. 158.

11. Ewart to Francis Jackson, Secretary of Legation in Berlin and thus Ewart's junior there, March 22, 24, 25, 27, 1791, Williamwood, Ewart papers.

12. Letters from Congress Protesting U.S. Coast Guard Budget Cuts, published on https://news.usni.org/2017/03/10/document-letters-congress-protesting-cuts-coast-guard-budget. Accessed on March 12, 2017.

13. Dean McFadden, "The Canadian Navy and Canada's National Interests in This Maritime Century," *NWCR* 63, no. 4 (2010): 53.

14. Williamson Murray and Peter Mansoor, eds., *Hybrid Warfare: Fighting Complex Opponents from the Ancient World to the Present* (Cambridge: Cambridge University Press, 2012).

Selected Further Reading

Bartlett, Merrill, ed. *Assault from the Sea: Essays on the History of Amphibious Warfare.* Annapolis, MD: Naval Institute Press, 1983.

Corbett, Julian. *Some Principles of Maritime Strategy*. London: Longmans, Green, and Co., 1911.

Dunnavent, Blake. *Brown Water Warfare: The U.S. Navy in Riverine Warfare and the Emergence of a Tactical Doctrine, 1775–1970*. Gainesville: University Press of Florida, 2003.

Elleman, Bruce A., and S. C. M. Paine, eds. *Naval Power and Expeditionary Warfare: Peripheral Campaigns and New Theatres of Naval Warfare*. New York: Routledge, 2011.

Gatchel, Theodore. *Defense at the Water's Edge*. Annapolis, MD: Naval Institute Press, 1996.

Lovering, Tristan. *Amphibious Assault: Manoeuvre from the Sea.* Woodbridge, UK: Seafarer Books, 2007.

Millett, Allan. *Semper Fidelis: The History of the United States Marine Corps*. New York: Free Press, 1991.

Moody, Wesley, and Adrienne Sachse, eds. *The Diary of a Civil War Marine: Private Josiah Gregg*. Madison, NJ: Fairleigh Dickinson University Press, 2013.

Polman, Norman, and Peter Mersky. *Amphibious Warfare: An Illustrated History*. London: Blandford Press, 1988.

Speller, Ian. *The Role of Amphibious Warfare in British Defence Policy, 1945–56*. Basingstoke, UK: Palgrave Macmillan, 2001.

Speller, Ian, and Christopher Tuck. *Amphibious Warfare: Strategy and Tactics from Gallipoli to Iraq*. London: Amber, 2001.

Trim, David, and Mark Fissel, eds. *Amphibious Warfare, 1000–1700: Commerce, State Formation, and European Expansion*. Leiden, Netherlands: Brill, 2006.

Index

About the Author

Jeremy Black graduated from Cambridge University with a Starred First and did graduate work at Oxford University before teaching at the University of Durham and then at the University of Exeter, where he is professor of history. He has held visiting chairs at the United States Military Academy at West Point, Texas Christian University, and Stillman College. He is a senior fellow of the Foreign Policy Research Institute. Black received the Samuel Eliot Morison Prize from the Society for Military History in 2008. His recent books include *Air Power: A Global History*; *War and Technology*; *Naval Power: A History of Warfare and the Sea from 1500 Onwards*; and *Rethinking World War Two: The Conflict and Its Legacy.*

Lightning Source UK Ltd.
Milton Keynes UK
UKHW041255010722
405244UK00009B/104